THE CAMBRIDGE
COMPANION TO
SALMAN RUSHDIE

THE CAMBRIDGE COMPANION TO
SALMAN RUSHDIE

EDITED BY
ABDULRAZAK GURNAH
UNIVERSITY OF KENT

CAMBRIDGE
UNIVERSITY PRESS

CAMBRIDGE UNIVERSITY PRESS
Cambridge, New York, Melbourne, Madrid, Cape Town, Singapore, São Paulo

Cambridge University Press
The Edinburgh Building, Cambridge CB2 8RU, UK

Published in the United States of America by Cambridge University Press, New York

www.cambridge.org
Information on this title: www.cambridge.org/9780521609951

First published 2007

Printed in the United Kingdom at the University Press, Cambridge

A catalogue record for this publication is available from the British Library

Library of Congress Cataloging in Publication data
The Cambridge companion to Salman Rushdie / edited by Abdulrazak Gurnah.
(Cambridge companions to literature)
Includes bibliographical references and index.
978-0-521-84719-3 hardback
978-0-521-60995-1 paperback
1. Rushdie, Salman – Criticism and interpretation. I. Gurnah, Abdulrazak, 1948– II. Title.
III. Series.

PR6068. U757Z585 2007
823′.914–dc22

ISBN 978-0-521-84719-3 hardback
ISBN 978-0-521-60995-1 paperback

Cambridge University Press has no responsibility for the persistence or
accuracy of URLs for external or third-party internet websites referred to
in this publication, and does not guarantee that any content on such
websites is, or will remain, accurate or appropriate.

CONTENTS

CONTENTS

CONTRIBUTORS

DEEPIKA BAHRI Emory University, USA

ABDULRAZAK GURNAH University of Kent, UK

IB JOHANSEN University of Aarhus, Denmark

JOEL KUORTTI University of Joensuu, Finland

VIJAY MISHRA Murdoch University, Australia

ANSHUMAN A. MONDAL Brunel University, UK

PETER MOREY University of East London, UK

BRENDON NICHOLLS University of Leeds, UK

RUVANI RANASINHA Brunel University, UK

MINOLI SALGADO University of Sussex, UK

AMINA YAQIN School of Oriental and African Studies, University of London, UK

CHRONOLOGY

1947	19 June: Born Ahmed Salman Rushdie in Bombay, Maharashtra to Anis Ahmed and Negis (née Butt) Rushdie.
1954–61	Attends Cathedral School, Bombay, an English Mission school.
1961–5	Sent to Rugby School, Warwickshire, England.
1962	Family moves briefly to England and then returns to Bombay.
1964	Family moves from Bombay to Karachi, Pakistan.
1965–8	Studies history at King's College, Cambridge, graduating with an MA with honours. During his time at Cambridge he develops his interest in the history of Islam. He also acts in the Cambridge Footlights review.
1968	Returns to Karachi in the summer to work briefly for Pakistan TV. Disenchanted by its heavy censorship, he returns to London.
1968–9	Becomes an actor with Oval House productions, Kennington, London. Also starts working in television, advertising and publishing.
1969	Starts work on an unpublished novel, *The Book of the Pir*.
1970	Meets Clarissa Luard.
1970–80	Works freelance as an advertising copywriter for Ogilvy & Mather in London.

1974   Travels around India with Clarissa Luard.

1975   *Grimus* published by Victor Gollancz. Starts work on *Midnight's Children*.

1976   Marries Clarissa Luard.

1977–83   Member of the Camden Committee of Community Relations working on projects in North London to help Bangladeshi immigrants.

1979   Son Zafar is born.

1981   *Midnight's Children* published by Jonathan Cape to critical acclaim. Wins the Booker Prize, as well as the James Tait Black Prize and the English Speaking Union Literary Award.

1983   *Shame* published by Jonathan Cape, shortlisted for the Booker Prize, wins *Prix du Meilleur Livre Etranger* in France. Starts work on *The Satanic Verses*. Is awarded fellowship of the Royal Society of Literature.

1984   Travels through Central Australia together with the author Bruce Chatwin. Meets Robyn Davidson.

1985   Produces the documentary film *The Painter and the Pest*.

1986   Travels to Nicaragua, invited by the Sandinista Association of Cultural Workers. Meets American author Marianne Wiggins.

1987   Publishes *The Jaguar Smile: A Nicaraguan Journey* detailing his journey the previous year. Marriage to Clarissa Luard dissolved.

1988   Marries Marianne Wiggins. Writes and produces *The Riddle of Midnight*, a documentary for Channel 4 television. September: Viking/Penguin publishes *The Satanic Verses*, shortlisted for the Booker Prize, wins the Whitbread award and, in Germany, the Author of the Year Award. In an interview in *India Today* Rushdie talks about the potentially offensive content of the book. 5 October: *The Satanic Verses* is banned in India; many other countries including Bangladesh, Sudan, Sri Lanka, South Africa, Kenya, Thailand, Tanzania,

Indonesia, Singapore, Venezuela and Poland follow suit. 10 December: first mass protest against the novel in London.

1989   14 January: public burning of *The Satanic Verses* at a rally in Bradford. 14 February: the Ayatollah Khomeini declares the *fatwa* on Radio Tehran sentencing Rushdie, his publishers and translators to death. 15 February: a bounty of £1.5 million is placed on his head. Rushdie goes into hiding. August: separates from Marianne Wiggins.

1990   February: publishes the essay 'In Good Faith' explicating the novel and 'Is Nothing Sacred?', the Herbert Read memorial lecture, given in his absence by Harold Pinter. *Haroun and the Sea of Stories* published by Granta. Meets Elizabeth West.

1991   *Imaginary Homelands: Essays and Criticsm 1981–1991* published by Granta. July: Rushdie's Italian translator Ettore Capriolo barely survives a stabbing attack in Milan. His Japanese translator Hitoshi Igarashi is stabbed to death in Tokyo.

1992   Publishes *The Wizard of Oz* for the British Film Institute's Film Classics series.

1993   *Midnight's Children* wins the Booker of Bookers, the prize for the best book to receive the award in the past twenty-five years. 11 August: Salman Rushdie walks on stage during a U2 concert at Wembley Stadium. Meeting with John Major. He visits the US and meets President Clinton. He becomes Honorary Vice President of PEN America and Honorary Professor at MIT, Cambridge, Massachusetts. Marriage to Marianne Wiggins dissolved. His Norwegian publisher William Nygaard is shot dead outside his home in Oslo.

1994   Publication of *East, West*, a collection of short stories, by Jonathan Cape.

1995   *The Moor's Last Sigh* is published by Jonathan Cape, shortlisted for the Booker Prize and wins the Whitbread Award for Best Fiction. 7 September: in London,

Salman Rushdie makes his first pre-announced public appearance since the inception of the *fatwa*.

1996   Receives the European Union's Aristeion Prize for Literature.

1997   Co-edits together with Elizabeth West *The Vintage Book of Indian Writing 1947–1997*. Rushdie marries Elizabeth West, birth of their son Milan.

1998   24 September: at the UN general assembly, the Iranian government officially distances itself from the *fatwa*.

1999   *The Ground Beneath Her Feet* is published by Jonathan Cape. India grants Rushdie a five-year visa. Publication of *The Screenplay of Midnight's Children* by Vintage. Meets Padma Lakshmi.

2000   Travels to India with his son Zafar for the Commonwealth Writer's Prize. Moves to New York.

2001   *Fury* published by Jonathan Cape.

2002   *Step Across This Line: Collected Fiction and Non-Fiction 1992–2002* published by Jonathan Cape.

2003   January: the Royal Shakespeare Company premiers the play adaptation of *Midnight's Children* at the Barbican Centre, London. Becomes President of PEN America. Marriage to Elizabeth West dissolved.

2004   April: marries Padma Lakshmi.

2005   *Shalimar the Clown* published by Jonathan Cape.

I

ABDULRAZAK GURNAH

Introduction

'The past is home albeit a lost home in a lost city in the mists of lost time.'[1] Salman Rushdie wrote that in 1982, in the early period of his new fame as the author of *Midnight's Children*, which had won the Booker Prize in 1981. The elegiac tone is striking. Many years before the *fatwa* threatened to make Rushdie's exile from India a permanent one, and at a time when he was 'enjoying the unique pleasure of having written ... a book that people liked',[2] he laments the loss of the city his novel celebrates. Clearly the present life, London and fame, have not displaced the memory of India and Bombay as a constitution of 'home'. Rushdie here describes a sense of being absent from his most intense reality that will be familiar to his migrant readers. The 'lost city in the mists of lost time' is Bombay in the 1950s, which is the period when Rushdie grew up, and which is the period of childhood in *Midnight's Children*. It is to this time and this city that Rushdie locates the best of India's possibilities, a time when Nehru's vision of a tolerant and plural India seemed achievable, and in a city which in some ways appeared to have made its own way towards that vision.

Salman Rushdie was born in Bombay in 1947, the year of India's partition and independence. He was born in June, some weeks before the date of India's independence (15 August), but the family joke was that the young Salman's appearance was the true cause of the departure of the British. This linking of the birth of a child and the birth of a nation provided 'the germ of a novel, *Midnight's Children*'.[3] In the meantime, he had plenty of other things to do before he got to write that novel. He attended Cathedral School in Bombay, an English Mission School, just like his narrator Saleem would do in the novel ('In my nearlyninth year I had begun to attend the Cathedral and John Connon Boys' High School'[4]). He was at the school until 1961, when he was sent to Rugby School, a famous boarding school in England. The period from 1947 until 1961, when Rushdie was thirteen, is the only continuous time of any length that Rushdie lived in Bombay, and is the period that figures most profoundly in the 'somewhat Proustian'[5] dimension of *Midnight's Children*, the part of it that is to do with retrieving the memory of a lost time. Rushdie was at Rugby from 1961 to 1965, a period rapidly passed over in the description of Saladin Chamcha's arrival in England in *The Satanic Verses*: 'Five years later he was back home again after leaving school, waiting until the English university term began.'[6] This sentence describing Saladin's return to Bombay is preceded by his first arrival in London, with the disappointment he felt after so much anticipation, and by the excruciating kipper-eating scene on his first outing at breakfast in Rugby. This scene succinctly acts as a metaphor for Saladin's simultaneous alienation from England and his perverse determination to be English, a precarious balancing act which is comically explored in the novel and which provides one of the narrative strands in the novel's migrant theme. But Rushdie himself did not return to Bombay after Rugby, because in the meantime his family had migrated to Karachi in Pakistan, and now Bombay was forever the lost city of childhood.

Rushdie studied History at King's College, Cambridge, graduating in 1968. While at Cambridge he studied Islamic history, and it was during this period that he first came across the story of the satanic verses which was later to be the source of the novel.[7] He also acted in the Cambridge Footlights review, something he was later to do professionally for a brief while, soon after his return from Pakistan. After graduation, Rushdie went to Karachi where his family now lived but only stayed for a few months, disenchanted by the crude and heavy censorship in the work he did with Pakistani TV during this period, and perhaps, as he makes Saleem Sinai say, because it was not Bombay. In any case, he was in London before the end of the year, working as an actor with Oval House productions and doing work in television, advertising and publishing. It was during this period that he started writing. For the next ten years, until the publication of *Midnight's Children*, he worked as a copywriter for an advertising agency, and he sums up his writing career until this point as follows: 'Before *Midnight's Children*, I had had one novel rejected, abandoned two others, and published one, *Grimus*, which, to put it mildly, bombed.'[8]

Most of Rushdie's readers and critics have also taken this view of his first novel and have mostly ignored it. Ib Johansen, in Chapter 6 in this volume, is one of the few who has written about the novel, and he shows here the sources and developments of its ideas. *Grimus* is also interesting, Catherine Cundy shows, for the way it points to Rushdie's later concerns:

> Viewed from the standpoint of *The Satanic Verses*, *Grimus* allows us to see areas of debate which are subsequently handled with greater depth and maturity in Rushdie's later work – ideas of personal and national identity, the

legacy of colonialism, the problems of exile and even the first signs of a tendency to demonise female sexuality.[9]

At the core of *Grimus* is a quest for knowledge or faith, or in another sense, the individual's need for meaning. These are central ideas in *The Satanic Verses* and, to some extent, in *Midnight's Children*. In *Grimus*, the narrative is dominated by its intertexts, Dante's *The Divine Comedy* and Farid Ud-Din Attar's *The Conference of the Birds*, from which it derives its title.[10] Perhaps it is the reliance on the ideas of its sources which makes *Grimus* seem stiff-jointed and abstract in style compared to the later Rushdie texts whose historical and cultural locations are explicit.

Compared to what was to follow, *Grimus* was a failure. Rushdie started work on *Midnight's Children* in the same year as *Grimus*'s publication, although it is very likely that some of the material from one of the earlier, abandoned novels found its way into it. *Midnight's Children* was published by Jonathan Cape in 1981 to huge acclaim in the United Kingdom, in North America, in India and elsewhere. It won the Booker Prize that year, the first time the prize was televised, turning it into the huge public event it has since become. It made Rushdie famous, and in the years that followed, ensured his frequent presence in the book pages of national newspapers: as novelist, reviewer and commentator on current events. Rushdie scholars and critics return to the novel repeatedly (as is evident in this collection of essays), and few quibbled when it was chosen in 1993 as the best novel to have won the Booker Prize in the Prize's first twenty-five years. Much has been written about the novel: its narrative inventiveness, its huge ambition, its intertexts, which more recently have been shown to be filmic as well as textual. Vijay Mishra in Chapter 2 of this *Companion* shows the significance of Indian popular cinema in reading Rushdie, and especially *Midnight's Children*.

In 1983 Rushdie published *Shame*, about which the novel's narrator, at times unmistakably the novelist himself, has this to say: 'I tell myself this will be a novel of leavetaking, my last words on the East from which, many years ago, I began to come loose.'[11] It turned out to be a mistaken prediction, of course, but it expresses a compelling and recurring desire in Rushdie's writing, to write 'the East' out of him and found new origins, yet finding himself not quite able to do so. The sentence just cited above is followed by: 'I do not always believe myself when I say this.' Aijaz Ahmad in his *In Theory: Classes, Nations, Literatures* took Rushdie thoroughly to task on his self-representation as an exile with the degree of agency that would enable him to deliver 'last words' on 'Pakistan'.[12] Ahmad's argument is complex and detailed, and perhaps its real emphasis lies in the representation of women in the novel, and of Sufiya Zenobia in particular. However,

Ahmad's discussion is valuable on the issue of 'self-representation' as it attempts to situate Rushdie's novel (and at times it seems Rushdie himself) in a modernist–postmodernist debate.

As we have noted above, Rushdie lived only very briefly in Pakistan,[13] and everything he had had to say about that country by 1983, in both *Midnight's Children* and in *Shame*, expressed his repulsion. If the former novel describes India's lost possibilities, its tolerant and plural ambitions squandered for expediency, the latter describes Pakistan as never having had such possibilities because it was constructed out of intolerance and narrow-mindedness. The failure of the state of Pakistan has a domestic allegory in the squabble between two powerful families, only thinly disguised to represent that of Zulfikar Ali Bhutto (Iskander Harrappa) and of Zia ul-Haq (Raza Hyder).[14] But the force of Rushdie's critique of Pakistan as an oppressive and authoritarian society is focused on the treatment of women.

Sufiya Zenobia is born a girl when Raza Hyder wanted a boy. At her birth, he rages at the medical staff as if somehow his anger will force them to change the baby's gender. Sufiya Zenobia blushes for shame. From the moment of her birth, Sufiya Zenobia is made inadequate, shamed by her gender. As the novel progresses she comes to represent an unavoidable capacity for feeling shame while the world that dictates to her, the world of men, cannot restrain itself from shamelessness. Rushdie's argument suggests a gendered sense of 'honour', a public sense in which men fraudulently disguise cynicism by investing honour in the conduct of women, in the process dictating to them, while conducting themselves with cruelty and self-indulgence. Women, who are required to submit to what has been invested in them and are made inadequate by this submission, feel shame. Sufiya Zenobia cannot prevent herself blushing for shame, and is a literal representation of this gendered condition, which is attenuated further by making her retarded by illness to a permanent mental age of a six-year-old. So her blushes, in other words, are not from a heightened moral sense but the metaphorical conditioning of her gender.

Rushdie's women in *Shame* are not mere cyphers, though they are given a problematic agency.[15] The novel's 'peripheral hero' has three mothers: three sisters who had spent their lives in a huge blank-walled house shut off from the outside world. The house is a metaphor, no doubt, for the detention of women in the medieval form of Islam which Rushdie ascribes to the idea of Pakistan. The house is called Nishapur, the birthplace of the eleventh-century Persian poet Omar Khayyam, and has rambling rooms with forgotten books which, perhaps, represent arrested learning. The three sisters rebel against their incarceration by going to a dance in the British 'lines' and returning with a joint pregnancy, whose outcome is Omar Khayyam Shakil, whose self-indulgence knows no shame. Rani Harrapa, Iskander Harrapa's wife, knits a shawl in which she records her husband's murders. Good News Hyder, Raza Hyder's other daughter, kills herself because she cannot prevent her husband fathering more babies on her. If all these are problematic and, to some extent, tragic forms of agency, it is Sufiya Zenobia who is given its most grotesque form.

In Rushdie's argument, humiliation and shame will inevitably lead to violence, which is as much about the oppression of women in Pakistan (and Islam) as about the whole society. It is Sufiya who demonstrates this argument. The first occasion is when she tears off the heads of 218 turkeys, 'then reached down into their bodies to draw their guts up through their necks' (*Shame*, p. 138). Later, in the novel's closing stages, she fulfils what this early outburst of prodigious violence promises. She tempts four nameless men to have sex with her, inverting the right of Muslim men to take four wives, then she pulls their heads off:

> Shame walks the streets of night. In the slums four youths are transfixed by those appalling eyes, whose deadly yellow fire blows like a wind through the lattice-work of the veil. They follow her to the rubbish-dump of doom, rats to her piper, automata dancing in the all-consuming light from the black-veiled eyes. Down she lies [...] Four husbands come and go. Four of them in and out, and then her hands reach for the first boy's neck. The others stand still and wait their turn. (*Shame*, p. 219)

Her humiliation at the hands of men who should have loved her, her father Raza Hyder and her husband Omar Khayyam Shakil, have turned her into a Beast. Rushdie celebrates Sufiya's violence as liberation, or makes Omar Khayyam Shakil ponder along these lines, but the real force behind this figuration of women is not so much to suggest a route to fulfilment, but to issue a warning to the rulers of Pakistan. Out of the encounter of shame and shamelessness will come violence. Not surprisingly, *Shame* was banned in Pakistan, although it was short-listed for the Booker Prize.

Rushdie's next novel, *The Satanic Verses* (1988), was also banned in Pakistan, as it was in India and in many other countries, including several Muslim countries. In Bradford in the United Kingdom, the novel was publicly burned by protesters and in Karachi, Pakistan, the police fired into a mass protest and killed ten people. The climax of these protests against the novel was the death 'sentence', the *fatwa*, declared by the Ayatollah Khomeini on Rushdie, his publishers and translators, with a bounty of £1.5 million offered to whoever would do the deed. It was a remarkable and shocking intervention by a head of state in response to a novel. If this found an echo in many countries whose opinion-leaders were also repelled by what they saw as the mockery of the Prophet, it also brought out writers, intellectuals and many others in support of Rushdie and his right to write freely. In any case, the invitation to murder drove Rushdie into hiding for several years and broke his life and career in two. A great deal has been written about the *fatwa* and its consequences on Rushdie's writing. This volume has two chapters on the subject, by Ruvani Ranasinha on the background to and consequences of the *fatwa* (Chapter 4), and by Joel Kuortti, who reads *The Satanic Verses* in the light of the *fatwa* (Chapter 9). There is little need here to add to what those two readings undertake. In addition, Rushdie published several defences of his novel and of his practice as a novelist, and these are alluded to in the chapters of this volume. All these essays were published in *Imaginary Homelands* (1991, 1992), including an essay in which Rushdie 'embraced' Islam as a way of getting out of the impasse. Rushdie withdrew this essay from later editions because he thought he had been ill-advised to publish what looked like an apology.[16]

During this period of great post-*fatwa* intensity, when Rushdie was involved in a campaign to make his case to officials and the public, when he was fêted as an emblem of the writer's freedom, he published the short novel *Haroun and the Sea of Stories* (1990). The novel is described as a children's book, yet it is one of Rushdie's most complete books, which gracefully manages his customary energetic comedy despite its dark subject, the imposition of silence on a story-teller. In 1994, he also published a collection of stories *East, West*; both these publications are discussed by Deepika Bahri in Chapter 10 in this volume. The following year, seven years after the publication of *The Satanic Verses* and the trauma that followed it, Rushdie published *The Moor's Last Sigh* (1995), in many ways the disillusioned sequel to *Midnight's Children*. Towards the end of the earlier novel, its narrator Saleem Sinai contemplates the possibility of 'new myths' being born after the failure, or the destruction, of Nehru's vision of a secular and tolerant India. That possibility is symbolically lodged in Aadam Sinai, the 'son' of Saleem and Parvati-the-Witch, although his real father was Saleem's potent rival, Shiva. Aadam is the 'son' of the children of midnight, but without Saleem's sense of significance. His silence while the Emergency lasted and his Ganesh-like features hint at a moral position and a modest persona, a more practical attitude to what lies ahead for India and for Bombay, which in its pluralism signifies India's best possibilities. In *The Moor's Last Sigh* this possibility is utterly lost. In the novel, Bombay's parallel allegorical site of tolerance and pluralism is Muslim Spain. Its title alludes to the place on the hill from which the last Muslim ruler of Granada turned to look on his beautiful city for the last time, after his and his people's expulsion by the fundamentalist Christian reconquista. Like Granada in its era, Bombay is now in the hands of fundamentalists and Aadam Sinai has fulfilled a wholly different future from that anticipated for him in *Midnight's Children*. He has found no new myths but has become a gangster in the service of organised crime. In this volume, Minoli Salgado discusses Rushdie's method in this later reading of India and shows the complex techniques the novel employs.

In 2000, Rushdie moved to New York and published the novel *Fury* which is set in New York. This novel and the earlier *The Ground Beneath Her Feet* (1999) signify a change of location for Rushdie's fiction, and in Chapter 12 in this volume, Anshuman Mondal discusses the significance of this change. After the September 11 attack on the World Trade Center in New York, which happened just before the publication of *Fury*, Rushdie took a pronounced pro-United States government position in support of 'the War on Terror', and this is evident in the essays and columns he has collected in *Step Across this Line* (2002). He has retreated from this support to some extent,[17] but his self-positioning on this issue opens up in an interesting way the subject with which this Introduction began, the location of 'home'.

In 2005, Rushdie published *Shalimar the Clown*, a novel in which the Indian sub-continent, with Kashmir as a central political event, features prominently, returning his writing to the location primarily associated with him. Clearly there are many more twists and turns to come from this writer, and it is too soon yet to be definitive about recent developments in his work.

This *Companion to Salman Rushdie* is organised in two parts. Part I contains four chapters on important themes of context necessary to reading Rushdie's work: Vijay Mishra on the influence of Indian popular cinema, Peter Morey on the English tradition in Rushdie's writing, Ruvani Ranasinha on the consequences of the *fatwa* and Amina Yaqin on the significance of gender and family. Part II studies the texts and offers readings of all the fictional texts available in volume form, except for *Shalimar the Clown*.[18] There are references to Rushdie's non-fictional writing throughout the book, and for the interested reader there is an extensive bibliography of further reading.[19]

NOTES

1 Salman Rushdie, 'Imaginary Homelands', *Imaginary Homelands* (London: Granta, 1991, 1992), p. 9.
2 Rushdie, 'Introduction', *Imaginary Homelands*, p. 1.
3 Rushdie, 'The Riddle of Midnight', *Imaginary Homelands* (1991), p. 26.
4 Salman Rushdie, *Midnight's Children* (London: Jonathan Cape, 1981), p. 153.

5 Rushdie, ' "Errata": or, Unreliable Narration in *Midnight's Children*', *Imaginary Homelands* (1991), p. 23.

6 Salman Rushdie, *The Satanic Verses* (London: Viking, 1988), p. 44.

7 See Chapter 9 in this volume, Joel Kuortti, '*The Satanic Verses*: "To be born again, first you have to die" ', for a discussion of the sources of the story of the verses.

8 Rushdie, 'Introduction', *Imaginary Homelands* (1991), p. 1. *Grimus* was the winner of the Victor Gollancz Science Fiction Prize, and the prize was its publication. The novel's editor at Gollancz was Liz Calder, who later moved to Jonathan Cape, and whom Rushdie followed there with *Midnight's Children* and later *Shame*. Liz Calder went on to found the independent publisher Bloomsbury.

9 Catherine Cundy, *Salman Rushdie* (Manchester: Manchester University Press, 1996), p. 12.

10 The birds' quest in Attar's poem is for their ruler Simurg, a sufi conceit for God, and Grimus is, of course, an anagram of this name.

11 Rushdie, *Shame* (London: Jonathan Cape, 1983), p. 28.

12 Aijaz Ahmad, *In Theory: Classes, Nations, Literatures* (London: Verso, 1992), pp. 123–58.

13 The narrator of *Shame* says: 'Although I have known Pakistan for a long time, I have never lived there for longer than six months at a stretch' (p. 69).

14 The high drama played out by these two figures is too well known to be repeated here. For some discussion of the feud see Chapter 5 in this volume, Amina Yaqin, 'Family and gender in Rushdie's writing' (pp. 61–74).

15 For a detailed discussion of Rushdie's women in *Shame*, see Ahmad, *In Theory* (1992), pp. 139–52.

16 Rushdie, 'Why I have Embraced Islam', *Imaginary Homelands* (1991), pp. 430–2.

17 For example, on 8 November 2005, he participated in the protests against the detention centre at Guantanamo Bay, where 'terror' suspects are held and tortured, and in April 2005, he criticised President Bush for his failure to engage with 'the international community' in pursuit of 'the War on Terror'.

18 Rushdie has also written a story 'The Firebird's Nest', which appeared in *The New Yorker*, 23 and 30 June 1997, pp. 122–7. The story is also published in a special limited edition (Las Vegas, Nev.: Rainmaker Editions, 2004), and is reportedly to be made into a film scripted by Rushdie himself with his wife in the leading female role.

19 I am grateful to Florian Stadtler, who compiled the chronology and the bibliography.

PART I

Themes and issues

2

VIJAY MISHRA

Rushdie and Bollywood cinema

'nobody from Bombay should be without a basic film vocabulary'
Midnight's Children[1]

I

Any study of Rushdie remains incomplete, indeed deficient, if not seen through the literature of migration and cinema. To read Rushdie through these – demographic shift and artistic form – simply means that we are more likely to get our understanding of him right than if we do not. The fact of diaspora, of the trauma of migration, explains many facets of Rushdie's reading of culture: his emphasis on the mongrelisation of our lives, delight in the chutnification of history, and importance given to the moment when 'newness' enters the world. Indeed, some, like Timothy Brennan, have found Rushdie's anti-nationalist, non-foundational reading of the nation state particularly prescient.[2] The fact of cinema explains a number of matters of representation in the Rushdie corpus which without an understanding of cinema would be lost. Given the brief of this chapter, though, we may want to set aside the theme of migration and diaspora, referring to it only in as much as it impinges on our reading of Rushdie's engagement with cinema, in particular Bollywood/Bombay cinema.

When Rushdie writes about Indian urban culture as a culture 'full of fakery and gaudiness and superficiality and failed imaginations' but also full of 'high vitality, linguistic verve'[3] and metropolitan excitement, he reads Indian urban culture through the eyes of his beloved Bombay and its dominant art form, the Bollywood cinema. The homage to Bombay and its cinema began early as is evident from Rushdie's tribute to *The Wizard of Oz*.[4] We note that Rushdie saw the film at the Metro Cinema in 1957 at the age of ten, a crucial age at which he also saw, as it seems from his novels, two Bollywood films which had a decisive influence on him: *Shree 420* ('Mr 420', 1955) and *Funtoosh* ('The Madhatter', 1956). Metro Cinema, now decrepit, is at the corner of First Marine Street (Anandilal Podar Marg) and the Esplanade (Mahatma Gandhi Road), next to Cinema Lane and not too far away from the Dhobi Talao area. The child of ten experiencing this classic Hollywood fantasy may have been ignorant of foreign countries and 'about growing up' but he came with a better understanding of the 'cinema of the fantastic than any Western child of the same age'.[5] Rushdie was a Bombay boy and like any other Bombay boy, regardless of class, he knew his Bollywood, a cinema in which fantasy figures prominently. He confesses that it is easy to satirise Bollywood, but then he continues: 'gods descending from the heavens to meddle in human affairs, supermen, magic potions, superheroes, demonic villains and so on have always been the staple diet of the Indian filmgoer'.[6] The fantasies of Bollywood were forever lodged in the young child and films, beyond *Shree 420* and *Funtoosh*, which the young Rushdie would have found appealing around the time he saw *The Wizard of Oz* would have included *Baghdad Ka Chor* ('The Thief of Baghdad', 1955), *Jungle Ka Jadoo* ('The Magic Forest', 1955), *Udan Khatola* ('The Aeroplane', 1955), *Hatimtai* (1956), *Mother India* (1957), *Patal Pari* ('The Underworld Fairy', 1957), *Tumsa Nahin Dekha* ('There's No One Like You', 1957), *Alladin Ka Chirag* ('Aladdin's Lamp', 1958) and *Chalti Ka Naam Gadi* ('When the Jalopy is King', 1958). Except for two, these were all black-and-white movies. Rushdie notes this fact and recalls the impact the one-reel colour sequence – the suggestively defiant dance of Anarkali in Emperor Akbar's court – in the film *Mughal-e-Azam* (1960) had on the audience. K. Asif, the maker of the film, had intended to make his epic, like the other epic, Mehboob Khan's *Mother India* (1957), in colour but could not because of financial constraints. The film itself took a full seven or eight years to complete. So what is given colour is not a battle scene or a formal state occasion but the dance of the courtesan, the dance that connects directly with male spectatorial desire. When Rushdie returns to this film in his novels, it is invariably to invoke the allure of Anarkali, to suggest that great moments of history are in fact moments of passion, of love, of desire unrequited and entombed.

I pause to take in two films already mentioned – *Shree 420* and *Funtoosh* – since they are films whose magic is singularly felt in the Rushdie corpus. Both these films rework the picaro hero towards a distinctly Indian cosmopolitanism. In *Shree 420*, the simpleton traveller on the road saves a city's underclass from exploitation and transfers a term applied to absconders and cheats ('Mr 420') to a city as a whole. The second film, *Funtoosh*, touches on the fine line dividing the sane from the insane, the real from the magical. A man called Ramlal 'Funtoosh', the latter an attribute rather than a name, insane due to a personal trauma, is located in an 'International Madhouse'. In the establishing shots the inhabitants of this madhouse are from all over the world (poetic licence is necessary here for the spectator), and the man to be released, our Funtoosh, will now carry this cosmopolitanism. His story will be written down by an out-of-work writer; his life will be transformed into an item to be insured and from which profit may accrue should he, in his madness, decide to die. Funtoosh, of course, escapes all attempts at suicide at the behest of a shady industrialist who had insured him and made himself the sole benefactor. He manages to win the heart of the industrialist's daughter, and drives the industrialist himself insane as he in turn ends up in the International Madhouse. Although the use of the word 'funtoosh' in *Midnight's Children* implies that a person is 'finished, washed-up, or in our own expressive word, funtoosh'[7] (which is not its meaning in the film from which the word is derived), the narrative of the film and its style shadow Rushdie's writings and indeed provide an insight into the ways in which Rushdie indigenises the western picaro.

2

'Bollywood' has finally made it into the *Oxford English Dictionary*. The 2005 edition defines it as: 'a name for the Indian popular film industry, based in Bombay. Origin 1970s. Blend of Bombay and Hollywood.' The acceptance of the word by the *OED* is certainly a plus for Bollywood which between 1931, when the first talkie was made in India, and 2006 had produced some 10,000 films (which must not be confused with the output of Indian cinema generally, which would be five times more). What is less evident is the way in which the word has acquired its current meaning and has now displaced the earlier descriptors (Bombay Cinema, Indian Popular Cinema, Hindi cinema) functioning, horrifyingly perhaps, as an 'empty signifier' that may be used for any particularist reading of popular Indian cinema. The triumph of the word is nothing less than spectacular, and although Indians continue to feel uneasy with it (the vernacular press came around to using it very reluctantly) its ascendancy has been such that *Bombay Dreams*, the Andrew Lloyd Webber musical, finds its match in the home-grown *Merchants of Bollywood*.

The best critic of Indian cinema, Ashish Rajadhyaksha, suggests that the word first appeared as a joke in the journal *Screen* on its 'Bollywood Beat' page, with the 'companion words Tollywood for the Calcutta film industry based in Tollygunge and even, for a while, Mollywood for the Madras industry'.[8] The reference to 'Tollygunge'/'Tollywood' is an interesting one and may well point to a more local origin of the term 'Bollywood' itself and one that may de-link its usage from a more generalist reading of it as a signifier of a much larger process of globalisation. On this point the highly original film critic Madhava Prasad located the first usage of 'Tollywood' in a telegram that Wilford E. Deming, an American working on films, received as he was about to leave India: 'Tollywood sends best wishes happy new year to Lubill film ...'.[9]

Rajadhyaksha distinguishes between the political economy of the Indian popular cinema based in Mumbai/Bombay and the hype around it. This hype has led to a real confusion between 'Bollywood' as a fad, a taste, an Indian exotica, and 'Bollywood' as a global phenomenon in the way in which say the Beatles and Hollywood are. The hype and the confusion is most noticeable in generalist magazines such as *Newsweek* and *Time* which tend to celebrate Bollywood as a pervasive, global form, based on the sometimes exaggerated claims of both film producers and critics alike.[10]

Against the *OED* definition, which links Bollywood with popular Indian cinema produced in Mumbai, Bollywood actually functions as something more. Although cinema is central to its definition, Bollywood is, as Rajadhyaksha says, 'a more diffuse cultural conglomeration involving a range of distribution and consumption activities from websites to music cassettes, from cable to radio'.[11] The film industry may well be a small part of this culture which is, as Bombay cinema, much older than Bollywood, going back as it does to the 1930s and, if one has to be fastidious, even to Phalke's first silent movie in Hindi, *Raja Harishchandra* (1913). In this reading Bollywood, as distinct from Bombay cinema, is very much an early 1990s phenomenon and hence just over a decade old. 'The term today refers to a reasonably specific narrative and a mode of representation', writes Rajadhyaksha (p. 28). Its features, some of which are not as new as they are made out to be, include love stories couched in family values and presented as staged musicals; stories that do not unsettle cultural presumptions (inter-caste or inter-religious marriage); representations that are framed within Hindu iconography; a form that fetishises high tech values; a cinema whose target audience is increasingly the Indian diaspora.

Rushdie's own writings acquire added meaning when we recognise that they began as Bollywood made inroads into the late modern Indian diaspora increasingly located in Europe and in white settler nations. This new global diaspora turned to Bollywood for a commodified 'feel-good' version of their own culture and began to provide 'more than 60 percent of overseas revenues' for it.[12] By the 1990s, Bollywood cinema had become such an indispensable cultural form in the lives of the global Indian diaspora that British mainstream weeklies such as *Time Out* began to carry news about Bollywood cinema. Diasporic cultural productions such as plays, films and music in dance halls too paid direct homage to Bollywood. So when the Indian diaspora began to intervene in British cultural productions with an eye to its own distinctive artistic traditions, Bollywood became the indispensable form to imitate (as in Mira Nair's *Monsoon Wedding*), parody (Kaizad Gustad's *Bombay Boys*), deconstruct (Gurinder Chadha's *Bhaji on the Beach*), creatively re-write (Gurinder Chadha's *Bride and Prejudice*) or simply imitate (Tamasha Theatre Company's *Fourteen Songs, Two Weddings and a Funeral* based on the 1994 Bollywood film *Hum Aap ke Hain Koun*). Listening to the latter musical with the original Bollywood film in mind, parallel texts emerge but also an awareness of a sense of a slight dissonance, because the original can never be adequately replaced. The original remains the sign of the lost homeland that in the end defies complete reclamation. As Rushdie presciently observed: 'we will not be capable of reclaiming precisely the thing that was lost'.[13] With Andrew Lloyd Webber's *Bombay Dreams*, which began at Apollo Victoria in 2002 after *Starlight Express* ended its eighteen-year run there, a diaspora fetish (Bollywood cinema) has found a different, mainstream translation. Here the procedures are similar to those adopted by Tamasha but the audience is cross-cultural, which was not the case with *Fourteen Songs* where the audience were all Bollywood cinema buffs. In *Bombay Dreams*, the art form that has the highest currency in the Indian diaspora is repackaged for a much wider audience because the form itself is seen as another element in Western aesthetic modernity: for Western culture always adapts artistic forms on the ascendant, and in so doing liberates art from generic exhaustion.

How and why Bollywood is to so many a signifier of the cultural logic of Indian modernity are questions whose answers may be discovered in the Rushdie corpus. For what Rushdie did was to read Bombay cinema as 'Bollywood' (which as we have seen is more than just Bombay cinema) even before it acquired that meaning. In his treatment, Bombay cinema was both film and a particular logic of culture. It was, finally, a form that mediated how Indians, both homeland and diaspora, read quotidian life.

3

'Nobody from Bombay should be without a basic film vocabulary', Saleem Sinai had declared as he narrated his story in *Midnight's Children*. And all Rashid had to do as the teller of tales in *Haroun and the Sea of Stories* was to 'part his lips in a plump red smile and out would pop some brand-new saga, complete with sorcery, love-interest, princesses, wicked uncles, fat aunts, moustachioed gangsters in yellow check pants, fantastic locations, cowards, heroes, fights, and half a dozen catchy, hummable tunes'.[14]

So both in terms of controlling narrative structure and representation, Bombay cinema, 'that raddled old tart',[15] invades the Rushdie text.

In *Midnight's Children* Saleem Sinai confesses, 'I accept my life has taken on, yet again, the tone of a Bombay talkie'[16] because like many Bollywood films, he too has a double in Shiva. If we believe Saleem, albeit only on this point, we begin to understand why Bollywood is so pervasive. Two features in particular of this cinematic practice come across powerfully in Rushdie's first major novel: the synchronicity of the form (the Bombay film makes sense regardless of when you enter it as a spectator/viewer), and its generic capaciousness. In Rushdie, cinema functions as *the* aesthetic of India, as the dominant cultural form of the country. India is recalled through it and its mode of representation mediates the diaspora's understanding of India. At times in *Midnight's Children*, direct stylistic connections are made between film and novel: at one point, for instance, 'a Bombay-talkie-style close-up' is inserted.[17] What is the Bombay-talkie-style close-up? One suspects the style refers to the way in which the camera focuses on the face of the actor, lingers on her for a while, absorbs her look, and then cuts to a flower or a gushing waterfall. The montage technique referred to here is a predictable form, since the cuts to the natural object are always thoroughly systemic and capture, in segmental shots often, the juxtaposition of images that one finds in Indian calendar and related art, including their chromolithograph forerunner. In a massive metaphorical conceit (which, after Dr Johnson, is the violent yoking of disparate images together) for which Rushdie is famous, we are told it was in Homi Catrack's film *The Lovers of Kashmir* that the famous 'indirect kiss'[18] was introduced to Indian cinema. The indirect kiss is a special use of montage where a cinematic cut to flowers or birds or a half-eaten apple just before the lovers' lips meet is meant to indicate the actual kiss that has taken place but which the spectator is forbidden to see. In this way Rushdie brings to his writing, indeed to his representational apparatus (for this is what the novel has to do), a discourse that connects directly with this cultural form. The link between Rushdie's narrative discourse and the Bollywood film semiotic becomes clearer when we look at the manner in which the reference to the indirect kiss is built into a playful mode of narration:

> In those days it was not permitted for lover-boys and their leading ladies to touch one another on screen, for fear that their osculations might corrupt the nation's youth ... but thirty-three minutes after the beginning of *The Lovers*, the premiere audience began to give off a low buzz of shock, because Pia and Nayyar [the lover-boy] had begun to kiss – not one another – but *things*.
>
> Pia kissed an apple, sensuously, with all the rich fullness of her painted lips; then passed it to Nayyar; who planted, upon its opposite face, a virilely passionate mouth. This was the birth of what came to be known as the indirect kiss –[19]

and thereby dishonestly induces the person deceived to deliver any property to any person, or to make, alter or destroy the whole or any part of a valuable security, or anything which is signed or sealed, and which is capable of being converted into a valuable security, shall be punished with imprisonment ...'[27] Section 420 has come to be associated with petty cheats and small-scale frauds but also with people who may simply abscond with other people's belongings, or even an unreliable person. Its use in Raj Kapoor's film as a description of both the hero and the city of Bombay brings both people and the city together: one of the early scenes of the film is a road sign which reads 'Bombay 420', which may be read as defining Bombay or as indicating that Bombay is 420 miles away. Of course, the whole point of the film is that through the love of the innocent Vidya, the hero quickly learns to distinguish between the urban 'villainy of politicians and businessmen'[28] and the hero's own personal desire to be successful in the city. Raj Kapoor's *Shree 420* was released in 1955 and, as we have already suggested, it is one of two films of the period (the other being *Funtoosh*) that Rushdie probably saw at the age of ten. We may also want to note that *Shree 420* is the first Bollywood film that he can fully recall, and one with which he reads Bombay, the magical metropolis of his novels. The film, along with *Funtoosh*, after all, are very much films about Bombay, its streets, its buildings, its underworld, its colonial definition of a unit of labour by 'time-in' and 'time-out' clocks, and so on.

If Gibreel Farishta's initial entry into the novel is heralded through a song (a song which is also heard in Mira Nair's *Mississippi Masala* as a kind of diasporic homage to both Raj Kapoor and Salman Rushdie), the character himself is coded through the lives of N. T. Rama Rao, a successful actor in mythologicals, and Amitabh Bachchan, arguably Indian cinema's most endurable actor and a towering figure since the mid-1970s. The latter's near death on the sets of *Coolie* (1983) is transformed into Gibreel's own collapse at the hands of the stunt-man Eustace Brown. Rushdie writes:

> The whole of India was at Gibreel's bedside. His condition was the lead item on every radio bulletin, it was the subject of hourly news-flashes on the national television network ... The Prime Minister cancelled her appointments and flew to visit him. Her son the airline pilot sat in Farishta's bedroom, holding the actor's hand. A mood of apprehension settled over the nation, because if God had unleashed such an act of retribution against his most celebrated incarnation, what had he in store for the rest of the country? If Gibreel dies, could India be far behind.[29]

The passage ends with an echo of Percy Shelley's concluding line in 'Ode to the West Wind': 'If Winter comes, can Spring be far behind?'. There is hope in Shelley; in Rushdie there is despair, or at any rate ironic despair, for the nation is rendered in terms of a film star whose near fatal illness brought the nation itself close to death. The logic of the 'serpent' announcing, metaphorically, the death of a nation during *The Lovers of Kashmir* is repeated as the actor's life itself becomes theatre. The 'real' gets theorised through fiction, the latter informing the former, changing the normal hierarchy of archive and commentary. For, as the novel proceeds, it is Farishta, the Mr 420, the fabulist, who dreams the text of Islam, reprojecting belief as desire, rendering the archive indirectly as if it were the kiss of the lovers of Kashmir.

'Why be afraid of love?' sings Anarkali in the film *Mughal-e-Azam*, which, along with *Shree 420* and *Funtoosh* has a very special place in the Rushdie corpus.[30] This film, and its earlier prototype, the artistically more unified *Anarkali* (1953), find their way into *The Satanic Verses*. Gibreel, walking through the city streets, recalls songs sung by Rekha Merchant (modelled on the 1970s and 1980s Bollywood megastar Rekha):

> Rekha ... serenaded him with the sweetest of love songs ... singing everything from the gazals of Faiz Ahmed Faiz to the best old film music, such as the defiant air sung by the dancer Anarkali in the presence of the Grand Mughal Akbar in the fifties classic *Mughal-e-Azam*, – in which she declares and exults in her impossible, forbidden love for the Prince, Salim, – 'Pyaar kiya to darna kya?' – That is to say, more or less, *why be afraid of love?*[31]

K. Asif's *Mughal-e-Azam* (1960) is one of the two great film epics of India, the other being Mehboob Khan's *Mother India* (1957). It is a story about Salim (Jehangir), Emperor Akbar's son, and his love for the dancing girl Anarkali, in the legend a daughter of a courtesan. The story had been made into films before: a silent version in 1928, versions with sound in 1935 and 1953, with the 1953 film setting the standard for songs that K. Asif followed. The 1953 *Anarkali* remained true to the legend as Anarkali is entombed alive. It also had the haunting song *Ye zindagi usi ki hai jo kisi ka ho gaya/pyaar hi me kho gaya* ('Life is for those who love; who lose themselves in it') sung by Lata Mangeshkar, the voice heard on All India Radio in *Midnight's Children*.[32] The K. Asif version transforms this song, which is a private, somewhat melancholic paean, into a song of defiance sung in Akbar's court in the presence of both the Emperor and his son. The song marks the transition from accommodation of youthful enthusiasm on the part of Salim to the latter picking up the defiant challenge in the song and transforming it into an act of disloyalty towards the Emperor as Salim takes arms against his father. All this adds to the drama. But the K. Asif version also parts company with the legend and the earlier filmic versions on another crucial point. It overcodes the text with the principle of righteousness or dharma; it transforms, on this point, Akbar into the father of the God Rama, Dasaratha, who too had declared in the *Ramayana* that truth and his word were more important than political expediency. And so in this version of the story, Anarkali is entombed, but a hidden sub-terranean passage enables the Emperor to save her life and give Anarkali, alive, to her mother. The law of dharma has to be followed because it was Anarkali's mother who had brought the Emperor news of the birth of Salim, a son that he had yearned for but who came his way only after years of religious penance. Upon receiving this news the Emperor had, in an unguarded moment, declared, 'Woman you bring wonderful tiding, here is my royal ring, ask of me whatever you wish and it shall be granted.' The mother of Anarkali did not ask then, but she does just before Anarkali is taken away to be entombed.

For Rushdie, the story acts as a cinematic spectacle, as an evanescent moment that reminds him of the special syncretic quality of Indian culture, the triumph of multiplicity over oneness. As a text about diaspora and migration interwoven into the narrative of the arrival of a great world religion which chose the law of austere oneness over the many, *The Satanic Verses* uses cinema as a means of imparting an alternative, parallel narra-tive of cosmopolitanism. In that narrative the discourse of Bollywood brings an erstwhile vision before fundamentalism began to shake India's liberal democratic and philosophically open culture.[33]

In Rushdie's next major novel after *The Satanic Verses*, *The Moor's Last Sigh* (1995), his interest in films (now available to him only on video and not in public theatres because of the Iranian *fatwa*) is extended and the references to them brought forward to the early 1990s. The novel also takes up references, at times fictitious, to films in his earlier works as a means of conflating the real with the postmodern hyperreal. The ubiquitous *Gai-wallah*, transformed into an ongoing conceit, resurfaces: 'cinemas [are] showing the widescreen remake of the old classic Gai-Wallah'.[34] Two things strike us: the first is the word 'remake' which clearly situates *The Moor's Last Sigh* (at this moment in the narrative) at a time closer to our own; the second is that there has been a technological advance. The old classic was probably a black and white 35mm film. The new version is widescreen and therefore in colour. The use of cinematic moments as part of the novel's *histoire* is a powerful endorsement of the enormous cultural significance of Bollywood, especially if we also read this to mean that life in India is indeed measured by dates of particular films. Cinema therefore acts as a marker of history, providing the reader with implicit dates. So a *Shree 420* song places the narration after 1955 but also suggests that the character at that juncture in the narrative would have seen the film. The same relationship is underlined by Sammy 'Tin Man' Hazaré's rendition of a song as he holds the photo of Nadia Wadia (the Australian Mary Evans who played lead roles in many of Homi Wadia's action movies in the 1940s and 1950s under the film name of Nadia). He sings Madhuri Dixit's *Khalnayak* (1991) song: '*What is under my choli? ... What is under my blouse?*'[35] The song was a breakaway hit both in India and in the diaspora.

The more sustained use of cinema in *The Moor's Last Sigh*, however, has a different aesthetic motive. The magical narratives of Indian cinema, captured in all their gaudiness and excess in films like *Mr India* (1987), become entry points into the competitive claims of magic and realism in the novel itself. Although in describing *Mr India*, the narrator doesn't spare the film from being subjected to a critical idiom of irony, the engagement with this film suggests that for Rushdie it is films like *Mr India* that carry the real deconstructive capacities of art, and through the popular 'provide us with an image of the National father after all ... In Mr India's struggle against Mogambo I recognize the life-and-death oppositions of many movie fathers and sons.'[36]

The debate between realist and magical texts gets a deeper focus when Rushdie considers the humane values that the Bengali realist film-maker Sukumar Sen (Satyajit Ray) brings to Indian cinema. His achievement is seen to be the only one on a par with that of the painter Aurora da Gama, the key female character of the novel. It is clear, though, that Aurora's own realism, the aesthetic demanded by the nationalist 'spirit of the age' as the narrator suggests, was of a different order for she secretly preferred those series of films by Sen 'in which fish talked, carpets flew and young boys dreamed of previous incarnations in fortresses of gold'.[37]

Aurora da Gama's 'instinctive dislike for the purely mimetic' which 'turned her back towards the epic-fabulist manner'[38] is also the author Rushdie's own preference in the battle between Bollywood and the realists. Abraham Zogoiby, in fact, admonishes Aurora's flirtation with 'naturalism' with a clear reference to those Bombay films that were more realistic:

> Will you spend your life painting boot-polish boys [*Boot Polish*, 1954] and air-hostesses and two-acres of land [*Do Bigha Zamin*, 1953]?[39]

The narrator's/Rushdie's sympathies clearly lie with Abraham Zogoiby for to him too 'life [was] fantastic'[40] and 'realism confused him'.[41] The genre of Bombay cinema – as ' "Epico-Mythico-Tragico-Comico-Super-Sexy-High-Masala-Art" '[42] – invades the Rushdie text as the magical genre of Indian modernity.

A key cinematic trope that *The Moor's Last Sigh* returns to is 'Mother-ness' as the 'big idea in India'.[43] To make his case the narrator, Moor

Zogoiby, begins by connecting the canonical Bombay cinema text, *Mother India*, with the year of his own birth (1957).[44]

> The year I was born, Mehboob Productions' all-conquering movie *Mother India* – three years in the making, three hundred shooting days, in the top three all-time mega-grossing Bollywood flicks – hit the nation's screens.[45]

The towering figure in this film, which is also a response to Katherine Mayo's antagonistic but immensely influential critique of Hindu casteism in her book *Mother India* (1927), is, of course, Nargis who played the part of Mother India in the film:

> And as for its leading lady – O Nargis with your shovel over your shoulders and your strand of black hair tumbling forward over your brow! – she became, until Indira-Mata supplanted her, the living mother-goddess of us all.[46]

Aurora da Gama's interest in Nargis, however, is more personal. She knew her, of course, but couldn't quite understand how she could have married her own son, the actor Sunil Dutt who played the role of Birju, Mother India's younger son in the film: 'And now look – you have gone and marry-o'ed him!'[47]

Beyond asserting the cultural valency of a canonical Bollywood film, Rushdie uses *Mother India* as the intertext for 'Moor' Zogoiby's own rebellion against his mother Aurora. And in so far as the real life relationship of Nargis and Sunil Dutt shadows the mother–son fictive relationship in the film, this composite text of actor, wife and mother shapes the world of Rushdie's 'Moor' Zogoiby as well. Recounting the episode, 'Moor' Zogoiby also establishes two further connecting threads. First, that like the husband of Mother India in the film, who is made symbolically impotent because his arms are crushed by a rock, his own father too may have become impotent. Second, Birju's desire for his mother in the film may be 'Moor' Zogoiby's own: 'I have been keeping my secret for too long', he says.[48]

4

What the characters say about each other is perhaps not as important as the way in which Bollywood cinema is actually deployed by Rushdie toward a postmodern aesthetic. In collapsing the real with the virtualité of cinema we get not only the collapse of the real/nonreal divide but also the 'device' of characters walking out of their filmic frames. In this sense Rushdie's fiction shows the complex ways in which stars operate in and out of cinema. As an instance of creative appropriation of this cinematic practice, my point is that the Rushdie aesthetic uses the archive of Bollywood to negotiate India itself. What is significant is that there is a cinematic point-of-view, a cinematic organisation of the magical, of hybrid lives, that Rushdie uses for his own project.

Whether as a huge conceit or as kitsch, Bollywood tends to serve post-modernist ends for Salman Rushdie. Cinema functions as a text within a text and cinematic characters enter into the body of his works. Rushdie raises important questions about the role of the spectator in an artistic form that constantly deconstructs the principle of the gaze and its unproblematic consumption by the spectator. Rushdie's spectator here is often the dia-sporic spectator for whom, along with defamiliarisation and critical coding, comes voyeuristic pleasure and consumption. In Rushdie's postmodern poetics, Bollywood is both an evanescent presence and a structural refer-ence point as well as, for the diasporic reader, an empowering mode of corporeal identification and self-representation. What Rushdie anticipates is the current redefinition of Bollywood as something more than a con-venient term that unproblematically displaces Hindi/Bombay Cinema. Bollywood is in fact a way of thinking through a cultural shift directly linked to Indian (post)modernity. Bollywood, for Rushdie, is like an empty signifier into which is poured a number of things: diasporic idioms and cultural practices, the English language which, as the universal tongue of cyberculture, will gradually strip the genre of its historicity and Indian-specific foundations, and a growing cosmopolitanism. Bollywood then is integral to Rushdie's style, both as source of discourse and of genre. In its generic openness Bollywood, recalling the great epic texts, claims that what is not there is nowhere else to be found. The Rushdie corpus insinuates a similar capaciousness.

NOTES

1 Salman Rushdie, *Midnight's Children* (First published London: Jonathan Cape, 1981; all page references will be to the Picador edition, 1982), p. 33.
2 Timothy Brennan, *Salman Rushdie and the Third World* (New York: St Martins Press, 1989).
3 Salman Rushdie, *Imaginary Homelands* (London: Granta, 1991, 1992), p. 110.
4 Salman Rushdie, *The Wizard of Oz* (London: British Film Institute, 1992).
5 *Ibid.*, p. 11.
6 *Ibid.*, p. 11.
7 Rushdie, *Midnight's Children*, p. 64.
8 Ashish Rajadhyaksha, 'The "Bollywoodization" of the Indian Cinema: Cultural Nationalism in a Global Arena', *Inter-Asia Cultural Studies* 28 (2003), pp. 25–39.
9 M. Madhava Prasad, 'The Name of a Desire: Why They Call It Bollywood', *Unsettling Cinema. A Symposium on the Place of Cinema in India*, Issue 525 (May 2003). www.india-seminar.com/2003/525

10 The producer of the Bollywood film *Taal* (1999) in fact declared that this film would be noted by the 'whole world' (Rajadhyaksha, 'The "Bollywoodization" of the Indian Cinema', p. 26). For a few days this seemed like being the case as in the first three days of its release, over the weekend of 13–15 August 1999, the film raked in $591,280 making it, in those few days, among the top ten films in the American market.

11 Rajadhyaksha, 'The "Bollywoodization" of the Indian Cinema', p. 27. In the pages of the *Sydney Sun Herald* (11 September 2005, S34) the pop culture journalist Clara Laccarino uses Bollywood in a number of ways: Bollywood fever, Bollywood industry, Bollywood bonanza, 'hot'n'spicy Bollywood fever', a Bollywood fix, Bollywood shakedown, Bollywood romp, Bollywood breaks, Bollywood dancing, Bollywood calendar. And there is of course Planet Bollywood, the restaurant.

12 Suketu Mehta, *Maximum City: Bombay Lost and Found* (New York: Alfred A. Knopf, 2004), p. 57.

13 Salman Rushdie, 'Imaginary Homelands', in *Imaginary Homelands*, p. 10.

14 Salman Rushdie, *Haroun and the Sea of Stories* (London: Granta, 1990), pp. 16–17.

15 Salman Rushdie, *The Moor's Last Sigh* (First published London: Jonathan Cape, 1995; all references to the Vintage edition, 1996), p. 173.

16 Rushdie, *Midnight's Children*, p. 350.

17 *Ibid.*, p. 346.

18 *Ibid.*, p. 142. In Subhash Ghai's *Taal* (1999) the indirect kiss takes the form of lovers sipping Coca-Cola from the same straw, and then drinking from the same bottle. The indirect kiss is alive and well in Bollywood.

19 Rushdie, *Midnight's Children*, p. 142.

20 *Ibid.*, p. 143.

21 *Ibid.*, pp. 32–3.

22 Sergei Eisenstein, *The Film Sense*, trans and ed. Jay Leyda (London: Faber and Faber, 1968), pp. 55–6.

23 Rushdie, *Midnight's Children*, p. 36.

24 *Ibid.*, p. 49.

25 Salman Rushdie, *Shame* (London: Jonathan Cape, 1983), p. 62.

26 Rushdie, *Midnight's Children*, p. 216.

27 Quoted in Srinivas Aravamudan, 'Being God's Postman Is No Fun, Yaar: Salman Rushdie's *The Satanic Verses*', *Diacritics* 19 (1989), pp. 3–20; this citation p. 7.

28 Aravamudan, 'Being God's Postman', 7.

29 Salman Rushdie, *The Satanic Verses* (London: Viking, 1988), pp. 28–9.

30 See also M. G. Vassanji, *The Book of Secrets* (Toronto: McClelland and Stewart, 1994) where the Anarkali story is again part of the fabric of the novel.

31 Rushdie, *The Satanic Verses*, p. 334.

32 Rushdie, *Midnight's Children*, p. 70.

33 See also Salman Rushdie, *Shalimar the Clown* (London: Jonathan Cape), 2005, p. 132 where Boonyi Kaul Noman (or Mrs Shalimar the Clown) performs 'the dance number from *Anarkali*, a new play devised by the group after the immense success of the film *Mughal-e-Azam*'. Later Shalimar, the actor, proposes that the Anarkali play should be reworked to show the dancing woman as a

Vietnamese peasant woman bricked up in her wall by American soldiers (p. 231). This, Shalimar felt, would be readily seen as an allegory of India's treatment of Kashmir/Anarkali.

34 Rushdie, *The Moor's Last Sigh*, p. 374.

35 *Ibid.*, p. 357.

36 *Ibid.*, pp. 168–9.

37 *Ibid.*, p. 173.

38 *Ibid.*, p. 174.

39 *Ibid.*, p. 174.

40 *Ibid.*, p. 174.

41 *Ibid.*, p. 175.

42 *Ibid.*, pp. 148–9.

43 *Ibid.*, p. 137.

44 Released during Diwali week, October 1957, *Mother India*, directed by Mehboob Khan (1909–74), son of a Gujarati policeman with strong agrarian roots, ran for a whole year at Liberty Cinema, Bombay. It received rave reviews in key film journals such as *Filmfare* and *Filmindia* and in *Bharat Jyoti* and went on to become the Bollywood film dubbed and subtitled more than any other. The usually acerbic Baburao Patel noted in his *Filmindia* review '[*Mother India*] is the greatest picture produced in India during the forty odd years of film-making', to which he also added in a later paragraph 'Remove Nargis and there is no *Mother India*.' See Bunny Reuben, *Mehboob … India's DeMille* (New Delhi: HarperCollins, 1999), pp. 261–8.

45 Rushdie, *The Moor's Last Sigh*, p. 137.

46 *Ibid.*, p. 137.

47 *Ibid.*, p. 137.

48 *Ibid.*, p. 139.

3

PETER MOREY

Salman Rushdie and the English tradition

At the turn of the millennium, Salman Rushdie left London, his home for the previous thirty years, for New York, declaring the English literary scene to be bitchy, insular and smug. The move was portrayed in some quarters as a desertion of the country that had sheltered him during the dark years of the Ayatollah Khomeini's *fatwa*, with the popular press particularly acerbic in some of its comments. Even the liberal broadsheet newspaper the *Guardian* joined the personalised attacks, merging Rushdie's complex private life with the plot of his ill-received 2001 novel *Fury* in a spoof 'condensed account' of the novel: 'Self-regarding fiftysomething man dumps his wife, moves to New York, meets the most beautiful woman in the world and writes about it.'[1]

As the latest in a long line of controversies accompanying the author, the storm over Rushdie's relocation might serve as anecdotal evidence of the fraught relationship between the writer and the British cultural establishment, and as an instance of the inherent difficulty of placing Rushdie in relation to Britishness in general, and the English literary tradition in particular. Moreover, attempting to characterise 'the English tradition' itself is an exercise beset with snares. Looking back into the recent history of literary criticism the picture appears to have been clearer, at least to cultural conservatives. Writing in an essay entitled, 'The Englishness of the English Novel' (1981), Q. D. Leavis – with enviable certainty – described an 'instinctive national preference' leading to a 'demand on creative writers for inwardness, understanding, and the Shakespearian "fullness of life"': something which was, for her, attainable only when English authors chose 'to write from their roots'.[2] With its attendant emphasis on social and individual particularity, realism and psychological interiority, Leavis's co-ordinates of English writing marry the task of moral education with the philosophical tenets of empiricism, valorising sensory experience above theories and clarity above style. However, with its dependence on the notion of roots, her prognosis might not be expected to be as congenial to a writer like Rushdie, for whom roots are a conservative myth designed to keep us in our places, and whose writing – like his life – has consistently celebrated the fraught delights of journeys and migrations. Indeed, Rushdie's great contribution to the English tradition might be said to be the way he opens up this comforting but rather parochial vision, with its low-key mode of address, to international influences and concerns, as part of his postcolonial revision of Englishness. Against the national, Leavisite 'Great Tradition', Rushdie has identified for himself an international lineage, 'selected half consciously, half not', which includes 'Gogol, Cervantes, Kafka, Melville, Machado de Assis; a polyglot family tree, against which I measure myself, and to which I would be honoured to belong'.[3]

Nevertheless, as I wish to argue, Rushdie does not refuse or refute the English tradition. Rather his work interacts intertextually with those elements of it he finds most concordant. The imprint of numerous writers from the canon of English literature – which, for the sake of convenience in this essay can be extended to include those Irish and American-born artists who have enriched it from time to time – can also be seen in Rushdie's work. Famously, F. R. Leavis's canon, emphasising verisimilitude and moral seriousness, was set out in 1948 with the declaration: 'The great English novelists are Jane Austen, George Eliot, Henry James and Joseph Conrad', a list to which Leavis subsequently added D. H. Lawrence.[4] Rushdie's 'tradition', by contrast, has a place for Swift, Fielding, Sterne – whose inventive, bawdy *Tristram Shandy* was described by Leavis as 'irresponsible (and nasty) trifling'[5] – Blake, Lewis Carroll (who is especially important for *Haroun and the Sea of Stories*), Dickens – initially dismissed by Leavis as merely 'a great entertainer' – Joyce and Beckett. Rushdie responds to the experimental, the playful and the flamboyant in these writers, and these qualities characterise his own fiction. It is a lineage that makes room for the epic and the fantastic. It also opens up to admit aspects of narrative from different genres such as science fiction: as in the frequent device of over-lapping dimensions or levels of reality in *Grimus*, *The Satanic Verses* and *The Ground Beneath Her Feet*. At the same time, I wish to argue, by reacquainting the English tradition with its partly suppressed elements, Rushdie is offering a critique of a particular kind of imagined Englishness, sanctified by time and codified in certain notions of 'the literary'. He achieves this through a kind of radical intertextual decentring.

Postcolonial intertextuality takes a variety of forms: strategically deployed quotations or allusions; intertexts as structuring frameworks for plot and thematics; the juxtaposition of many intertexts to create a parti-cular effect and, thus, to generate meaning; and a dialogic engagement between the novel and aspects of broader cultural discourse, such as the grand narratives of history, science and progress. From the beginning, Rushdie's texts have always inscribed a recognition of how literary representations of place and identity operate in a discursive field that is always haunted by, and in dialogue with, authoritative constructions which precede and to some extent determine the cast of those representations. In *Grimus* the authoritative intertexts are those of world mythologies, in *Midnight's Children* they are the established accounts of postcolonial Indian history, and so on. His technique amounts to what Keith Booker has described as 'encyclopedic allusiveness',[6] borrowing from different cultures and traditions. His often satirical intent is likewise well served by such borrowings, allowing the narrative voice to inhabit but at the same time contest the common view.[7]

Thus, despite Rushdie's own famous journalistic epigram, the empire does not merely 'write back' to the metropolitan centre in terms of overturning hackneyed tropes and contesting stereotypes. Rather it recognises that, to a certain extent, the self-constitution of the text and sometimes of its characters takes place through intertextuality and the 'second-hand': Saladin Chamcha in *The Satanic Verses* carries around an ideal of a 'picture postcard' England, composed of the Royal Family, cricket and the Houses of Parliament; and the England of Sir Darius Cama in *The Ground Beneath Her Feet* is a retrospective, aristocratic dream, allegorising the Parsi community's close association with the British during the Raj.[8] Intertexts may be small or large: nods in the direction of Kipling occur in the frequent use of the Kim and Mowgli tropes, and to E. M. Forster in Saleem Sinai's grandfather, the Westernised Dr Aadam Aziz, in *Midnight's Children*, while Shakespeare's *Othello* and *The Merchant of Venice* provide strategic quotations and intertextual structuring principles for *The Moor's Last Sigh*.[9] Rushdie is not afraid of importing, verbatim, whole passages of dialogue from a source text if it helps to encapsulate a point about narrative and authority: as when the local police chief – himself a facsimile of Kipling – has Aurora Zogoiby's father and uncle arrested in *The Moor's Last Sigh*, and admonishes his charges with the very same words Kipling's narrator uses to describe the operations of colonial power in the short story 'On the City Wall'.[10] (One of his most enjoyable intertextual forays is the short story 'Yorick', from *East, West*, which is a twentieth-century pastiche of an eighteenth-century-style retelling of a supposed incident from the life of Shakespeare's posthumous jester in *Hamlet*.[11])

There was a time in Rushdie criticism when justifiable offence was taken by some at the tendency of critics only to bother to identify those Western intertexts that dot the novelist's work. Since then, a number of works have emerged which acknowledge and explore those influences from Hindi,

Urdu, the languages and texts of South India, the Persian inheritance and the visual style and argot of Bollywood cinema.[12] It should now be possible to acknowledge that all these traditions are mutually fructifying and, in fact, impossible to disentangle. Taken together they constitute the fabric of Rushdie's writing, and exist in a creative tension that lends the work its distinctive hybridity. It is also possible to suggest, however, that the nature and insistency of Rushdie's English sources betrays an ambivalence at the heart of his attitude to those cultural values the fiction ostensibly sets out to interrogate.

Englishness remains notoriously difficult to define, and the English tradition can, therefore, seem equally elusive. Despite this, some defining characteristics have been acknowledged. For example, the central philosophical principle in the English tradition has often been identified as empiricism. Empiricism is the theory that one gains knowledge and learns to evaluate truth through sensory data. Deriving from the work of Hobbes and Locke in the seventeenth century, and forming the mainstream of English philosophy through at least to Bertrand Russell in the twentieth century, empiricism presupposes a complete separation between the perceiving subject and the object of perception. It is an epistemology which privileges 'being objective', which believes that language can render sensory impressions directly, and which therefore requires of language that it be as transparent as possible in relation to that which it describes. Hobbes and Locke famously viewed language essentially as a nomenclature – a system of naming – thereby privileging nouns as the key units by which clear communication might best be ensured.[13] Anything that distracted from the direct communication of impressions and ideas – such as clever wordplay or ornate description – was to be strictly avoided. In Book Three of his *Essay Concerning Human Understanding* (1689), Locke attacked stylistic flourishes:

> But yet, if we would speak of Things as they are, we must allow, that all the Art of Rhetorick, besides Order and Clearness, all the artificial and figurative applications of Words Eloquence hath invented, are for nothing else but to insinuate wrong *Ideas*, move the passions and thereby mislead the Judgement; and so indeed are perfect cheat.[14]

Clearly, this emphasis on directness and truth cannot be applied wholesale to the more imaginative and to some extent adjectival art of fiction. Nevertheless, the idea of a transparent 'styleless' style does loom large in the history of English novel criticism.

It was perhaps given its most celebrated shape by Ian Watt in *The Rise of the Novel* (1957), where it was traced in the distinctive narrative qualities of that group of eighteenth century novelists, Defoe, Richardson and (less securely) Fielding, conventionally seen as the fathers of the novel form. The term Watt coined for these shared techniques was 'formal realism': novels – as opposed to the fanciful continental romances which preceded them – were distinguished by the particularity accorded to plot, character and setting, something which contributed to the defining effect of verisimilitude, of being true to life.[15] Yet Watt is merely one of a long line of critics whose identification of English writing with the central tenets of empiricism have led them to privilege the devices that make for realism. It is a view that exalts the best writing of the late nineteenth and early twentieth centuries – before the supposed depredations of 'High Modernism' – as the apogee of the novel form (as witnessed by Leavis's canon). Such preferences include the close marriage of content and form, and the idea that the novel ought to present incident and moral reflection dramatically, rather than having the narrator intervene to direct us, thereby breaking into the illusion of reality the novelist has set up.[16] Walter Allen has usefully summarised this formalist, empiricist ideal behind what he calls the 'pure novel':

> The writer of the pure novel sets out to delight us not by prodigality of invention, the creation of a large gallery of characters, ... but by attention to the formal aspects of composition, to design, to the subordination of the parts to the whole ... Readers who rejoice in the fiction of the great extroverts, Fielding, Balzac, Tolstoy, commonly find an impoverishment when they turn to the work of the pure novelists. Perfection, however, which is what the pure novelist is after, demands the recognition of severe limits. Dickens recognizes no limits at all; the art of Jane Austen is made possible precisely by the recognition of limits.[17]

It should be remembered, of course, that this is merely one facet of the English tradition, and that realism itself as an aesthetic category is far more overtly 'impure', open to, and composed of highly artificial devices and conventions, than this account allows. None the less, it is clear that Salman Rushdie is, in these terms, anything but a 'pure' novelist. He prefers the epic, the external and the fantastic to the realist, the internal and the domestic, and throughout his work – especially in *Grimus* and *Haroun and the Sea of Stories* – his puns, anagrams, loaded names, double meanings and interjections from different languages problematise the simple correspondence between signifier and signified. Similarly, Rushdie's writing tends to shy away from that close identification, born of believability and a developing imagined relationship, that is used to establish a bond between reader and central protagonist, preferring to keep us at arm's length and making frequent narratorial interventions. Where he does seek to explore the psychological coordinates of character it is usually through the outward confluence of history, race and nation, and takes the form of obsessive behaviour and grotesque transformations.

It is no coincidence, then, that Rushdie chooses to bypass the classic realism of the nineteenth century and draws inspiration from the diverse practices of the previous era. He has said:

> I think the eighteenth century is the great century for English literature, and it's no secret that I've been very affected by *Tristram Shandy* or *Tom Jones* and because they are those things that Henry James called 'loose baggy monsters' – I actually don't think they're that loose or baggy ... Kundera has this essay ... about how the novel has two parents, one of which is Richardson and Clarissa Harlow, and the other of which is Sterne and Tristram Shandy and he says, and I think he's right, that broadly speaking the children of Clarissa Harlow have populated the earth, and there are not that many children of Tristram Shandy.[18]

In his fiction Rushdie exploits the greater freedom of the Shandian tradition to mix genres, styles and registers, and revels in the unfettered power of the well-told tale. Nowadays, postmodern and postcolonial literary theories acknowledge the power of story – decried among some modernist practitioners as a distraction from the proper aesthetic preoccupations of the novel – for its own sake, and because it encodes alternative visions of the world to those sanctioned by authoritative discourses. Peter Ackroyd has remarked that: 'Eighteenth century fiction is hybrid and various, part realistic and part allegorical, combining heroism and farce in equal measure; it conflates epic with romance, and even includes critical theory.'[19] The novel wherein this miscellany is most memorably displayed is Laurence Sterne's *Tristram Shandy* (published serially 1759–67).

Digressive and episodic, *Tristram Shandy* offers a striking alternative to what was emerging as the dominant mode of eighteenth-century novel writing, using techniques now familiar to the modern reader. There are the many asides on writing itself which gleefully expose the artifice of a set of conventions rapidly solidifying into orthodoxy. Sterne never lets us forget that there are many different ways in which the story could be told: as many ways as there are characters and incidents. In particular, the experimentation with the disjunction between 'novelistic time' (the time of writing) and 'real time' (the time of living) is conducted in a strikingly sophisticated and self-aware manner.

As is well known, numerous elements of *Tristram Shandy*'s style and thematics have been borrowed by Rushdie in *Midnight's Children* to tell the story of his miraculous child, born on the stroke of midnight on

15 August 1947, and destined to live his life 'handcuffed to history'. Like his eighteenth-century forebear, Saleem Sinai feels obliged to approach the narration of his birth by providing copious antenatal details – in his case, concerning the history of India leading up to independence – so that the central protagonist has to wait to make an entrance into his own story. The run up to his birth is punctuated by the proleptic 'tick tock' of an imagined clock counting down to 15 August, just as Tristram's story really begins with the parental coitus that is to conceive him being interrupted by the necessity of winding the clock. Both books are unstintingly excursive. Sterne, like his own literary progenitor Jonathan Swift, introduces digressions on subjects as various as philosophy, dress, military, obstetric, educational and other matters, recommending them to the reader as 'the sunshine ... the life, the soul of reading' without which the book would be as cold as winter. Likewise, Rushdie's Saleem 'destroying the unities and conventions of fine writing', pauses to muse on meaning versus contingency, to attempt the categorisation of various smells, and to advance a theory of how best to read his own narrative.[20] It is the conviction of both narrators that to tell the story of one life it is necessary to try to encapsulate the whole of experience; Tristram's comment, 'nothing which has touched me will be thought trifling in its nature',[21] is matched by Saleem's assertion that 'To understand just one life, you have to swallow the world.'[22] Like that other great eighteenth-century novelist Fielding – who was also given to flights of erudition and authorial intervention – Rushdie is writing a 'comic epic'.[23] *Midnight's Children* has been compared to Fielding's *Tom Jones* (1749) and described as 'a postmodern version of the picaresque', incorporating incident-filled journeys 'from Kashmir to Amritsar, Agra, Delhi, Bombay, Lahore, Dacca and back again'.[24] Echoes of other late eighteenth- and early nineteenth-century novelists such as Tobias Smollett and Thomas Love Peacock can also be detected in Rushdie's exuberant, exaggerated style.

However, the writer with whom Rushdie can be most closely compared is Charles Dickens, one who often drew his inspiration from eighteenth-century sources such as Fielding and Smollett. Rushdie says of Dickens: 'I was particularly taken with what struck me as his real innovation: namely his unique combination of naturalistic backgrounds and surreal foregrounds' – almost a definition of Rushdie's own brand of magic realism.[25] Critics have been quick to note the Dickensian qualities of Rushdie's imagined capital city, Ellowen Deeowen in *The Satanic Verses*, with its juxtaposition of slick, multi-channel postmodernity and the downtrodden existence of the migrant communities, and its invocation of *Our Mutual Friend* (1865). However, I would argue that the Dickensian strain is most prevalent in *Shame* (1983). The note is struck from the start in the three sisters, Chhunni, Munnee and Bunny, who are joint-mothers of Omar Khayyam Shakil. Compared at various points to the three graces and the three wise monkeys, and carrying echoes of the weird sisters from *Macbeth*, they also recall the four Miss Willises from Dickens's earliest work, *Sketches by Boz* (1836–7). Dickens's women too 'seemed to have no separate existence', doing everything together and never being seen apart, to such an extent that when a Mr Robinson begins visiting, it is unclear whether he is courting one of the Miss Willises or all of them. The wedding day arrives:

> Who shall depict the perplexity of the clergymen, when *all* the Miss Willises knelt down at the communion table, and repeated the responses incidental to the marriage service in an audible voice – or who shall describe the confusion when ... all the Miss Willises went into hysterics at the conclusion of the ceremony, until the sacred edifice resounded with their united wailings.[26]

Dickens achieves the effect of ambiguity by keeping us outside the house at the crucial moments, as does Rushdie with the uncertain maternity of Omar Khayyam.

The Dickens novel that has the greatest affinity with *Shame*, and that shares its interest in the corruption of power and the inevitable violence it engenders, is *A Tale of Two Cities* (1859). Both texts explore what happens when a rotten political system is confronted by the newly awakened power of the long-oppressed. Throughout Rushdie's text there are echoes of Dickens's French Revolution novel: the shawls made by Rani Harappa to record the iniquities of her husband's regime resonate with Madame Defarge's knitting which acts as a register of crimes against the people by the French aristocracy. She claims to be knitting 'shrouds', like the burqas stitched by Rani Harappa in which her husband eventually flees. In *Shame* the retributive dimension is mainly saved for the ending, when the people, inspired by 'the human guillotine' that Sufiya Zinobia has become, take control of their destinies and storm the 'bastille' of Nishapur:

> All day a crowd has been gathering around the compound walls, growing angrier as it grows larger ... How will it end ... with the mob surging into the palace, lynchings, lootings, flames – or in the other, stranger way, the people parting like waters ... allowing her through, their champion to do their dirty work: the Beast with her fiery eyes?[27]

Rushdie's use of the word 'mob' here seems almost preprogrammed to conjure the frantic revolutionaries of Dickens's Paris: 'changed into wild beasts by terrible enchantment long persisted in'.[28] The message of both novels may be summarised in Dickens's valedictory observation: 'Crush humanity out of shape once more, under similar hammers, and it will twist itself into the same tortured form.'[29]

However, there is a revealing ambiguity at the heart of both novels. Dickens understood the motives of the revolutionaries but deplored the merciless violence of their methods. Rushdie too, despite his recognition of the colonial roots of nepotism and corruption and the neocolonial strategic considerations that sustain them, opposes brutality and religious fundamentalism with an appeal to the watchwords of the Enlightenment radical tradition: 'liberty; equality; fraternity'.[30] Such an invocation might appear out of keeping with postcolonialism's usual deep suspicion of Enlightenment values. Yet it is of a piece with Rushdie's invocation of freedom of speech and the autonomy of art elsewhere: in his spirited defence of *The Satanic Verses* in the essay 'In Good Faith', for example.[31] It can be seen as part of that valorised Romantic individualism and elevation of the writer that is a feature of his work: one thinks of the urgent endeavours of Saleem Sinai, the Joycean hero-as-writer of *Midnight's Children*, and his counterpart Moraes Zogoiby in *The Moor's Last Sigh*. Damian Grant has commented persuasively on Rushdie's latter-day commitment to the principles of the Romantic imagination, likening his belief in art and the imagination as central to our humanity to that of Shelley in his *A Defence of Poetry* (1840).[32] In fact, the Shelleyan connection can also be read back into *Shame*, where the transformed Sufiya Zinobia, confronting her husband and jailer Omar Khayyam at the end, performs a similar role to Demogorgon in Shelley's *Prometheus Unbound* (1820) when he drags the tyrannical Jupiter down into Hell: 'Descend, and follow me down the abyss/ I am thy child ... / Mightier than thee: and we must dwell together/ Henceforth in darkness.'[33]

Despite the Romantic valorisation of the artist as creator, it has been convincingly argued, as Easthope has shown, that the continued quest to find a significant relationship between subjective and objective worlds means that Romanticism can still be understood as part of the empiricist enterprise.[34] The tensions between the constituent parts of Rushdie's aesthetic – secular Islam, aspects of Hinduism, third world liberationism and a rather lukewarm socialism – are brought most sharply into relief in *The Satanic Verses*, where a centrifugal migrant hybridity pulls at a text structured on a Miltonian fall motif and ideas of Romantic inspiration drawn extensively from William Blake.

The distinctive quality of *The Satanic Verses* is its recognition of the location of some of the deepest modes of identification in religious and cultural, rather than specifically national paradigms. As the carrier of culture, language is seemingly up for grabs in the novel. This is made explicit both by the text's hybrid linguistic style and when the poet Jumpy Joshi, as part of his attempts to appropriate English, muses on the 'real language question' for the postcolonial subject: 'how to bend it, shape it, how to let it be our freedom, how to repossess its poisoned wells'.[35] However, as the controversy around the novel's so-called 'blasphemy' might in part suggest, the lodestar of Rushdie's exploration – for all its flights of fantasy – can be said to be the familiar glow of empiricist and Romantic verities.

This can be seen most clearly in the controversial revelation scene, where Gibreel Farishta, in the guise of the angel of annunciation, discloses Allah's decrees to the prophet Mahound. Even setting aside the critical factor of Gibreel's incipient schizophrenia, Rushdie's account of the revelation owes less to divine authority than to the established lexicon of Romantic inspiration. It is unclear whether the power that rends Gibreel emanates from within or without him. There is a fusion of prophet and angelic intercessor; Mahound says, 'Often, when Gibreel comes it's as if he knows what's in my heart. It feels to me, most times, as if he comes from within my heart: from within the deepest places, from my soul.'[36] The scene is constructed on the notion of the prophet-as-poet, the intuitive seer who is able to process, distill and articulate powerful emotions, thereby performing the central empiricist task of bridging the gap between external impressions and the poet's immortalising apparatus. The origin of the divine vision is, thus, beside the point. Rushdie's characters seem to be participants in a process akin to that described in Coleridge's 'Apologia Pro Vita Sua' (1822), where: 'The poet in his lone yet genial hour/ Gives to his eye a magnifying power,/ Or rather he emancipates his eyes/ From the black shapeless accidents of size', until, 'His gifted ken can see/ Phantoms of sublimity'.[37] Compare this to Rushdie's description of the artistic process: 'Literature is made at the frontier between the self and the world, and in the act of creation that frontier softens, becomes permeable, allows the world to flow into the artist and the artist to flow into the world.'[38] A secular mystery has replaced the sublime Romantic muse, but the process appears essentially the same.[39] The true home of the 'divine' lies in the human imagination, something that is reiterated by the many references to Blake and his visions in the text. When Gibreel immerses himself in a copy of Blake's *Marriage of Heaven and Hell*, his eye is drawn to a significant passage: '*I saw no God, nor heard any, in a finite organical perception; but my senses discover'd the infinite in every thing.*'[40] Later we are reminded of Blake's dinner conversation with the prophet Isaiah wherein he asks: '*does a firm perswasion that a thing is so, make it so? He* [Isaiah] *replied. All poets believe that it does. & in ages of imagination this firm perswasion removed mountains.*'[41] Different cultural readings and Blake's unique afflatus notwithstanding, to some extent Rushdie is utilising definitively

English tools to lay the foundations of a novel which is also, in part, an attempt to critique Englishness.

Rushdie launches his exploration of conservative constructions of Englishness by inhabiting its discourses in the guise of Rosa Diamond, the octogenarian revenant into whose garden Gibreel and Saladin plummet at the start of their adventures. Her house on the Sussex coast is the prime site of English history, where the spectral arrival of William the Conqueror's invasion fleet is re-enacted for her private delectation on moonlit nights:

> Best place to see 'em come, she reassured herself, grandstand view. Repetition had become a comfort in her antiquity: the well-worn phrases, *unfinished business*, *grandstand view*, made her feel solid, unchanging, sempiternal, instead of the creature of cracks and absences she knew herself to be.[42]

With the evocation of T. S. Eliot's elegiac 'Little Gidding' in the word 'sempiternal', and Rosa's childhood psychic experience of being part of the battle – its immediacy conjuring Dan and Una's time-travelling historical peregrinations in Kipling's *Puck of Pook's Hill* (1906) – the nostalgic, palimpsest-world where the past overlaps with, and invades the present, is matched in the palimpsest of intertextual resonances by which it is conjured. However, the converse fact of this Romantic conservative construction is that, 'in an ancient land like England there was no room for new stories': the anti-immigrant argument in a nutshell.[43]

Into this scene of atavistic torpor tumble Gibreel Farishta, soon to metamorphose into the Angel Gibreel, and Saladin Chamcha, whose diabolic horns and 'sizeable erection' will make him the embodiment of the fetishised social and sexual threat posed by the outsider. His transformation symbolises the cost of being an immigrant in 1980s Britain. As Jumpy Joshi observes, he becomes but another victim of: 'Wrongful arrest, intimidation, violence ... Illegal detention ... psychological breakdown, loss of sense of self, inability to cope. We've seen it all before.'[44] The physical transmogrification belies his desperate attempts at cultural assimilation to the Britishness he so admires, and gives Saladin a salutary taste of the exclusionary tactics of Thatcher's Britain, with its nostalgia for imperial glory, amoral free market capitalism, racism and police brutality. His uncritical adulation of all things British means that he is initially ill-equipped to cope with contemporary reality, unlike Anahita and Mishal Sufyan, fashion-conscious teenage daughters of the Shaandaar Café owner, and second generation Britons for whom their parents' country of origin means nothing and whose name they cheerfully travesty as 'Bungleditch'.

Inevitably, the focus of this frenetic activity is the metropolis itself. London figures in the text as a place of danger and thwarted dreams. Gibreel travels to the city excited by the promise of 'Proper London'. However, as his hallucinations take hold it becomes an apocalyptic landscape, a slippery, shifting wasteland, 'a confusion of languages. Babel: ... "the gate of God." Babylondon'.[45] Several critics have noted the Dickensian qualities in Rushdie's depiction of the capital. Yet his London is also the fictional descendant of the chaotic and threatening cityscapes of Defoe, Fielding and Hogarth.

By the end of the novel Gibreel is dead by his own hand and Saladin – cured of his unthinking anglophilia – has made the return journey to India to be with his dying father. The change of register in this last section of the novel, 'The Wonderful Lamp', allows for the intrusion of an uncharacteristic degree of interiority and psychological realism, and brings the text to rest in the uncharacteristically cathartic space of a return to roots, rounded off by a moving deathbed reconciliation and an optimistic turning towards the future. As Antony Easthope has remarked, pathos in the empiricist tradition functions essentially to record personal, individual loss, and several critics have remarked that this denouement appears to owe more to the sentimental conventions of the Victorian novel than to the rumbustious postmodern playfulness that has preceded it.[46] However, it can also be argued that the resolution of *The Satanic Verses* is in fact consistent with the novel's dissection of the idea of home in its many guises, which, while exposing the intertextual nature of the postcolonial migrant's construction of belonging, nevertheless is always already indebted to the larger philosophical structures framing that endeavour. In certain respects *The Satanic Verses* is the most English of Rushdie's novels, and not merely because of its subject matter.

This is not to say that Rushdie's aesthetic is somehow compromised in its commitment to cosmopolitan ideals, since the cosmopolitan is a category that must by definition include England, and Englishness, as one of its ports of call. In the same way, the explosion of writing from the former colonies and their diasporas now categorised as postcolonial, coupled with the diversification of the reading public in the years since the Second World War, mean that the English tradition itself has undergone radical change.[47] In any case, Peter Ackroyd has claimed that historically: 'Englishness is the principle of appropriation. It relies upon constant immigration, of people or ideas or styles, in order to survive'; it is, in short, a 'mongrel' tradition.[48] Ultimately, it is impossible to separate the English tradition from a wider literary inheritance across cultures and ages. Like his exile forebears Swift, Conrad and Joyce, Rushdie takes a body of works and a set of conventions and appropriates them for new purposes. Seamus Deane's observation about Joyce might, therefore, be equally applicable to Rushdie: 'The British imperium was overcome by parody, taking the tradition of literature as it had expressed itself in the novel, and scrutinizing its silent assumptions.'[49] Tracing the English tradition in Rushdie always, in the end, brings us back to the global perspective.

NOTES

1 *Guardian*, Saturday, 8 September 2001.
2 Q. D. Leavis, *Collected Essays: Volume I, The Englishness of the English Novel*, ed. G. Singh (Cambridge: Cambridge University Press, 1983), pp. 314, 315, 322.
3 Salman Rushdie, 'Imaginary Homelands', *Imaginary Homelands: Essays and Criticism 1981–1991* (London: Granta, 1991, 1992), p. 21.
4 F. R. Leavis, *The Great Tradition* (London: Chatto and Windus, 1948), p. 1.
5 *Ibid.*, p. 2, note 3.
6 M. Keith Booker, '*Finnegans Wake* and *The Satanic Verses*: Two Modern Myths of the Fall', *Critique* 32.3 (1991), p. 190.
7 See John Clement Ball, *Satire and the Postcolonial Novel: V. S. Naipaul, Chinua Achebe, Salman Rushdie* (New York and London: Routledge, 2003), p. 5.
8 Salman Rushdie, *The Satanic Verses* (London: Viking, 1988); this citation from the paperback edition (Dover, Del.: The Consortium Inc., 1992), p. 175. *The Ground Beneath Her Feet* (London: Cape, 1999); this citation from the Vintage edition (2000), pp. 28–30, 86–7. All subsequent references will be to these editions.
9 See Salman Rushdie, *The Moor's Last Sigh* (London: Cape, 1995), pp. 114–15 for reference to *The Merchant of Venice*, and pp. 224–45 for reference to *Othello*. Page citations and all subsequent references will be to the Vintage edition, 1996.
10 Rushdie, *The Moor's Last Sigh* (1995), pp. 39–40. See also, Rudyard Kipling, 'On the City Wall', in *Soldiers Three* (London: Macmillan and Co., 1895), pp. 307–38.
11 Salman Rushdie, 'Yorick', in *East, West* (London: Jonathan Cape, 1994), pp. 61–83. The story is also, in its own way, a testament to Rushdie's own sense of filial indebtedness to these earlier writers.
12 Vijay Mishra and Bob Hodge famously took Linda Hutcheon to task for listing in detail *Midnight's Children*'s Western influences but failing to name any Indian intertexts; see Vijay Mishra and Bob Hodge, 'What is Post(-)colonialism?', in Patrick Williams and Laura Chrisman (eds.), *Colonial Discourses and Post-colonial Theory: A Reader* (Hemel Hempstead: Harvester Wheatsheaf, 1993), pp. 276–90. For an interesting account of some of Rushdie's overlooked South Asian literary sources see D. C. R. A. Goonetilleke, *Salman Rushdie* (Basingstoke: Macmillan, 1998).
13 For an account of empiricism as central to the English tradition, see R. S. Woolhouse, *The Empiricists* (Oxford: Oxford University Press, 1988); Peter Ackroyd, *Albion: The Origins of the English Imagination* (London: Chatto and Windus, 2002); Antony Easthope, *Englishness and National Culture* (London: Routledge, 1999).
14 Locke quoted in Easthope, *Englishness*, p. 77.

15 Ian Watt, *The Rise of the Novel* (London: Hogarth Press, 1987), pp. 9–34.

16 See for example George Henry Lewes, 'The Novels of Jane Austen', *Blackwood's Edinburgh Magazine* 86 (1859) pp. 99–113; George Eliot, 'John Ruskin's *Modern Painters*, Vol. III', in *Selected Critical Writings*, ed. Rosemary Ashton (Oxford: Oxford University Press, 1992), p. 251; Henry James, *The Critical Muse: Selected Literary Criticism*, ed. Roger Gard (London and New York: Penguin, 1987); Percy Lubbock, *The Craft of Fiction* (London: Jonathan Cape, 1921); E. M. Forster, *Aspects of the Novel* (Harmondsworth: Penguin, 1990).

17 Walter Allen, *The English Novel: A Short Critical History* (Harmondsworth: Penguin, 1958), pp. 108–9.

18 'Salman Rushdie talks to Alistair Niven', *Wasafiri* 26 (1997), p. 55; reprinted in *Salman Rushdie Interviews*, ed. Pradyumna S. Chauhan (Westport, Connecticut: Greenwood Press, 2001) pp. 231–42.

19 Ackroyd, *Albion* (2002), p. 327.

20 See Laurence Sterne, *The Life and Opinions of Tristram Shandy, Gentleman* (serially published 1759–67), this citation from the Oxford University Press edition, 1983, p. 58; Jonathan Swift, *The Tale of a Tub* (1704), this citation from the Penguin edition, 2004, pp. 107–8; Salman Rushdie, *Midnight's Children* (London: Jonathan Cape, 1981), this citation from the Picador edition, 1982, pp. 78–9, 236, 238.

21 Sterne, *Tristram Shandy*, p. 10.

22 Rushdie, *Midnight's Children* (1982), p. 109.

23 Damian Grant quotes Rushdie's use of this phrase in interview; see Damian Grant, *Salman Rushdie* (Plymouth: Northcote House and British Council, 1999), p. 53. The term 'comic epic' was originally coined by Henry Fielding in his Preface to *Joseph Andrews* (1742).

24 Goonetilleke, *Rushdie*, p. 46.

25 Salman Rushdie, 'Influence', *Step Across This Line: Collected Non-Fiction 1992–2002* (London: Vintage, 2003), 1999, p. 71.

26 Charles Dickens, *Sketches by Boz* (London: Hazell, Watson and Viney Ltd., Undated), p. 19.

27 Salman Rushdie, *Shame* (London: Jonathan Cape, 1983); all citations from the Picador edition, 1984, pp. 261–2.

28 Charles Dickens, *A Tale of Two Cities* (1859), all citations from the Penguin edition, 1970, p. 263.

29 *Ibid.*, p. 399.

30 Rushdie, *Shame*, p. 251.

31 Rushdie, 'In Good Faith', in *Imaginary Homelands* (1992), pp. 393–414.

32 Grant, *Rushdie*, p. 1. Grant reads *Grimus, The Satanic Verses*, and *Haroun and the Sea of Stories* as essentially allegories of the operation of the imagination (pp. 11–12).

33 P. B. Shelley, *Poetical Works*, ed. Thomas Hutchinson (Oxford: Oxford University Press, 1970), p. 243.

34 Easthope, *Englishness*, p. 104.

35 Rushdie, *The Satanic Verses*, p. 281.

36 *Ibid.*, p. 136.

37 Samuel Taylor Coleridge, *Poetical Works*, ed. Ernest Hartley Coleridge (Oxford: Oxford University Press, 1969), p. 345.

38 Rushdie, 'Is Nothing Sacred', in *Imaginary Homelands*, pp. 415–29; this citation p. 427.
39 For more on these and other Romantic echoes, see Fiona Louise Richards, 'Literary Irreverence in Selected Works of James Joyce and Salman Rushdie', unpublished Ph.D. thesis, University of Leeds (2002).
40 Rushdie, *The Satanic Verses*, p. 305.
41 *Ibid.*, p. 338.
42 *Ibid.*, p. 130 (original italics).
43 *Ibid.*, p. 144.
44 *Ibid.*, pp. 252–3.
45 *Ibid.*, p. 459.
46 Easthope, *Englishness*, p. 154. See also Michael Gorra, *After Empire: Scott, Naipaul, Rushdie* (Chicago: University of Chicago Press, 1997), p. 147; Goonetilleke, *Salman Rushdie*, p. 91; Sara Suleri, 'Contraband Histories: Salman Rushdie and the Embodiment of Blasphemy', in D. M. Fletcher (ed.), *Reading Rushdie: Perspectives on the Fiction of Salman Rushdie* (Amsterdam: Rodopi, 1994), p. 235.
47 For a fuller account of this process see Steven Connor, *The English Novel in History: 1950–1995* (London and New York: Routledge, 1996).
48 Ackroyd, *Albion*, p. 237.
49 Seamus Deane, *Celtic Revivals* (Winston-Salem, North Carolina: Wake Forest University Press, 1987), p. 100.

4

RUVANI RANASINHA

The *fatwa* and its aftermath

'A poet's work,' he answers. 'To name the unnameable, to point at frauds, to take sides, start arguments, shape the world and stop it from going to sleep.' And if rivers of blood flow from the cuts his verses inflict, then they will nourish him.[1]

I

Few novels have had such an influence on world affairs, or engendered such divergent, interpretive communities and views that have continually changed. Gayatri Spivak identified the implied multi-levelled readers of Rushdie's novel *The Satanic Verses* as the international, postcolonial migrant readerships:

> This is not the Christian enlightenment person for whom British literature is written; nor the jaded European of 'The Wasteland' ... if you read it from the point of view of a 'secular Muslim' (Rushdie) is trying to establish a (post) colonial readership – already in existence – who will share a lot of the echoes in the book from Hindi films ... that you and I might miss.
> ... Rushdie was trying to create a post-colonial novel, from the points of view both of migration – being in Britain as Black British – and of decolonization.[2]

Yet some of the contradictions of the term 'secular Muslim' emerged in the diverse responses to the publication of the novel, as we shall see. Those who interpret the novel as blasphemy object chiefly to two chapters in the book. One of the protagonists of the novel is the Indian actor Gibreel Farishta, who suffers schizophrenic dream-sequences in which God reveals his will to the Prophet. A scribe named Salman writes down God's commands as they come from the lips of Mohammed, and he decides to play a trick by changing some of the divine words. Rushdie here retells an old legend that some of the Qu'ran's original verses originated with Satan and were later deleted by Mohammed, and Rushdie offended some Muslims by associating the Qur'ān, which Muslims see as the revealed word of God, with the work of Satan. The Jahilia section of the novel probably outraged these Muslims the most. The whores of Jahilia take the names of the prophet's wives revered by many Muslims as the 'mothers of all believers'. For some,

Rushdie's use of quotations and allusions from the Qu'ran and choice of the name 'Mahound' (a medieval demonisation of Mohammed) indicates his wish to insult Islam.[3]

While some Muslims world-wide read *The Satanic Verses* as a betrayal of their faith by a writer who writes from within and to a cultural context primed to disparage the Islamic faith, the most vociferous protest was voiced by the British Muslims anxious to separate themselves from the intellectual hitherto constructed as their representative.[4] Some felt particularly betrayed by the very person they had once admired as an ally. In an article on the subject Yasmin Alibhai-Brown cites a young Muslim woman's response: 'And what hurts so much is that one of our own, someone I really used to admire, someone who stood up on television and told the white British how racist they were, has let us down so badly.'[5] In the academic sphere some postcolonial critics such as Feroza Jussawalla read *The Satanic Verses* as evidence of Rushdie's participation in orientalist disparagement of Islam, arguing that he uses the genre of myth in order to debase native mythic traditions.[6] In her book *Letter to Christendom* (1989) Rana Kabbani similarly criticises Rushdie for taking over Western forms of orientalist prejudice against Islam.[7] Conversely, Fawzia Afzal-Khan (1993) argues that Rushdie uses 'Mahound' to debunk the use of the term and thus to reverse its meaning.[8] Vijay Mishra and Bob Hodge (1991) read the use of the genre of myth as 'stylistic nuances that mark the text's post-coloniality'.[9] The debate divided Muslim intellectuals. Prominent Muslim writers in Iran, Algeria, Palestine and Lebanon wrote in support of Rushdie in the volume *For Rushdie*.[10] While this contradictory literary reception was the subject of much discussion, the vocal 'non-readers' who constitute a significant interpretive community remain routinely sidelined in literary and sociological discussions of the Rushdie Affair. The mass protests and public book burnings by mostly non-readers in Bradford, Islamabad and India partly inspired, and were in turn backed up by the ageing Ayatollah Khomeini's politically motivated, infamous *fatwa*. The *fatwa* was pronounced against Rushdie and all those involved with the publication of *The Satanic Verses* on 14 February 1989, driving Rushdie into hiding and 'deforming' almost a decade of his life. Khomeini's move grew out of the decline of the revolution he led, the war against Iraq ended but not won, and a bitter conflict underway in Tehran between the 'pragmatists' (desiring a freer economy with more trade links with the West) and the 'radicals'. By rekindling the fervour of the revolution Khomeini sought to shift the balance of power, ensure a 'radical' successor, and unite disparate Muslim sects and communities. Today, the *fatwa* remains officially dormant (although not rescinded) as it has been since 1998, and it is as interconnected to global warfare and political events as it was in 1989. The September 11 and July 7 attacks and the global 'war on terror' inflame and conflate questions of Islam, immigration and security. The current supreme leader Ayatollah Ali Khamenei revived the *fatwa* in a lengthy tirade against Western and Zionist capitalists in the context of the US-led war on Terror: 'They talk about respect towards all religions, but they support such a *mahadour al-damn mortad* as Salman Rushdie.'[11]

The Ayatollah's incitement to murder turned what had been seen by Western readers as a cheerful, anti-Thatcherite polemic and comic postmodern novel into a beacon of freedom of expression against religious intolerance. This view was made more credible after the assassinations of a Belgian imam and his assistant who spoke in Rushdie's defence, the assassination of Rushdie's Japanese translator Hitoshi Igarashi, and the attacks on Rushdie's Norwegian publisher William Nygaard and Italian translator Ettore Capriolo. Rushdie met with uneven support within Western nations. Backed by the liberal press and most writers, including those such as Farrukh Dhondy, Hanif Kureishi and Tariq Ali who interrogated and explored the *fatwa* and its impact in their own writing, some conservative commentators argued Rushdie should have been more sensitive, or that he had brought this on himself. A climate of fear prevailed. With the ban in place in forty-five countries with large Muslim populations, and fire-bombings and threats to shops that displayed the novel in Western countries, many European publishers delayed publication. The publisher Collins dropped Lisa Appignanesi and Sara Maitland's collection of essays cataloguing worldwide support for Rushdie, *The Rushdie File*, for 'security reasons'.[12]

The Satanic Verses and its contradictory reception began to be seen as a metaphor for 'the clash of civilisations' with 'dogmatic Islamic certainties' pitted against the 'free enquiry of Western liberalism'. It was examined in such schematic terms by Malise Ruthven in *A Satanic Affair: Salman Rushdie and the Rage of Islam* (1990) and Fay Weldon's *Sacred Cows* (1989).[13] The Muslims' mass peaceful protests were often elided with the murderous violence of the killings. There were crude examples of intolerance, rehearsing dominant fears of 'intemperate minorities taking over', and anticipating the move beyond 'an assertion of a Muslim subjectivity to a full-blooded attempt to reconstruct society on Islamic principles', putting 'fundamentalist' principles into practice.[14] At the other end, there was the 'awkward' liberal dilemma of how a 'tolerant society' deals with an 'intolerant' one, as articulated by Charles Taylor:

> ... all societies are becoming increasingly multicultural, while at the same time becoming more porous. ... [M]ore of their members live the life of

diaspora, whose center is elsewhere. In these circumstances, there is something awkward about replying simply, 'This is how we do things here.' This
reply must be made in cases like the Rushdie controversy, where 'how we
do things' covers issues such as the right to life and to freedom of speech.
The awkwardness arises from the fact that there are substantial numbers of
people who are citizens and also belong to the culture that calls into question
our philosophical boundaries. The challenge is to deal with their sense of
marginalization without compromising our basic political principles.[15]

As Taylor's comments suggest, minority Muslim protests against Rushdie's
The Satanic Verses provoked debates on multiculturalism, definitions of
Britishness and highlighted the gap between citizenship and integration.
While there has been a development of a significant communitarian strain
within liberalism, it is by no means flawless. Tariq Modood critiqued both
Taylor's and Will Kymlicka's exclusion of Muslims from their conceptions
of multiculturalism, particularly Taylor's implicit assumption above that
excludes mainstream Muslims from 'the politics of recognition'.[16] Several
commentators interrogated the post-*fatwa* homogenising of Muslims, and
the equation of Islam with intolerance that overlooked the differentiated
nature of Muslim responses.[17] Devout Muslims were not unequivocal
about either Rushdie or the Ayatollah's *fatwa*, despite the high-profile
media projection of extreme Muslim voices such as the self-appointed
champion Kalim Siddiqui. Nor was it the case that all of those offended by
Rushdie's text supported the *fatwa* and the book burnings. While the book
burnings attracted immense media coverage at the time, no detailed discussions appeared as to why some Muslims took offence at certain passages
of the novel, suggesting to some Muslims other Britons' inability or
unwillingness to understand their values.

Academics such as Bhikhu Parekh, Akbar Ahmed and Tariq Modood,
called upon to act as cultural interpreters, consider why British Muslims'
mass protests provided a focal point for anti-Muslim racism within Britain
and elsewhere. Referring to 'the denunciation of the demonstrators as
Nazis', Modood argued: 'the blend of anti-Muslim prejudice and colour-
racism in the hysterical over-reaction to the anti-*Satanic Verses* demonstrators brought to the surface a highly specific form of cultural racism'.[18]
Ahmed adds: 'in their turn Muslims never appreciated the full impact in the
West of their death threat to the author and the burning of his book'.[19]
Modood shows how in the context of the Rushdie Affair and the first Gulf
War in 1990, Muslims were portrayed as a 'radical assault upon British
values, a threat to the state and an enemy to good race relations'.[20]
Modood identifies the demonising of Islamic beliefs as problematic and
'divisive' in terms of the wider assumption that 'religion divides, the secular

unites ... religion is "backward" and negative, secularism is progressive; religious people are the problem and secular rule is the solution'.[21]

Homi Bhabha goes further, problematising the equation between secularism with non-belief and alerting us to the limits of liberalism as evidenced in some liberal responses to fundamentalism that emerged in the wake of the Rushdie Affair. In his essay 'Unpacking my Library ... Again', Bhabha observes that the 'trouble with concepts like individualism, liberalism or secularism' is that 'they seem "natural" to us: it is as if they are instinctive to our sense of what civil society or civil consciousness must be'.[22] Bhabha suggests that it is the 'complex, self-contradictory history of "universal" concepts like liberalism, *transformed through their colonial and post-colonial contexts*, that are particularly important to our current social and cultural debates in a multicultural and multi-ethnic society'. Signalling the dangers implicit in the opposition between fundamentalism and traditional notions of secularism, Bhabha unpacks such constructions of secularism and suggests they can be imperialistic. He argues that the term secularism has been abused 'by many spokespersons of the Eurocentric liberal "arts" establishment who have used it to characterise the "backwardness" of migrant communities in the post-*Satanic Verses* cataclysm. Great care must be taken to "separate" secularism from the unquestioned adherence to a kind of ethnocentric and Eurocentric belief in the self-proclaimed values of *modernisation*.' Bhabha argues that the traditional claim to secularism is based on an 'unreconstructed liberalism' that presupposes an even playing field, a utopian notion of the self as sovereign and '"free" choice as inherent in the individual'. This bears no relation to the situation of the marginalised. Such a 'secularism of the privileged' is differentiated from the secularism claimed by minority groups who struggle against inequities of race, class, gender or generation, which are 'exerted by state institutions against minority groups, or by patriarchal and *class* structures within minority communities themselves'. Bhabha argues that 'we need to "secularise" the public sphere so that, paradoxically, we may be free to follow our strange gods or pursue our much-maligned monsters, as part of a collective and collaborative "ethics" of choice'.[23]

2

The *fatwa* provoked a widespread discussion of issues of freedom and responsibility in writing, both in the West and among Muslim intellectuals. The most prominently articulated response insisted that freedom of speech should be defended as vigorously as religious freedom.[24] However, as Webster argues in *A Brief History of Blasphemy* (1990), a civilised society should have constraints on freedom to act in ways that have adverse effects on others, and that freedom without responsibility is dangerous especially if offensive and damaging to a community.[25] He observes: 'If we push the liberal idea of artistic freedom to its logical extreme the inevitable consequence would be an "amoral society" ... absolute freedom of speech is ultimately no more desirable than absolute freedom to murder.' Citing the Race Relations Act and tracing the history of internalised censorship he shows the limits for artists set in the freest societies, and argues that freedom of speech is not an absolute, nor equivalent to democracy.[26] Other commentators such as Melanie Phillips have argued that the Race Relations Act and curbs on artistic expression are qualitatively different, making clear how literature is seen as exempt from the criteria applied to other forms of discourse.[27]

Webster's critique of 'the freedom to blaspheme' implicitly supports the group of Muslims who sought unsuccessfully to invoke blasphemy laws, which applied only to Christianity, against the novel in Britain in 1989. Article 19, a free speech pressure group who formed the International Committee for the Defence of Salman Rushdie, also began to campaign against blasphemy laws, which remained unchanged after much discussion. The legacy of this conflict emerged in the recent debate over the law against 'incitement to religious hatred' strongly contested by Rushdie and many other influential writers. In the context of this debate and the closure of Gupreet Kaur Bhatti's controversial play *Behzti* in December 2004 due to Sikh protests, Rushdie wrote in a letter to the *Guardian* published on 6 January 2005: 'The continuing collapse of liberal, democratic, secular and humanist principles in the face of the increasingly strident demands of organised religions is perhaps the most worrying aspect of life in contemporary Britain.' In response, Home Office minister Ms McTaggart's argument echoes Webster's:

> Free speech is a crucial right for everyone, faith groups as well as artists. For many years the law has established that free speech rights do not licence people to stir up hatred of others on the basis of their race. Now we are seeking to offer the same protection to people targeted because of their faith. This is not religious appeasement, but a responsible reaction to the tactics of those, especially from the extreme right, who would foster community tension by stirring up hatred of members of a faith group.[28]

One argument against this form of literary censorship circulating around the time of the *fatwa* (and articulated by Rushdie himself) is that the Affair amounted to the suppression of intellectual debate or reasoned dissent, proving Islam's inability to endure criticism or change. Acknowledging that 'there are those within Islam ... who do not like criticism and seek to suppress it', Webster suggests that 'such a view is based on a reluctance to attend closely to the actual terms of Muslim protest. For Muslims have gone out of their way to distinguish between criticism and abuse ... against use of obscene and violent language in relation to their religious traditions.'[29] Yet the Rushdie Affair brought to the fore the divisions amongst anti-racists and liberal multiculturalists particularly over the oppression of women that permeates fundamentalist religions. The feminist group Women Against Fundamentalism, founded in the wake of the *fatwa*, countered an anti-Rushdie march with the slogan 'Rushdie's right to write is ours to dissent'. The WAF allowed feminists to protest against religious fundamentalism of all faiths, and in this context provided a space for Asian feminists to distance themselves from religious leaders, such as those whose demands for separate Muslim schools for girls intensified in the aftermath of the *fatwa*.[30] Similarly in 2005 Rahila Gupta warned that the proposed law against religious incitement would choke women's right to dissent.[31]

In his defence, Rushdie argues: 'What is freedom of expression? Without the freedom to offend it ceases to exist.'[32] He also defends himself against accusations of insults and abuse, and distances himself from the internalised racism and 'self-hating, deracinated Uncle Tomism' he has been accused of. He draws attention to the text's sympathetic portrait of the dislocations of migration experienced by characters such as Hind, and moreover points to the fictionality of the text, not to be confused with the real opinion of the author. He argues:

> *The Satanic Verses* was never intended as an insult ... the story of Gibreel is a parable of how a man can be destroyed by the loss of faith ... the dreams in which the so-called 'insults' occur are portraits of his disintegration ... the dream figures who torment him with their assaults on religion are representative of this process of ruination, and *not* representative of the point of view of the author.[33]

In reply to some Muslims' objections that the issue was not Rushdie's exploration of Mohammed's humanity or the nature of Islamic revelation, but the offensive language, Rushdie has argued that the strong, meaty language is in keeping with his characterisation of Gibreel.[34]

Commentators such as Bhikhu Parekh question Rushdie's retreat into fiction as 'disingenuous' given the text's close historical resemblance to Islam.[35] This kind of response raises questions of genre and style: Rushdie's hallmark interweaving of history and fiction proved more explosive than pure invention and fantasy. Umberto Eco has observed that the mass media brings novels to people who have not read them and who do not share the fictional agreement, and for whom the novel's fictional status does not make it immune from causing offence.[36] Rushdie himself similarly discredits non-readers, implicitly dismissing their objections whilst making a distinction between those who share the fictional agreement, the suspension of disbelief and 'a sense of humour' and those who do not.[37] Yet as David Bowen points out, some Muslim readers 'were so nauseated' they stopped reading, and that even if they were to read the novel it does not mean they would not be insulted,[38] as Rushdie seems to assume when he observes: 'It has been bewildering to learn that people, million upon millions of people, have been willing to judge *The Satanic Verses* and its author, without reading it, without finding out what manner of man this fellow might be.'[39]

In the novel, Rushdie's character Bhupen says that to deny the ubiquity of faith is elitist. Ironically, this is the very accusation levelled at Rushdie. As Rushdie eloquently argues, his novel is not anti-faith: 'What is the opposite of faith? Not disbelief. Too final, certain, closed. Itself a kind of belief. Doubt.'[40] Indeed the novel thematises spirituality, and questions a monologic God. Rushdie argues that he set out to subvert repressive orthodoxies promoted throughout human history by 'the apostles of purity, those who have claimed to possess a total explanation, have wrought havoc among mere mixed-up human beings' as exemplified in his characterisations of the Imam and Ayesha. He writes: 'What does the novel dissent from? Certainly not from people's right to faith, though I have none. It dissents most clearly from imposed orthodoxies *of all types*.'[41] In place of religious certainties, Rushdie wrote, 'Doubt it seems to me is the central condition of a human being in the twentieth century.'[42] Yet, despite this apparent rejection of 'certainties' and 'orthodoxies', the fictional agreement is a literary judgement entrenched as normative and universal in liberal discourse. This subverts the widely received perception of the Rushdie Affair as embodying the battle between dogmatic certainties and liberal questioning.

Rushdie is unequivocal on the issue of blasphemy, as he states in 'In Good Faith': 'I do not accept the charge of blasphemy, because, as somebody says in *The Satanic Verses*, "where there is no belief, there is no blasphemy".'[43] However, the defiant, secular voice that recognised a 'God-shaped hole' in a postmodern world, which could be filled with art and literature, opposing imaginative writing with religion, faltered under the pressure of his extreme circumstances. Rushdie reaffirmed the Islam of his birth in an essay 'Why I Have Embraced Islam' in 1990 and offered to suspend publication of the paperback and not to issue any more translations.[44] He backtracked on this essay a few months later, and subsequently omitted it from later editions of *Imaginary Homelands*, which suggests a desire to erase this problematic episode from his self-conscious, crafted account of 'the plague years'.

3

> The best defence of literary freedoms lies in their exercise, in continuing to
> make untrammelled, uncowed books.[45]

After almost a year in hiding, 'impelled by necessity to keep on writing',
Rushdie produced the two lengthy essays cited above in defence of his
work, 'In Good Faith' and 'Is Nothing Sacred?' In October 1990, eighteen
months after the *fatwa*, *Haroun and the Sea of Stories* appeared. *Haroun* is
a children's fairy tale offering an allegorical defence of *The Satanic Verses*
with the stifling of freedom of expression as its subtext. Some critics saw the
novel's key issues debated in schematic terms. Others commented on the
significance of the representation of the Land of Gup, a place of foolish
prodigality for words, lack of care for them and lack of sense: 'The world is
not so clear, right and wrong, black and white. Forced to rethink everything, I've thought about everything.'[46]

When he was asked in an interview if the *fatwa* had scared him off
certain topics, Rushdie replied by commenting on his short story 'The
Prophet's Hair' (1994).[47] The story depicts in the manner of a spoof
Jacobean tragedy the havoc wreaked in the name of religious symbols.
Rushdie said, 'I think "The Prophet's Hair" is the answer to the intimidation question. If I was scared off writing about Islam it wouldn't be in
the [*East, West*] collection, would it?'[48] Talking about *The Moor's Last
Sigh*, the first large novel about India published seven years after *The
Satanic Verses*, Rushdie described the challenge of writing as an exile
entirely from memory: 'it is painful, but the country is inside you forever ... you just need to be aware of the pitfalls of sentimentality'.[49] Yet
as Maya Jaggi observes, the novel is suffused with the nostalgia of
the exiled writer who loves intensely but may not safely and freely
visit India again. The narrator invokes the names of a dozen Bombay
localities 'that have slipped away from me forever. All I possess is memory.
Forgive please if I yield to the temptation to conjure them up.'[50] The novel
mourns the greater loss of the plural, secular Bombay of Rushdie's childhood, now threatened by religious extremism and the rise of Hindu
fundamentalism.

The Moor's Last Sigh and Rushdie's other novels were censored in the
subcontinent and other countries in the wake of the *fatwa*. Similarly, the
proposed filming of Rushdie's screenplay of his novel *Midnight's Children* in
India had to be abandoned. The project then failed in Sri Lanka with
the government initially keen but later fearful of offending the Muslim
electorate in the context of the introduction of sensitive legislation. Rushdie

observed: 'The rejection of *Midnight's Children* changed something profound in my relationship with the East. Something broke and I am not sure it can be mended.'[51]

Rushdie identifies other shifts in his post-*fatwa* writing. In jest he talks about his renewed zest for humour and happy endings. He also reflects that where he used to identify with both positions now 'in the struggle of insiders and outsiders ... I've come down on the side of those who by preference, nature or circumstance simply do not belong.'[52] The darkness of the *fatwa* years gave him 'Time to reflect upon the countervailing value of love. Love feels more and more like the only subject',[53] and both *The Ground Beneath Her Feet* (1999) and *Fury* (2001) demonstrate this.

Step Across this Line (2002) includes letters, articles and reflections of life under the *fatwa* and describes Rushdie's sharp, angry response both to the threat and to the personal attacks which he faced in Britain from the right-wing press. He felt they reinforced in their readers the perception that he was 'the villain of the Rushdie affair', and this treatment alongside 'smaller, but still wounding slights' clearly influenced his decision to move to New York in 2000. The implied readership of the collection *Step Across this Line* is palpably post-September 11 US, particularly in those essays that endorse secularism.

These essays mark the impact of the *fatwa* on Rushdie. In contrast to the earlier privileging of doubt, he now celebrates non-belief in stronger terms:

> ... values and morals are independent of religious faith, ... good and evil come before religion ... it is perfectly possible, and for many of us even necessary, to construct our ideas of the good without taking refuge in faith.[54]

Faith, not only religious extremism, is now dismissed. In an essay originally written in 1993, Rushdie lamented that 'If the worst, most reactionary, most medievalist strain in the Muslim world is treated as the authentic culture, so that the bombers and the mullahs get all the headlines while progressive, modernizing voices are treated as minor and marginal "Westoxicated" ... the fundamentalists are being allowed to set the agenda.'[55] Now he subscribes to monolithic versions of Islam, and some of his pronouncements serve to polarise the debate: 'When murder is ordered in the name of god you begin to think less well of the name of god.'[56] Rushdie has long feared the 'absolutism of the Pure', forging a link between his contestation of notions of purity (particularly of origins) and his contestation of the absolutism of religious faith. For Rushdie, if hybrid identities contest or destabilise claims to mono-cultural identities, this is a parallel process to undermining the monologism of faith central to most understandings of Islam. In the author-narrator's imagined Pakistan in

Shame (1983), Islam, unlike multi-cultural Bombay or London, cannot bear the weight of the nation. Its monotheism and absolutism do not allow hybridity. Post-*fatwa* Rushdie seems more emphatically dismissive of those who resist his vision of liberal multiculturalism. In a letter to the *Independent* in defence of Bosnian Muslims, he describes them as 'indeed secularised and humanistic, representing an attractive blend of Muslim and European culture'. He privileges their multiculturalism against their British counterparts who he assumes *all* 'sneer at this hybrid culture'.[57]

The most striking shift is in Rushdie's politics. He now supports the 'authority of the United States' as 'the best current guarantor' of 'freedom' against 'tyranny, bigotry, intolerance, fanaticism'.[58] This position sharply contrasts with his critique of American imperialism in his non-fictional work *The Jaguar Smile* based on a three-week stay in Nicaragua in 1986.[59] Commenting in February 2002 on the US-led invasion of Afghanistan, Rushdie argues, 'America did in Afghanistan, what had to be done, and did it well.'[60] Supportive of American 'intervention' and regime change, he remains critical only of its selective imperialism:

> Apparently Osama bin Laden and Saddam Hussein are terrorists who matter; Hindu fanatics and Kashmiri killers aren't. This double standard makes enemies. ... And it is in Iraq that George Bush may be about to make the biggest mistake and to unleash a generation-long plague of anti-Americanism.[61]

By November 2002 he appears to support the US-led invasion of Iraq: 'a war of liberation might just be one worth fighting'.[62]

In the wake of September 11 he is outraged by the left-liberal, '*bien-pensant* anti-American onslaught' that followed.[63] While we can read the trauma of the *fatwa* into this shift, and his perception of his fate as a foretaste of the Islamic terrorism unleashed on a massive scale in 2001, such ideological changes are evident amongst other commentators of Rushdie's generation, notably Christopher Hitchens whose politics has swung more emphatically, and to whom Rushdie dedicates *Step Across this Line*. Ambivalence over the anti-war protests is echoed by another of Rushdie's contemporaries Ian McEwan in his novel *Saturday* (2004) about a day in the life of a neurosurgeon as anti-war demonstrators gather in London.

This is not to say Rushdie has become an uncritical supporter of US action or of the Bush administration's 'hard-line, ideologue right-wing regime'.[64] In the words of his New York-based protagonist Solanka in *Fury* Rushdie plays with the idea that:

> Might this new Rome actually be more provincial than its provinces; might these new Romans have forgotten what and how to value, or had they never known? Were all empires so undeserving, or was this one particularly crass?[65]

Instead, contesting the 'easy condemnation' of the dissemination of American culture, Rushdie argues that rather than call America the tyrant, 'Out there are real tyrants to defeat'.[66] Written significantly before the huge civilian losses in Iraq and the emergence of the Abu Ghraib atrocities, we await our foremost commentator's response.

NOTES

1 Salman Rushdie, 'Mahound', *The Satanic Verses* (London: Viking, 1988), p. 97.
2 Gayatri Chakravorty Spivak, *The Spivak Reader: Selected Works of Gayatri Chakravorty Spivak*, eds. D. Landry and G. M. Maclean (London: Routledge, 1996), p. 22.
3 See Shabbir Akhtar, *Be Careful with Muhammad! The Salman Rushdie Affair* (London: Bellew, 1989).
4 For examples of this response see *The Satanic Verses: Bradford Responds*, ed. David Bowen (Bradford: Bradford and Ilkley Community College, 1992).
5 Yasmin Alibhai, 'Satanic Betrayals', *New Statesman and Society*, 24 February 1989, p. 12.
6 Feroza Jussawalla, 'Resurrecting the Prophet: The Case of Salman, the Otherwise', *Public Culture* 2 (1989), pp. 106–17.
7 Rana Kabbani, *Letter to Christendom* (London: Virago, 1989).
8 Fawzia Afzal-Khan, *Cultural Imperialism in the Indo-Anglian Novel: Genre and Ideology in Narayan, Desai, Markandaya and Rushdie* (Pennsylvania: Pennsylvania State University, 1993).
9 Bob Hodge and Vijay Mishra 'What is Post-Colonialism?', *Textual Practice* 5.2 (1991), pp. 399–413.
10 *For Rushdie: Essays by Arab and Muslim Writers in Defense of Free Speech*, ed. Anouar Abdallah (New York: George Braziller, 1994).
11 'mahadour al-damn' refers to someone who has committed apostasy by leaving Islam, 'mortad' applies to someone 'whose blood can be shed with impunity'. Phillip Webster, Ben Hoyle and Ramita Navai, 'Ayatollah Revives Death Threat on Salman Rushdie', *The Times*, 20 January 2005, p. 4.
12 It was later published by Fourth Estate: *The Rushdie File*, eds. Lisa Appignanesi and Sara Maitland (London: Fourth Estate Limited, 1989).
13 Malise Ruthven, *A Satanic Affair: Salman Rushdie and the Rage of Islam* (London: Chatto and Windus, 1990), and Fay Weldon, *Sacred Cows* (London: Chatto and Windus, 1989).
14 Bobby Sayyid, *A Fundamental Fear: Eurocentrism and the Emergence of Islamism* (London: Zed Books, 1997), p. 17.
15 See Charles Taylor, 'The Politics of Recognition', in *Multiculturalism: Examining the Politics of Recognition*, ed. Amy Gutman (Princeton: Princeton University Press, 1994), p. 63. See also Will Kymlicka, *Multicultural Citizenship: A Liberal Theory Of Minority Rights* (Oxford: Clarendon Press, 1996), especially pp. 154–5.
16 See 'Introduction', in *The Politics of Multiculturalism in the New Europe*, eds. Tariq Modood and Pnina Werbner (London, New York: Zed Books, 1997),

pp. 3–4. See also Gayatri Chakravorty Spivak's succinct critique of recent works on liberalism and liberal multiculturalism in Gayatri Chakravorty Spivak, *A Critique of Postcolonial Reason: Towards a History of the Vanishing Present*, (Cambridge, Mass.: Harvard University Press, 1999), pp. 396–7, n. 113.

17 Nikos Papastergiadis, 'Ashis Nandy: Dialogue and Diaspora', *Third Text* 11 (1990), p. 100. See also Homi Bhabha, 'The Third Space', in *Identity: Community, Culture, Difference*, ed. J. Rutherford (London: Lawrence & Wishart, 1990), p. 214, who argues that 'within the Shi'ite sect (which is too easily and too often read as "fundamentalist") there are a number of other positions' on the Rushdie affair. These make a 'claim for a kind of hybridisation which exists no matter whether you keep asserting the purity of your origins'. See also Akbar Ahmed, *Postmodernism and Islam: Predicament and Promise* (London: Routledge, 1992), p. 176.

18 Tariq Modood, *Not Easy Being British: Colour, Culture and Citizenship* (London: Trentham Books, Ltd, 1992), pp. 29 and 81. Other commentators also point out the flaws in such a parallel, including Richard Webster, *A Brief History of Blasphemy: Liberalism, Censorship and the Satanic Verses*, (Southwold: The Orwell Press, 1990).

19 Ahmed, *Postmodernism and Islam*, p. 170.

20 Modood, 'British Muslims and the Rushdie Affair', in *Race, Culture and Difference*, eds. J. Donald and A. Rattansi (London: Sage Publications in association with the Open University, 1992), pp. 260–77, p. 268.

21 Modood, *Not Easy Being British* (1992), p. 87.

22 Homi Bhabha, 'Unpacking my Library … Again', in *The Post-Colonial Question: Common Skies, Divided Horizons*, eds. Iain Chambers and Lidia Curti (London: Routledge, 1996), p. 208.

23 *Ibid.*, all quotations pp. 209–11.

24 See for example, *The Rushdie Letters: Freedom to Speak, Freedom to Write*, ed. Steve McDonough (Dingle, Co. Derry: Brandon, 1993).

25 Webster, *A Brief History of Blasphemy*, p. 46.

26 *Ibid.*, p. 46. See also Simon Lee, *The Cost of Free Speech* (London: Faber, 1990). He argues that Rushdie supporters often invoke free speech to the disadvantage of minority groups.

27 Melanie Phillips, cited in Bhikhu Parekh, 'The Rushdie Affair and the British Press', in *The Salman Rushdie Controversy in Interreligious Perspective*, ed. Dan Cohn-Sherbok (Lampeter: Edward Mellon Press, 1990), p. 82.

28 Mark Oliver, 'Home Office to Meet Rushdie over Censorship Fears', *Guardian*, Thursday, 13 January 2005. A watered-down Racial and Religious Hatred Bill was passed in 2006.

29 Webster, *A Brief History of Blasphemy*, p. 90.

30 For a discussion of these issues, see *Refusing Holy Orders: Women and Fundamentalism in Britain*, eds. Nira Yuval-Davis and Gita Sahgal (London: Virago, 1992).

31 Rahila Gupta, 'Too High a Price to Pay', *Guardian*, 12 March 2005.

32 Salman Rushdie, 'In Good Faith', in *Imaginary Homelands* (London: Granta, 1991), p. 396.

33 Rushdie, 'Why I Have Embraced Islam' (1990), *Imaginary Homelands*, p. 431.

34 *Ibid.*, pp. 434–7.

35 Parekh, 'The Rushdie Affair and the British Press', p. 93. See also Bhikhu Parekh, 'Between Holy Text and Moral Word', *New Statesman*, 24 March 1989, pp. 29–33. Ziauddin Sardar and Merryl Wyn Davies make a similar point, arguing that dreams are a way for Rushdie to 'present his own ideas … without having to acknowledge the limits of propriety, respect for the sensitivities of others or the complexities of historical records' in Sardar and Davies, *Distorted Imagination: Lessons from the Rushdie Affair* (London: Grey Seal, 1990), pp. 157–8.

36 Cited in Editorial, *Economist*, 10 February 1990, online edition.

37 Rushdie interview with Alastair Niven (1994) in *Writing Across Worlds: Contemporary Writers Talk*, ed. Susheila Nasta (London: Routledge, 2004), p. 134.

38 Bowen (ed.), *The Satanic Verses: Bradford Responds*, p. 14.

39 Rushdie, 'In Good Faith', in *Imaginary Homelands*, p. 397.

40 Rushdie, *The Satanic Verses*, p. 92.

41 Rushdie, 'In Good Faith', in *Imaginary Homelands*, p. 396.

42 *Ibid.*, p. 396.

43 *Ibid.*, p. 405.

44 Rushdie, 'Why I Have Embraced Islam' (1990), in *Imaginary Homelands*, pp. 430–2.

45 Salman Rushdie, 'February 1999: Ten Years of the Fatwa', *Step Across this Line: Collected Non-Fiction 1992–2002* (London: Jonathan Cape, 2002), p. 294.

46 Cited in Review, '*Haroun and the Sea of Stories*', *Economist*, 10 March 1990, online edition.

47 'The Prophet's Hair', *East, West* (London: Jonathan Cape, 1994), pp. 33–58.

48 Rushdie (1994) in Nasta (ed.), *Writing Across Worlds*, p. 134.

49 Rushdie interview with Maya Jaggi, 'The Last Laugh', *New Statesman and Society*, 8 September 1995, pp. 20–1.

50 *Ibid.*, p. 21.

51 Rushdie, 'Adapting *Midnight's Children*' (1999), in *Step Across this Line*, p. 87.

52 Rushdie, 'February 1999', in *Step Across this Line*, p. 294.

53 *Ibid.*, p. 295.

54 Rushdie, 'From an address delivered in King's College Chapel, Cambridge, on the morning of Sunday 14 February 1993', in *Step Across this Line*, p. 252.

55 Rushdie, first published in the *New York Times* in July 1993 under the title 'The Struggle for the Soul of Islam', in *Step Across this Line*, p. 258.

56 Rushdie, 'First published on 7 February 1993, under the title "The Last Hostage"', *Step Across this Line*, p. 235.

57 Rushdie, 'From a letter to *The Independent*, July 1993', in *Step Across this Line*, p. 262.

58 Rushdie, 'March 1999: Globalisation', in *Step Across this Line*, p. 297.

59 Salman Rushdie, *The Jaguar Smile* (London: Picador, 1986).

60 Salman Rushdie, 'Anti-Americanism Has Taken the World by Storm', *Guardian*, 6 February 2002.

61 Salman Rushdie, 'Ironic if Bush Himself Causes Jihad', *Sydney Morning Herald*, 10 September 2002, online edition.

62 Salman Rushdie, 'A Liberal Argument for Regime Change', *Washington Post*, 1 November 2002, A35.

63 Rushdie, 'October 2001: The Attacks on America', in *Step Across this Line*, p. 392.
64 Rushdie, in a note added to 'December 2000: A Grand Coalition?' on its appearance in *Step Across this Line*, p. 361.
65 Rushdie, *Fury* (London: Jonathan Cape, 2001), pp. 86–7.
66 Rushdie, 'March 1999: Globalization', in *Step Across this Line*, p. 298.

5

AMINA YAQIN

Family and gender in Rushdie's writing

In his comfortable, Upper West Side sublet, ... Professor Malik Solanka nursed a glass of red Geyserville Zinfandel and mourned. The decision to leave had been wholly his; still, he grieved for his old life. Whatever Eleanor said on the phone, the break was almost certainly irreparable. Solanka had never thought of himself as a bolter or quitter, yet he had shed more skins than a snake. *Country, family, and not one wife but two had been left in his wake. ... He told them – each of his women in turn – that friendship was what he had instead of family ties, and, more than friendship, love.*[1]

Thus writes Salman Rushdie of his protagonist Professor Malik Solanka who resigns from his job at King's College, Cambridge opting out of the academy and cashing in on the lucrative world of television to make a series of 'popular history-of-philosophy' programmes. The programme is eventually a success and is aired under the title 'The Adventures of Little Brain'. It stars his collection of 'outsize egghead dolls', all made by himself, representing great thinkers. The chief 'knowledge-seeker' is the 'female time-travelling doll Little Brain' – echoing other Rushdie characters who journey through space and time, including Gibreel Farishta in *The Satanic Verses*, shuttling between twentieth-century Britain and seventh-century 'Jahilia', and Flapping Eagle in *Grimus* who falls through a hole in the Mediterranean into a different dimension. Little Brain is a 'hip, fashion-conscious, but still idealistic Candide, his Valiant-For-Truth in urban-guerrilla threads, his spiky-haired girl Basho journeying, mendicant bowl in hand, far into the Deep North of Japan'.[2] She is the only doll he falls in love with and who breaks his heart. Appropriated by popular television she is turned into a celebrity and her intellect dumbed down for the mainstream viewing public. The producers move her to 'Brain Street' in 'Brainville' and Solanka decides to let her go. The more successful she becomes the more Solanka hates her. Eventually his obsession about the doll drives an unbridgeable gap in the marital home, sends him out on his life-changing peregrinations and, thus, sets up the pattern of family and alienation that marks the writer's œuvre.

This is one of the many examples of the themes of gender and the family in Rushdie's novels. I will examine these, drawing in part on Edward Said's ideas of filiation and affiliation which describe a movement away from the natural bonds of home to those associative connections made in the modern world: something which is particularly suggestive in the context of migrancy. I will also consider the significance of a historicised understanding of the shifting category of woman and interrogate discursive and ideological family networks which serve to allegorise the postcolonial nation as much as they offer sites of love and belonging.

Fury encapsulates the themes of migration, separation from the family, a crisis of masculinity and the search for love. Like most of Rushdie's novels, it is a narrative centrally concerned with 'the idea of home'.[3] Paradoxically, Solanka leaves his North London home for New York in search of peace, to be a sanyasi, to get rid of the murderous mid-life 'fury' stirring inside him. But he cannot rid himself of the paternal love he feels for his son Asmaan, who symbolises his need for natural ties and who 'twisted in him like a knife'. Meanwhile, in New York Solanka finds himself next to Mila Milo, a young woman in her twenties with a father fixation who Solanka initially recognises as 'his angel of mercy, his living doll'. She says to the Professor after she has discovered that he is the creator of Little Brain, 'your L. B., this little lady right here, has been my like total *obsession* for most of the last ten *years* .... And as you spotted, she's only the *basis* and *inspiration* for my whole current *personal style*.'[4] So the Professor has his ambivalent vanity piece. He has made a connection in New York City by means of the very life he thought he had left behind. Mila becomes his confidante and he confesses to her the reasons for his departure from England. He tells her of the knife that he wielded over his sleeping wife and son, an act which he connects to the murderous rage he felt over Little Brain's desertion.

Mila becomes his secret sharer; she will save him from his sinister fantasies. Solanka, uncomfortably aware of Mila's sexuality, is torn between paternal feelings toward her and a desire to possess her sexually. As Mila tells him the story of her father, their relationship progresses into an ambiguous intimacy. The father–daughter resonance heightens Mila's fascination with Solanka while he imagines an incestuous past being relived by her through him. In the process she is transformed from his rescuing angel to the spider 'caught in her own necrophiliac web, dependent on men like Solanka to raise her lover very, very slowly from the dead'.[5] During their furtive meetings he cuddles Mila in his lap, treating her like a doll and acting out the play of his inner fantasies. However he denies himself the pleasure of sexual gratification as suspicions about the father–daughter relations continue to dog him. Eventually, Solanka rationalises his relationship with Mila by choosing to recognise her as his creative muse giving him the 'breath of life' on his workbench and falls in love with the beautiful Neela Mahendra instead, a third generation Indian immigrant and his friend's lover. Rather predictably she cures Solanka's fury. She unlocks the story of his unhappy childhood in India, growing up with a stepfather who had sexually abused him. Then, dolls had provided him comfort like 'blood kin: the only family he could bring himself to trust'.[6] Eventually, the three women, Eleanor, his wife, Mila and Neela turn on him in an absurd scene where they all confront him with his betrayals. The only love that remains in the novel is what Solanka feels for his son, his 'blood kin'.

Fury has not had the critical acclaim of other Rushdie novels. One of the reasons for its weakness as a narrative can be attributed to the characterisation which regurgitates gender stereotypes and hence lacks the interesting ambivalence toward family, friendship and love which we find in his earlier novels. The psychoanalytic account of Solanka's character is in the end too formulaic to engage the reader. Nevertheless, this whole episode in *Fury*, which re-enacts the crisis of the male within the family, who leaves home to find himself and eventually returns in a search punctuated by the need for love, is characteristic of Rushdie's novels. His protagonists are often in search of a more meaningful sense of home and are doubly displaced as outsiders within their own countries because they occupy the border spaces of minority identity. As Rosemary Marangoly George has argued: 'Homes are not about inclusions and wide open arms as much as they are about places carved out of closed doors, closed borders and screening apparatuses.'[7] Rushdie's narratives too are about those *unheimlich* 'at home' places but are situated often within satirical treatments of the postcolonial nation as in *Midnight's Children, Shame* and *The Moor's Last Sigh*.

It can be argued that in these novels his characters are searching for those connections between filiation and affilation as described by Edward Said, who refers to filial relationships as those which are fostered through natural bonds 'involving obedience, fear, love, respect and instinctual conflict' and affiliative links as ones which are formed by 'transpersonal forms' including 'guild consciousness, consensus, collegiality, professional respect, class, and the hegemony of a dominant culture. The filiative scheme belongs to the realm of nature and "life" whereas affiliations belong exclusively to culture and society.'[8] In *The Satanic Verses* Saladin Chamcha and Gibreel Farishta are literally thrown out of their filiative units and have to construct their affiliative bonds without the helping hand of family while Saleem Sinai, Omar Khayyam Shakil and Moraes Zogoiby (in *Midnight's Children, Shame* and *The Moor's Last Sigh* respectively), have to negotiate their affilations in the face of smothering parental intrusions and the arduous networks of the family. All three are shadowed by confusion over their paternity: Saleem, the son of Wee Willie Winkie's wife Vanita and William Methwold, is swapped at birth with his dark double Shiva and is unwittingly taken into the bosom of the family of Amina and Ahmed Sinai; Omar Khayam Shakil is effectively born of three mothers and may or may not have been sired by an English army officer; and Moraes Zogoiby – living and dying twice as quickly as everyone around him – teasingly holds out the possibility that his father might not have been Abraham but Jawaharlal Nehru, the Prime Minister of India himself. Likewise, in various ways the three protagonists are caught in an oedipal relationship with their mothers: in particular, Moraes Zogoiby who is tricked by his duplicitous lover Uma into fantasising an incestuous scenario involving his mother Aurora. Thus, filial relationships are never straightforward for Rushdie's characters, and it is in these intricate relationships that he interweaves those patterns of gender and sexuality that have come to define his writing.

In his study of the history of sexuality in European culture, Michel Foucault shows the multiplicity of institutional discursive traditions which feed into the larger discourse of sexuality. He argues that sexuality should not be considered as a pre-existing phenomenon but should instead be thought of as a 'historical construct'. This reflection on sexuality, he argues, opens up the possibility of examining different discourses around the body and pleasure, 'the strengthening of controls and resistance', which give us a deeper understanding of how sexuality has been deployed in the struggle of 'knowledge and power'. Foucault references the family as an institution which has been used to 'anchor sexuality' since the eighteenth century. For him, the husband–wife and parents–children alliance of the family historically represents a regulatory model of sexuality that both exercises a control over the female body and conveys the law.[9]

Foucault thus asks us to review our understanding of sexuality as a fixed concept and to investigate the historicity of the subject in order to reflect on the present. However, he bases his reading of 'the truth of sex' on an East–West binarism of 'ars erotica' for the former and a 'scientia sexualis' for the latter, around which he unpacks his analysis of sexuality. The family which he deconstructs is a European Christian one and this one-sided approach makes it difficult to import his argument wholesale to another context. Foucault's model of study has since been critiqued by many scholars. The Marxist critic Aijaz Ahmad regards Foucault's poststructuralist historiographical model as one which does not allow the subject a 'stable belonging and subject position' and sees it as complicit with the project of 'elite' postmodernism. Ahmad introduces a consideration of gender into his reading of *Shame*. He focuses on four points: the major role women play in the novel; Rushdie's publicly stated reason for giving women such prominence in the book which is to redress fictively their oppressed status in Pakistan; the presence of alleged misogyny in their portrayal; and the lack of male figures from the oppressed sections of society.[10] Ahmad performs a useful task in drawing our attention to the class bias in this novel and in Rushdie's writing more generally where the spotlight usually falls on members of the elite, politically aware middle and upper classes. Yet his interpretation appears to be informed by a fixed understanding of sexuality and women and also a slightly simplistic reading of women as a substitute for the absent underclasses. By contrast Rushdie is concerned to highlight the specificities of gender oppression in his version of Pakistani society, which are to do with women's domestic roles, child-bearing and socially enforced passivity in relation to active male characters. For example, Good News Hyder commits suicide because of her unending arithmetical progression of children, none of whom are male. As John Clement Ball observes: 'This image of grotesque excess ... enables a vivid satiric admonishment of patriarchal ambition fearsomely imposed on the functional female body.'[11] Likewise Iskander Harappa's discarded lover, Pinkie Aurangzeb, becomes prematurely decrepit and eccentric without him, satirising the notion of a woman's utility being bound up with her sexual desirability:

> *If a great man touches you, you age too quickly, you live too much and are used up.* Iskander Harappa possessed the power of accelerating the ageing processes of the women in his life. Pinkie at fifty was ... beyond even the memory of her beauty.[12]

In contrast to Ahmad, the feminist critic Joan Wallach Scott recommends Foucault's style of scholarship to feminist historians so that they may demythologise the idea of an 'inherent timeless, agency of women'.[13] She recommends that in writing about the identity of 'women', the historian should trace the specificities of the term in given contexts, and in that process discover that '*women* refers to so many subjects, different and the same'.[14] It is therefore interesting to juxtapose Scott with feminist rereadings of Rushdie's novels which, on the basis of a shared feminism, try to reclaim women's histories from the clutches of the male narrator, particularly in *Shame*, without sufficiently allowing for experiential differences to do with geographical context and class.

The novel lends itself to feminist interpretations of suppressed women's histories when the narrator comments more than halfway through:

> I had thought, before I began, that what I had on my hands was an almost excessively masculine tale, a saga of sexual rivalry, ambition, power,

patronage, betrayal, death, revenge. But the women seem to have taken over; they marched in from the peripheries of the story to demand the inclusion of their own tragedies, histories and comedies, obliging me to couch my narrative in all manner of sinuous complexities, to see my 'male' plot refracted, so to speak, through the prisms of its reverse and 'female' side.[15]

It would seem on the surface that what is being attempted is a fictional revision which will clear a space for the (supposedly unified) female voice: just as Rani Harappa's shawls, contradicting the official narrative of her husband's regime, reinterpret Pakistani history from a woman's angle. However, despite the narrative's playfulness – the narrator in *Shame* is unreliable and given to digression and personal intervention – the narratorial claim of female agency has been taken literally by some critics. For example, in the often cited feminist reading of the novel by Inderpal Grewal we find that while she applauds Rushdie's commitment to gender equality, she finds his methodology wanting and complains that 'the novel instead subverts these [female] voices, indicating thereby that the male writer and his narrator fail to carry through their participation in the concerns and lives of women'.[16] Catherine Cundy finds the project of voicing the female narrative a problematic one because it is 'undercut by the representation of women themselves'. She finds the 'innocent/whore binarism' to be characteristic of the gendering in the novel and Sufiya Zinobia 'the ultimate manifestation of the destructive capabilities of female sexuality'.[17] Again, Cundy has a very fixed interpretation of Sufiya as female here. By contrast, while Jenny Sharpe suggests re-reading the women in *Shame* through a consideration of the instability of gender roles, she sees Sufiya Zinobia as a positive character because she encapsulates the anger and self-pride of shame instead of being its vessel of embarrassment and family honour.[18] As the narrator tells us, she is the 'collective fantasy of a stifled people, a dream born of their rage' producing the violence to cleanse the shameless society.[19]

Sharpe's reading is based on the silenced stories of British Asian immigrant women given voice in *Shame* through the incident of the Asian girl, Anahita Mohammed, killed by her father because she had sexual relations with a white boy. The narrator of *Shame* reflects on this Pakistani father's murder of his daughter in this way:

> We who have grown up on a diet of honour and shame can still grasp what must seem unthinkable to peoples living in the aftermath of the death of God and of tragedy: that men will sacrifice their dearest love on the implacable altars of their pride.[20]

Sharpe claims that the narrator is guilty of ignoring the role played by British racism in the way the community structures itself around notions of honour and shame. It is this concern with 'honour and shame' amongst the immigrant community that Sharpe focuses on. In her view, Rushdie's reversal of the effects of shame and violence in the character of Sufiya Zinobia fails to alter the traditional gendering of violence as an 'active, masculine response to Shame, and silence as a passive, feminine one' whereas in contrast the work of numerous black women's organisations in contemporary Britain challenges those stereotypical male–female binarisms. Sharpe sees the work done by these groups as key toward reforming the societal representations of conventional masculinity such as those framed in Rushdie's narrative. However, Sharpe's 'fantasy echo' of 'British Asian immigrant women' too easily runs together 'real' and fictionalised female experience, and takes no account of the primary location of the story or the elite class structures mirrored in *Shame* which have very little to do with the working classes in Britain. In Pakistan, the family has been a prominent feature of the state's political discourse from the period of Field Marshal Ayub Khan's martial law in the 1960s, during which he introduced the liberalisation of family laws, to the military regime of General Zia ul-Haq in the 1980s which implemented the Shariah laws. Zia deployed the media-led *Nizam-e Mustafa* (The law of Muhammad) campaign, making sex a public mattter mediated by religious law.[21] It is this aspect of Pakistani postcolonial politics that is satirised in *Shame*: a fact of which most feminist readings appear unaware.

In order to problematise the rather fixed view of such interpretations I wish to argue that gender in *Shame* can only be understood in relational terms: the roles of females and males are mutually constitutive and interdependent. In order to understand Sufiya Zinobia it is necessary first to understand the character and narrative function of Omar Khayyam Shakil. Sufiya is desired by Shakil, thirty-one years her senior, who falls in love with her while she is under his care as an immunologist. As a peripheral hero he suffers from vertigo attacks which seem to be cured by his love for her. Underlying his condition is the absence of a father figure in his upbringing and his hatred of his mothers. They are the ones who first explain shame to him:

> 'What does it feel like?' he asked – his mother, seeing his bewilderment, essayed explanations. 'Your face gets hot,' said Bunny-the-youngest, 'but your heart starts shivering.'
>
> 'It makes women feel like to cry and die,' said Chhunni ma, 'but men, it makes them go wild.'
>
> 'Except sometimes', his middle mother muttered with prophetic spite, 'it happens the other way around.'[22]

Sufiya is the embodiment of that shame and it is significant that she is initially treated by Shakil after her first violent outburst against Pinkie's turkeys:

> What seems certain is that Sufiya Zinobia, for so long burdened with being a miracle-gone-wrong, a family's shame made flesh, had discovered in the labyrinths of her unconscious self the hidden path that links *sharam* to violence.[23]

Shakil represents the symbolic order of language while for the mute Sufiya, actions speak louder than words. Allegorically, her rape of the four youths in the slums is a dark reversal of the *Hudood* Ordinances passed in the 1980s in Pakistan which require the witness of four adult males in order to register a rape crime.[24] On the motif of rape itself Rushdie has recently written about the honour and shame cultures that prevail in India and Pakistan, commenting that:

> [M]ale honour resides in the sexual probity of women, and the 'shaming' of women dishonours all men. ... The 'culture' of rape that exists in India and Pakistan arises from profound social anomalies, its origins lying in the unchanging harshness of a moral code based on the concepts of honour and shame. Thanks to that code's ruthlessness, raped women will go on hanging themselves in the woods and walking into rivers to drown themselves.[25]

Whether Sufiya is one of those women is debatable but *Shame* constantly returns to the cultural phenomenon of honour and shame. Omar Khayyam Shakil is Sufiya's foil and his masculinity is an unstable construct in the novel fluctuating from one extreme to another. At first he is associated with the hyper-masculine carousing and fornicating antics of the unreconstructed Iskander Harrapa. After Isky's conversion to sobriety and statesman-like behaviour he transfers his allegiance to the coming man Raza Hyder, only to find himself fleeing the Presidential compound with the deposed dictator dressed in the burqa, the very 'shroud' which has previously functioned as a symbol of female oppression. On arrival in Nishapur, he finds out from his mothers that Raza Hyder is the murderer of his brother. They attack him for his lack of a sense of family honour and taunt him with the familial legacy of fraternal betrayal: 'You know this is a family in which brothers have done the worst of things to brothers, and maybe you even know that you are just the same.'[26] Caught in feverish hallucinations, language is no longer able to sustain him and he is destined to wait for the Beast, 'like a bridegroom on his wedding night'. She will absorb him before exploding, because the 'Beast of shame cannot be held for long within any one frame of flesh and blood, because it grows, ... until the vessel bursts.'[27]

Families are notably foregrounded in *Midnight's Children*, *Shame* and *The Moor's Last Sigh* – the latter two texts beginning with a family tree mapping the complex genealogies of the Shakils and Hyders, and the Da Gamas and Zogoibys respectively. In these novels families are often a microcosm of the nation. In *Midnight's Children*, Saleem Sinai directly links himself to the birth of the nation:

> Newspapers celebrated me; politicians ratified my position. Jawaharlal Nehru wrote: 'Dear Baby Saleem, My belated congratulations on the happy accident of your moment of birth! ... We shall be watching over your life with the closest attention; it will be, in a sense, the mirror of our own.'[28]

It has been argued in this discussion that Rushdie uses the family as a discursive device to critique the postcolonial nation. In *Shame*, the family unit plays out in miniature the corruption and nepotism that lead to the breakdown of civil society. In *Midnight's Children* and *The Moor's Last Sigh* the family can be mapped onto political developments such as the attempt by Indira Gandhi to establish dynastic rule and, as a result of her policies, the increasing communalism which has since encroached on Nehruvian ideals of secularism.

In the Indian subcontinent, 1947 saw the longed-for independent nation-in-formation split in two. The bloody horrors of Partition permanently underscored the memories of the new nations. The movement of millions of people across the new borders had a direct impact on the structure of the family. Such family break-up is at the heart of *Midnight's Children*. After the Indo-Chinese war Ahmed Sinai prophetically observes to his wife, 'this country is finished'.[29] After the ceasefire his wife Amina persuades him to emigrate to Pakistan, to join her sisters.

Love, in these novels, often appears fragile and its tender affections are frequently overturned or even crushed altogether by the machinations of power and authority. This occurs both on the level of the national political elite and, frequently, in filial relationships. To understand how power operates in these families it is useful to understand them in the specific historical context of Indian nationalism and consider the broader political discourse of which they are a part.

According to Partha Chatterjee, the discourse of nationalism in nineteenth-century India depended on a binary view of the relationship between the coloniser and the colonised. Participation in the outer 'material domain' of politics was deemed to be a necessary move towards modernity defined in terms of the West, but with the retention of an authentic, inner 'spiritual self' seen to be essential for the preservation of a true Indian identity.[30] This ideology nominated women as keepers of tradition and also gave them the status of 'modern' participants in the new nation. Chatterjee argues that patriarchal nationalism gave women a new social status while at the same time it bound them to the 'historical goal of sovereign nationhood'.[31] However, Sangari and Vaid have suggested that 'modernising movements' including social reform and nationalism offered a much more 'liberal space' for middle-class women in colonial India while 'democratising movements' worked toward altering the 'social structures of patriarchal formations'. In their analysis the common denominator setting the agenda in both was the middle-class family.[32]

The middle classes are often the subject of Rushdie's novels, and women in these families are not always bound inside the home. In *Midnight's Children*, Amina Sinai conducts her affair with Nadir Khan, her ex-husband, in the public space of the Pioneer Café. Saleem, who follows her, hidden in the boot of the car, watches her betrayal in anguish and acts on the moral code of honour and shame. 'O shameless mother! Revealer of duplicity, of emotions which have no place in family life.'[33] Her shamelessness propels him into action: he punishes her by example, teaching her the lesson of honour. 'By umasking the perfidy of Lila Sabarmati, I hoped also to administer a salutary shock to my own mother. Two birds with one stone; there were to be two punished women, one impaled on each fang of my forked snake's tongue.'[34] But another negotiation of honour and shame takes place through the character of 'Reverend Mother', Naseem Aziz, who is initially shown to be in purdah 'at home', even to the Doctor, Aadam Aziz, who is later to be her husband, and who can only examine her through a perforated sheet. Naseem preserves tradition at home by holding on to her code of honour, but toward the end of the novel, with the progress of age, she too branches out into the public sphere as manager of a petrol pump which she runs with her daughter-in-law Pia Aziz on the busy Grand Trunk Road between Lahore and Rawalpindi. This is not to suggest that there is an easy liberation for women in these stories. The path to selfhood is not always smooth, as in the case of Brass Monkey who becomes Jamila Singer, a popular Pakistani chanteuse whose career is still managed by men and whose respectability in the scandalous world of entertainment is only salvaged by performing from behind the veil. Being a middle-class woman is by no means a guarantee of a cosmopolitan modernity. What is interesting about these middle-class families in *Midnight's Children* is that Saleem eventually leaves them behind for the earthy Padma, his 'goddess of dung'.

Amrita Chhachhi writing about secular identity politics and women in India reiterates that women have been 'crucial markers of identity – of the nation, community, caste group and religious group. They have been objects as well as agents.'[35] Drawing on Anderson's work on nationalism she too focuses on how nations utilise the 'language of kinship or the home' to further their ideology. As an example she refers to 'the merging of the nation/community with the selfless mother/devout wife' and makes the observation that discourses of communalism, nationalism and fundamentalism include 'notions of revenge for the "violation of our mothers and sisters"'. In *The Moor's Last Sigh* the narrator repeatedly invokes the motif of 'motherness' and describes how the Indian cultural tradition of a 'Mother India' became a household symbol with the release of the film *Mother India* in 1957: 'Nobody who saw it ever forgot that glutinous saga of peasant heroism, that super slushy ode to the uncrushability of village India made by the most cynical urbanites in the world.' 'Motherness', he says, 'is a big idea in India ... the land as mother, the mother as land, as the firm ground beneath our feet.'[36] Rushdie's satiric treatment of a classic paean to 'motherhood' attacks the idea of a benevolent motherland and explodes the myth of secular nationalism in India. Symbolically, Moraes Zogoiby, the narrator of the novel, was born on the day the film was released. The youngest of four, he is the only male child and also the only one his mother Aurora suckles at her breast while she is working on her first 'Moor' picture. In contrast to the idealisation of motherhood, Aurora Zogoiby's determined self-sufficiency allows her to be India's foremost woman artist. However, as Moraes observes, there is something of the traditional female deference in her toleration of the sexual infidelities of her husband, Abraham:

> [She] was still, in some deep recess of her heart, a woman of her generation, a generation that would find such behaviour tolerable, even normal in a man; whose womenfolk shrugged off their pain, burying it beneath banalities about the *nature of the beast*, and its need, periodically, to *scratch an itch*. For the sake of family, that great absolute in whose name all things were possible, women averted their eyes and kept their grief knotted in a twist of fabric at the end of a dupatta.[37]

It is significant that her sexual indiscretions occur *after* Abraham's betrayals. Her confessional paintings are supplements for her feelings toward Moraes but maintain the strong oedipal overtones that characterise their relationship. In her *To Die Upon a Kiss* picture, 'she portrayed herself as murdered Desdemona flung across her bed, while I was stabbed Othello, falling towards her in suicided remorse as I breathed my last'.[38] Rushdie mocks this mother–son intimacy through Moraes who gossips with his ayah, Miss Jaya Hé about the 'unhealthy' relationship between Indira and Sanjay Gandhi saying, '[t]he whole nation is paying for that mother–son problem'. In response, Miss Jaya 'snorted disgustedly. "You can talk", she said. "Your family. Perverts. Your sister and mother also. In your baby time. How they played with you. Too sick." [39] Their ambiguous relationship is thrown into relief by the arrival of Uma Sarasvati, also an acclaimed artist at the young age of twenty and Moraes's first love. She is a release for Moor's sexual passions but at a price. She encourages Moor's incestuous fantasies by inciting him to call his mother's name during intercourse. This marks the decline and eventual fall of Moraes's position in the Zogoiby family. Torn between two loves, he chooses the equivocating Uma who promises to be a replacement for his family but ends up betraying him and ironically dies in the trick suicide pact she engineers to get rid of him. Cast out from the family he is only reunited with his father after Aurora's death. But Abraham brings him back into the family not for the sake of love but for revenge.

The trajectory of *The Moor's Last Sigh* is characteristic of Rushdie's fiction in that familial betrayals are the springboard for the central protagonist's subsequent migrations. In *Midnight's Children* it is the revelation of Saleem's true identity as the changeling child rather than the true son of Amina and Ahmed Sinai that causes him to be cast out. In *Shame* the family home of Nishapur increasingly comes to be a prison for Omar Khayyam Shakil. He rampages through the rambling corridors in an orgy of destruction that symbolises his desire for escape, until he turns his gaze outwards to the release apparently promised by Farah Zoroaster, the customs officer's daughter. In *The Ground Beneath Her Feet*, both Ormus Cama and the narrator Rai rebel against the stifling attitudes of middle-class Bombay parents, the first through rock and roll and the second through photography.

But in *The Satanic Verses* an interesting variation takes place through the character of Saladin Chamcha. The novel has much to say about parent–child relationships: Saladin's socialist wife Pamela Lovelace has, to her chagrin, inherited the Home Counties plumminess of her parents; Allie Cone's private life is constantly dissected by her cosmopolitan mother; and the Sufyan girls, Mishal and Anahita, have little affinity with their parents' values and less still with the Bangladesh from which they have migrated. However, the unit in which we, as readers, are asked to invest most time and empathy is that of Saladin and his father Changez. Saladin is a troubled child, bullied and tricked by his father, who, like several other Rushdie protagonists, angrily abandons both his overbearing parent and his country of birth to gain an independent identity. His values are shaped by the Anglicised education his father has imposed on him. Saladin's adventures – including his miraculous escape from the Boeing plane and the painful lesson he must learn about the Britain he has come to idolise, but which is now disfigured by greed and racism – eventually bring him back to the home he has left as a child to attend to his dying father. Here he is nurtured back to the path of love by the interventions of Zeeny Vakil who begins the process of healing, which is also one of reconciliation between father and child, nation and prodigal son. Saladin must suffer a heart attack and face down bereavement, in the process recovering his old place in the world – symbolised by his re-adoption of his full name Salahuddin Chamchawalla. His father's lamp, which he had coveted as a boy, becomes the symbol of the welcoming light of home to which he has returned. He muses:

> To fall in love with one's father after the long angry decades was a serene and beautiful feeling; a renewing, life-giving thing, Saladin wanted to say, but did not, because it sounded vampirish as if by sucking this new life out of his father he was making room, in Changez's body, for death. ... How hard it was to find one's father just when one had no choice but to say goodbye.[40]

This uncharacteristically cathartic ending is nevertheless indicative of the importance of families and homes in Rushdie's fiction as contested ideals, the value of which can only be truly understood when they are taken away. Within these spaces both men and women occupy different roles, playing out their identities in a complex mix of ideological impositions and primal fantasies.

NOTES

1 Salman Rushdie, *Fury* (London: Cape, 2001), Vintage edition, 2002, pp. 29–30. Emphasis added. All further references will be to the Vintage edition.
2 *Ibid.*, p. 17.
3 See the Introduction to Rosemary Marangoly George, *The Politics of Home: Postcolonial Relocations and Twentieth-century Fiction* (Cambridge: Cambridge University Press, 1996).
4 Rushdie, *Fury*, p. 90, original emphasis retained.
5 *Ibid.*, p. 133.
6 *Ibid.*, p. 223.
7 George, *The Politics of Home*, p. 18.
8 Edward W. Said, *The World, the Text, and the Critic* (London: Faber and Faber, 1983), p. 20.
9 Michel Foucault, *The History Of Sexuality: Volume I An Introduction*, trans. Robert Hurley (London: Penguin, 1990 (1978)), pp. 105–12.
10 Aijaz Ahmad, *In Theory: Classes, Nations, Literatures* (London and New York: Verso, 1992), p. 143.
11 John Clement Ball, *Satire and the Postcolonial Novel: V.S. Naipaul, Chinua Achebe, Salman Rushdie* (New York and London: Routledge, 2003), p. 138.
12 Salman Rushdie, *Shame* (London: Jonathan Cape, 1983), p. 181, emphasis in the original.

13 Joan W. Scott, 'Fantasy Echo: History and the Construction of Identity', *Critical Inquiry* 27 (2001), pp. 284–304.

14 *Ibid.*, p. 292.

15 Rushdie, *Shame*, p. 173.

16 Inderpal Grewal, 'Salman Rushdie: Marginality, Women and Shame', *Genders* 3 (1988), pp. 24–42; this citation p. 25.

17 Catherine Cundy, *Salman Rushdie* (Manchester: Manchester University Press, 1996), pp. 51–6.

18 Jenny Sharpe, 'The Limits of What Is Possible: Reimagining Sharam in Salman Rushdie's *Shame*', http://social.chass.ncsu.edu/jouvert/vlil/sharpe.htm (accessed 15 December 2004).

19 Rushdie, *Shame*, p. 263.

20 *Ibid.*, p. 115.

21 For a detailed view of Pakistani political history, See Ian Talbot, *Pakistan: A Modern History* (Lahore: Vanguard, 1999).

22 Rushdie, *Shame*, p. 39.

23 *Ibid.*, p. 139.

24 See Asma Jahangir and Hina Jilani, *The Hudood Ordinances: A Divine Sanction?* (Lahore: Rohtas, 1990).

25 Salman Rushdie, 'Where is the Honour in this Vile Code that Condemns Women to Die in Shame?', *Times*, 18 July 2005, p. 16.

26 Rushdie, *Shame*, p. 278.

27 *Ibid.*, p. 286.

28 Salman Rushdie, *Midnight's Children* (London: Jonathan Cape, 1981; Picador edition, 1982), p. 122. All further references will be to the Picador edition.

29 Rushdie, *Midnight's Children*, p. 305.

30 Partha Chatterjee, *The Nation and its Fragments: Colonial and Postcolonial Histories* (New Jersey: Princeton University Press, 1993), p. 120.

31 See Partha Chatterjee, 'The Nationalist Resolution of the Women's Question', in *Recasting Women: Essays in Colonial History*, ed. Kumkum Sangari and Sudesh Vaid (New Delhi: Kali, 1999), pp. 233–53; p. 248.

32 See Kumkum Sangari and Sudesh Vaid, 'Recasting Women: An Introduction' in *Recasting Women: Essays in Colonial History*, Sangari and Vaid (eds.), p. 19.

33 Rushdie, *Midnight's Children*, p. 161.

34 *Ibid.*, pp. 260–1

35 Amrita Chhachhi, 'Identity Politics, Secularism and Women: A South Asian Perspective', in *Forging Identities: Gender, Communities and the State*, ed. Zoya Hasan (New Delhi: Kali for Women, 1994), pp. 74–95; p. 86.

36 Salman Rushdie, *The Moor's Last Sigh* (London: Jonathan Cape, 1995; Vintage edition, 1996), p. 137. All further references will be to the Vintage edition.

37 *Ibid.*, pp. 222–3.

38 *Ibid.*, pp. 224–5.

39 *Ibid.*, p. 197.

40 Salman Rushdie, *The Satanic Verses* (London: Viking, 1988); this citation from The Consortium (Delaware) 1992 edition, pp. 523–4.

PART II

Studies of individual texts

6

IB JOHANSEN

Tricksters and the common herd in Salman Rushdie's *Grimus*

I

Flapping Eagle, the Amerindian protagonist of Salman Rushdie's *Grimus* (1975), has many of the characteristics of the prototypical Native American *trickster*. He is both 'a creator of order out of chaos and a destroyer of order which represses creative energies, [as] an animal being and a spiritual force', and '[w]hatever else he may be, [he] is also a SURVIVOR who uses his wits and instincts to adapt to changing times'.[1] In her anthropological study *In Favor of Deceit* (1987), Ellen B. Basso points out that '[t]he widespread occurrence of trickster characters in folklore has long been an intriguing puzzle to anthropologists and folklorists, who have written insightfully – but exceedingly sporadically – about these mythological figures'.[2] Franz Boas was, for instance, impressed by 'the "troublesome psychological discrepancy" between the apparently incongruous attributes of the "culture hero" (who makes the world safe and secure for human life) and the "selfish buffoon" (who ludicrously attempts the inappropriate)'.[3] Others have emphasised the trickster's explicit status as an outsider – 'strikingly antisocial, marginal, or ambiguous' – and that he represents, in Karl Kerényi's words, the 'spirit of disorder, [as] the enemy of boundaries'.[4] Claude Lévi-Strauss in his preface to *The Raven Steals the Light* (1984) has commented on 'the Raven, a deity of the type called in English a trickster':

> The fact that the Amerindians placed a deceitful, insolent, libidinous and often grotesque character with a penchant for scatology at the forefront of their pantheon sometimes surprises people. But indigenous thought places the Raven at the turning point between two eras ... [and] [i]n a universe that is undergoing constant change, the Raven is both ... the ultimate rebel and the foremost maker of laws.[5]

Flapping Eagle, or as he is also called, Joe-Sue or Born-from-Dead, is from the very outset an outsider, and later literally an *outcast*, in the eyes of the other members of his tribe, the Axona (an imaginary Native American tribe belonging to the American South West). He is a pariah '[f]or three reasons: first, my confused sex [he has a hermaphrodite's name, even if he is, in all other respects, a full-grown male]; second, the circumstances of my birth [his mother dies moments before he is born and his father shortly afterwards]; and third, my pigmentation [he is white-skinned and taller than the rest of his tribe]'.[6] However, in spite of these circumstances, which are characteristic of his situation, he turns out to possess special gifts and qualities as an individual which compensate for his 'strikingly antisocial, marginal, or ambiguous' status. In the last resort these qualities make it possible for him to become, in a wider perspective, precisely a 'culture hero', that is, a person who is able to act not only on his own behalf, but on behalf of the whole community – struggling against and eventually over-coming the forces of evil.

According to Joseph Campbell in his classic study *The Hero with a Thousand Faces* (1949), the quest of the archetypal/mythical hero can ordinarily be divided into three phases: departure (1), initiation (2) and return (3).[7] In *Grimus*, Flapping Eagle definitely undergoes or fulfils the objectives of the first two phases whereas the third stage in his 'progress' can be said to represent a somewhat *modified* version of the last phase in Campbell's narrative, the 'return'. However, in this connection we must bear in mind that we may occasionally come across what Campbell terms the 'refusal of the return'. Ideally, '[w]hen the hero-quest has been accomplished, through penetration to the source, or through the grace of some male or female, human or animal, personification, the adventurer still must return with his life-transmuting trophy. The full round, the norm of the monomyth, requires that the hero shall now begin the labor of bringing the runes of wisdom, the Golden Fleece, or his sleeping princess, back into the kingdom of humanity, where the boon may redound to the renewing of the community, the nation, the planet, or the ten thousand worlds.'[8] But as it is pointed out by Campbell, 'the responsibility has been frequently refused ... Numerous are indeed the heroes fabled to have taken up residence forever in the blessed isle of the unaging Goddess of Immortal Being.'[9] Taking up residence 'forever [on] the blessed isle' of Calf is pre-cisely Flapping Eagle's long-term project in *Grimus*, after he has fallen through a 'hole in the Mediterranean, into that other sea, that not-quite-Mediterranean' where Calf Island is situated, 'and was carried towards the misty beach in the first light of dawn as Mr Virgil Jones rocked in his chair' (G, p. 38). In this case *Virgil Jones* – combining some of the traits of Dante's poet-hero in his *Divine Comedy* and some of Mr. Everyman's features – is eventually going to become Flapping Eagle's spiritual guide or *psycho-pomp*, when he attempts to explore the secrets and hidden recesses of this mysterious island. But the outcome of Flapping Eagle's quest in the last resort turns out to be disastrous, for it ends up with the wholesale annihilation of the sacred centre, the Island of the Blessed or the Island of Immortals, of Calf Island itself: 'Deprived of its connection with all relative Dimensions, the world of Calf Mountain was slowly unmaking itself, its molecules and atoms breaking, dissolving, quietly vanishing into primal, unmade energy. The raw material of being was claiming its own' (G, p. 270). Instead of saving the world Flapping Eagle – who has refrained from making use of his allegedly 'life-transmuting trophy' or magical tool *par excellence*, the so-called Stone Rose – has actually destroyed this would-be utopia. That is, he has desisted from using a powerful magical tool, capable of making its possessor fit for intradimensional travel and other preternatural feats, and instead employed the same Stone Rose to create a world that contained no Stone Rose. This quasi-suicidal act, both on his own behalf and on behalf of the other islanders seems synonymous with obeying the impulses of the death drive.

Like a would-be ontological trickster Flapping Eagle – in his capacity as a time- and space-traveller – can also be related to some of today's most important philosophical concerns. His ability to reshuffle or remodel our present three-dimensional world in unexpected ways reminds us of Nietzsche's focus on *philosophy as a game*, and the philosopher as a kind of foolhardy gambler, juggling metaphysical issues like balls in the air, as it were: '[the philosopher] can no longer *lead* as a man of knowledge ... , unless he wants to become a great actor, a Cagliostro and pied piper of the spirit, in short a mis-leader ... but the genuine philosopher ... lives "unphilosophically" and "unwisely", above all *imprudently*, and bears the burden and duty of a hundred attempts and temptations of life – he risks *himself* constantly, he plays *the* dangerous game ...'[10] As a matter of fact, from the very outset we notice Flapping Eagle's slippery status, his inability to maintain any kind of permanent or stable notion of personal identity. The protagonist's penchant for imitating or mimicking the behavioural codes of others is pointed out very early in the text: '[Flapping Eagle] noticed in himself, not for the first time, a tendency to adopt the speaking style and speech patterns of others' (G, p. 40). In this connection we might argue that the existential stakes may be interpreted in two diametrically opposed ways: either as simply a symptom of a weak ego, or as an indication of Flapping Eagle's status as a twentieth-century trickster, as an 'enemy of boundaries' (Kerényi), including in this case, the boundaries of the self. And this somewhat wavering self-image on the part of the main character can be related to the way in which the novel 'brings a whole series of different codes – associated with a number of literary genres and conventions – into play. The text is characterized by its very heterogeneity, its refusal to adhere to any *one* particular semiotic code, any *one* narratological scheme.'[11] The multiple personality disorder of the protagonist can be said to mirror or duplicate the multi-*generic* status of the narrative.

In section 2 below, I shall focus on the way in which Salman Rushdie in *Grimus* manipulates and deconstructs his various mainly European and Asian sources, thereby, to a certain extent, employing them for other purposes than those for which they were initially designed. In that context I shall take into consideration what intertextual links can be identified in the novel. In section 3, I shall focus on the question of genre and in section 4 on the manner in which theoretical considerations – postcolonial and postmodern – can be introduced into a reading of *Grimus*.

2

Grimus is Salman Rushdie's first novel, and in later years, after *Midnight's Children* (1981), the writer distanced himself to a certain degree from his literary firstling. In 1982 he commented on his own debut as follows: 'I think *Grimus* is quite a clever book. But that's not entirely a compliment. It's too clever for its own good ...'[12] In another interview in 1985 he said: 'I feel very distant from [*Grimus*], mainly because I don't like the language it is written in. It's a question of hearing your own voice, and I don't hear it because I hadn't found it then.'[13] In her article ' "Rehearsing Voices": Salman Rushdie's *Grimus*' Catherine Cundy has similar objections to the novel: '*Grimus* is clearly a novel from a period when Rushdie had not yet achieved the synthesis of diverse cultural strands and narrative forms. He rightly attributes the novel's failure to this lack of a defined voice at its heart, or even, to borrow from Sufism, a unified voice which expresses its own diversity', and she then reproduces the quote from the *Scripsi* interview above.[14] However this may be, I still consider it worthwhile paying attention to Salman Rushdie's subtle manipulation of his narrative materials in this novel, the way he – like a true literary trickster – disrupts or deconstructs what Jacques Derrida has called 'the law of genre'.[15]

Moreover, a number of different mythological systems intersect – and interact – in the novel. We can find traces of 'Western', Native American and Asian mythological elements embedded in various ways in the narrative structure of *Grimus*. According to Idries Shah in his study *Oriental Magic* (1956), '[m]any stories have been handed down in the East relating to the search for the Elixir of Life, by which immortality could be secured'.[16] In ancient China, the search for the Isles of the Blessed – where immortality might be acquired – was undertaken by more than one emperor. Thus the Emperor Wu Ti in the year 133 BC is advised by an alchemist ([Li] Shao-chün): 'When your powers of long life have been increased [by alchemical means] you will be able to see the *hsien* [immortals] who live on the Island of P'êng-lai that is in mid-ocean. When you have seen them, and have also performed the sacrifices in honour of heaven and earth, you will become immortal.'[17] But as is explicitly stated by Major Yetts in the article just quoted, overseas paradises have been envisaged both 'in the West and in the Far East'[18] – the Irish cleric St Brendan's voyage to the Islands of the Blessed in the Far West is just one obvious example of the way such fantasies have appealed to the 'Western' imagination.

In *Grimus*, however, immortality appears to be a highly problematic issue – for here immortality is no longer associated with spiritual Enlightenment and an initiate's mysterious approach to the divine or celestial realm. Even if both Flapping Eagle, his sister Bird-Dog, and everybody else on Calf Island have obtained immortality by means of the elusive Elixir of Life, eternal life in this case in the long run turns out to be synonymous with ontological loss and an altogether mediocre lifestyle. Here we may bear in mind what Yetts writes about the First Chinese Emperor, who 'grew so obsessed with the desire to attain hsienship and evade the common fate of mortals through the magic agencies to be found in the Isles of the Blest that he became an easy dupe in the hands of Taoist adventurers, who imposed upon his credulity to further their own ambitious designs'.[19] Immortality can thus inadvertently be associated with the dubious activities of professional swindlers and charlatans.

However, there is one literary parallel that bears a much more obvious resemblance to the portrayal of the search for immortality in *Grimus*, and that is Jorge Luis Borges's 'The Immortal' ('El inmortal') from his *El Aleph* (1949). The first-person narrator of the story, the antiquarian Josephus Cartaphilus from Smyrna, obtains immortality and visits the City of the Immortals in a remote African desert. But after almost 2,000 years on earth, he longs for death and finally finds it, when he crosses a river capable of counteracting the effects of the *other* river that gave him immortality in the first place, for '[a] *river can be found whose waters bestow immortality* [on humans]; *somewhere another river may be found whose waters cancel it*'.[20] In this case eternal life is experienced as a curse rather than a blessing, and the City of the Immortals appears to be built by deities who are stark raving mad: 'To the impression of enormous antiquity were added others: of the interminable, of the atrocious, of the completely insane. I had traversed a labyrinth, but the glorious City of the Immortals terrorized and repelled me.'[21] In *Grimus* eternal life in a similar manner turns out to be a curse rather than a blessing, and Flapping Eagle's final act – where he creates a world that contains no Stone Rose – ultimately leads to the wholesale annihilation of the Island of the Immortals (Calf Island). As in Borges's story, in *Grimus* we come across a thematic preoccupation with labyrinths (the labyrinth is one of Jorge Luis Borges's favourite topoi). When Flapping Eagle enters the Kafkaesque Grimushome, inhabited by the arch-wizard and power-crazed patriarch of Calf Island, Grimus himself, he and his female companion, the prostitute Media, also have to traverse a labyrinth: 'The house was a kind of rough triangular labyrinth, the face which it presented to the ascending steps being the jagged base of the triangle ... Inside, Flapping Eagle and Media found a bewildering series of interlocking rooms ...' (G, p. 241, my ellipses).

The labyrinth is the predominant topos in Rushdie's novel on a higher level of abstraction as well, insofar as it thematises what Virgil Jones, who is Flapping Eagle's host and his guide when he climbs Calf Mountain, terms 'the theory of potential existences'. What Virgil Jones asks Flapping Eagle to focus on is a somewhat extravagant conceptual *hypothesis*: 'So suppose there were, say, merely four potential pasts and futures for the Mediterranean sea. In one of them, there never was nor will be an island such as this. In another the island existed but no longer does. In a third the island does not exist but will at some time in the future. And in the fourth ... he gestured around him ... it has existed; and continues to do so' (G, pp. 55–6 (Rushdie's ellipses)). But as a matter of fact, all these dimensions 'come in several varieties ... There are a million possible Earths with a million possible histories, all of which exist simultaneously' (G, p. 56 (my ellipsis)). These cosmological speculations bear a certain resemblance to what we may come across in quantum theory or, for that matter, to the probabilistic model of the universe suggested in many of the new cosmologies. As a matter of fact, '[i]t is quite remarkable that from the microworld [i.e. the world of the atom] we can predict the possible existence of [a] host of other macro-worlds'.[22]

But such a 'many worlds' theory can be found as a decisive thematic element in many other literary contexts as well (for instance in Philip Pullman's *His Dark Materials* trilogy, 1995–2000). And once more Jorge Luis Borges offers a clear-cut example of this, namely in his short story 'The Garden of Forking Paths' (1941), where the learned sinologist Stephen Albert comments on the first-person narrator's ancestor, Ts'ui Pên, and the 'interminable novel' he bestowed on posterity: '*The Garden of Forking Paths* is a picture, incomplete yet not false, of the universe such as Ts'ui Pên conceived it to be ... He believed in an infinite series of times, in a dizzily growing, ever spreading network of diverging, converging and parallel times. This web of time ... embraces *every* possibility. We do not exist in most of them. In some you exist and not I, while in others I do, and you do not, and in yet others both of us exist. In this one, in which chance has favoured me, you have come to my gate. In another, you, crossing the garden, have found me dead. In yet another, I say these very same words, but am an error, a phantom.'[23] What is offered here is, in other words, once more a *probabilistic model of the universe* – similar to the one foregrounded in Rushdie's novel, with its speculative approach to twentieth-century cosmology and its focus on intradimensional travel.

3

Borges's speculative fiction is occasionally classified as science fiction. Calf Island on the other hand bears a certain resemblance to islands dominated – or terrorised – in one way or another by a powerful patriarchal mogul or a mad scientist, such as those portrayed by Jules Verne or H. G. Wells. Those somewhat ambiguously invested representatives of Victorian patriarchy could be essentially benevolent in their behaviour towards others – their subordinates and visitors to the island, for example – as turns out to be the case as far as Captain Nemo is concerned in Verne's *The Mysterious Island* (1874). Or they could be repressive and reckless in their fanatical pursuit of their destructive objectives – like Wells's scientist-villain in *The Island of Doctor Moreau* (1896).[24] Rushdie's Grimus, whose name anagrammatically refers to the fabulous super-bird Simurg(h) in Farid Ud-Din Attar's twelfth-century poem *The Conference of the Birds*, resembles both Nemo and Dr Moreau. For to begin with, Grimus's project appears to be beneficent, when he creates Calf Island as a quasi-paradisiacal environment; but eventually his misuse of so-called 'Conceptual Technology' (employing the Stone Rose for this purpose) turns out to lead to disastrous results. In the end, incessant *blinks* tend to dominate the whole setting, because the cosmic continuum is essentially destabilised. Here we may bear in mind what Brian McHale writes about postmodernist fiction and its 'flickering' symptomatology: 'Not only presented objects but, says [Roman] Ingarden, entire "ontic spheres", worlds, may flicker. The worlds projected by means of these strategies of self-erasure are precisely such flickering worlds.'[25]

We come across several references to Dante's *Divine Comedy* in *Grimus*, where the relationship between Flapping Eagle and Virgil Chanakya Jones bears a certain resemblance to the *liaison dangereuse* between Dante and Virgil in the medieval poem. In the latter, Virgil becomes the persona's guide in the Otherworld, all the way through Hell and Purgatory until they reach the Gates of Paradise. At the end of Canto I in Dante's Inferno the poet implores his 'master': ' " ... lead me where thou now hast said, so that

I may see the gate of St Peter, and those whom thou makest so sad." Then he moved; and I kept on behind him.'[26] And whereas Dante in the said Canto I loses his way 'in a dark wood',[27] Flapping Eagle 'was climbing a mountain into the depths of an inferno, plunging deep into myself' (G, p. 74). In other words, Flapping Eagle's journey seems essentially to be an *inner journey*, where he has to confront his own traumatic past and the demonic agents of his unconscious.

The distance between Rushdie's fictional world and that of his literary predecessors becomes particularly clear if we take into consideration the third part of *Grimus*, where Flapping Eagle finally gets access to Grimushome (corresponding to Dante's *Paradiso*) and where the Stone Rose (embodying the technological knowhow of a higher civilisation, that of the so-called Gorfs) replaces the 'white rose' of Canto XXXI of *Paradiso*: 'In form, then, of a white rose displayed itself to me that sacred soldiery which in his blood Christ made his spouse ...'[28] In *Grimus* Flapping Eagle at this point overcomes the antagonist of the novel (Grimus), and immediately afterwards the father-tyrant is killed by a local posse, representing in this context the Freudian brother horde, whose members 'united to overpower their father and, as was the custom in those days, devoured him raw'.[29]

As a matter of fact, quite a few twentieth-century science fiction texts/films operate with the idea of a superior extraterrestrial civilisation observing our own ('ET, call home!') – from Anna Kavan's *Ice* (1967) to Doris Lessing's *Briefing for a Descent into Hell* (1971) and her *Canopus in Argos* series (1979–83). In *Grimus*, 'the most intelligent life-form in any Galaxy' are the Gorfs. And after taking over some of Grimus's consciousness, Flapping Eagle encounters 'the second thought-form', that of 'the great thinker Dota himself' (G, p. 262). Everything in the world of the Gorfs (in this case called 'Thera' alias 'Earth') is expressed by means of anagrams ('Gorf' is 'Frog' and 'Dota' is 'Toad', etc.). What is interesting in this connection is that according to an eccentric French amateur linguist, Jean-Pierre Brisset (1837–1923), in his study *La Science de Dieu* (1900), all human languages can be traced back to our forefathers in the swamp, i.e. the frogs.[30] No wonder that the Gorfs in *Grimus* ('They look like frogs, I thought. Huge stone frogs')[31] can be represented as superior beings compared to us poor earthmen! In Brisset's perspective our predecessors thus belong to the animal kingdom, and Darwinian speculations about the biological descent of Man have been replaced by what looks like a purely linguistic aetiology.

Grimus himself refers anagrammatically to the legend of the Simurg: 'When I became Grimus, I took the name from a respect for the philosophy

16 Idries Shah, *Oriental Magic* (New York: E.P. Dutton & Co., Inc., 1973 (1956)), p. 87.

17 Major W. Perceval Yetts: 'Taoist Tales', Part III, *New China Review* 2 (1920), p. 297.

18 *Ibid.*, p. 290.

19 *Ibid.*, p. 295.

20 Jorge Luis Borges, *El Aleph* (Madrid and Buenos Aires: Alianza/Emecé, Decimonovena reimpresión, 1991), p. 23. My translation, Borges's italics: '*Existe un río cuyas aguas dan la inmortalidad; en alguna región habrá otro río cuyas aguas la borren.*'

21 *Ibid.*, p. 15. My translation: 'A la impresión de enorme antigüedad se agregaron otras: la de lo interminable, la de lo atroz, la de lo complejamente insensato. Yo haba cruzado un laberinto, pero la nítida Ciudad de los Inmortales me atemorizó y repugnó.'

22 John Taylor, *Black Holes: The End of the Universe?* (Glasgow: Fontana Collins, 1974), p. 174.

23 Jorge Luis Borges, *Fictions*, ed. and with an Introduction by Anthony Kerrigan (London: John Calder, 1985), p. 91 (Borges's italics, my ellipses).

24 See my reading of *The Island of Doctor Moreau* in 'The Rise of Science Fiction', *Inventing the Future: Science Fiction in the Context of Cultural History and Literary Theory*, ed. Ib Johansen and Peter Rønnov-Jessen, *The Dolphin* 11 (April 1985), pp. 19–21.

25 Brian McHale, *Postmodernist Fiction* (First published by Methuen in 1987; this edition London and New York: Routledge, 1989), p. 101.

26 *The Inferno of Dante Alighieri* (London and New York: Dent and Dutton, 1964), p. 11 (my ellipsis).

27 *Ibid.*, p. 3.

28 *The Paradiso of Dante Alighieri* (London: J.M. Dent & Sons, Ltd., 1965), p. 375 (my ellipsis).

29 Sigmund Freud, *Moses and Monotheism: Three Essays*, trans. and ed. James Strachey (London: The Hogarth Press and the Institute of Psycho-Analysis, 1974), p. 81. Freud's theory of original parricide was initially put forward in his *Totem and Taboo* (1912–13).

30 Cf. Jean-Jacques Lecercle, *Philosophy through the Looking-Glass: Language, Nonsense, Desire* (London: Hutchinson, 1985), p. 25.

31 Rushdie, *Grimus*, p. 261: the first-person narrator here is Flapping Eagle.

32 Jorge Luis Borges with Margarita Guerrero, *The Book of Imaginary Beings* (1967), revised, enlarged and translated by Norman Thomas di Giovanni in collaboration with the author (Harmondsworth, Middlesex: Penguin Books, reprinted with revisions 1974), p. 131.

33 Farid Ud-Din Attar, *The Conference of the Birds*, trans. S.C. Nott with brush drawings by Kate Adamson (London and New York: Continuum Publishing Inc., 2000), p. 147.

34 See Henry James, *The Tragic Muse*, ed. with an Introduction by Philip Horne (London: Penguin Books, 1995), p. 4. From the 'Preface': ' ... what do such large loose baggy monsters [like Thackeray's *The Newcomes*, Alexandre Dumas' *The Three Musketeers*, or Tolstoi's *Peace and War* (sic)], with their queer elements of the accidental and the arbitrary, actually *mean*?' (James's italics, my

ellipsis). In *The Literary Fantastic: From Gothic to Postmodernism* (New York: Harvester Wheatsheaf, 1990), Neil Cornwell groups Rushdie with Joyce and Pynchon in a literary company handling narrative materials in novels precisely as it is done in Henry James's 'large loose baggy monsters'. He also uses the term: *the portmanteau novel*.

35 *The Encyclopaedia of Islam*, Vol. IV (Leiden: E. J. Brill, 1973), p. 401 (my ellipsis).

36 See Mikhail Bakhtin, *Problems of Dostoevsky's Poetics*, ed. and trans. Caryl Emerson, Introduction by Wayne C. Booth (Minneapolis: University of Minnesota Press, 1984), pp. 114–16.

37 *Ibid.*, p. 124 (Bakhtin's italics).

38 Friedrich Nietzsche, *Thus Spake Zarathustra*, an adaptation based on the Thomas Common Translation, Prologue, § 5 (www.luminary.ns/nz/zarathustra. html-101k).

39 *Ibid.*, § 5.

40 Edward W. Said, *Representations of the Intellectual: The 1993 Reid Lectures* (London: Vintage, 1994), p. 47 (my ellipses, Said's italics).

41 Salman Rushdie, 'Is Nothing Sacred?', from *Imaginary Homelands: Essays and Criticism 1981–1991* (London: Granta Books/Penguin Books, 1991), p. 428.

42 Salman Rushdie, *Haroun and the Sea of Stories* (London: Granta Books/Penguin Books, 1990), p. 15.

43 *Ibid.*, p. 208.

7

ABDULRAZAK GURNAH

Themes and structures in
Midnight's Children

Midnight's Children is a grand book, in the ambition and the scope of its subject, and in the daring and dynamism of its method. It is also an intimate book, attentive to childhood memories of people and neighbourhoods. In both these respects, subject and method, the novel has sources which influenced and informed its construction, and these will be discussed in more detail below. One of them is the novel *The Tin Drum* by Günter Grass, first published in German in 1959. In 1985, Rushdie paid this tribute to Grass and to the novel:

> In the summer of 1967 ... when I was twenty years old, I bought from a bookshop in Cambridge a paperback copy of *The Tin Drum* ... There are books that open doors for their readers ... And then there are readers who dream of becoming writers ... [For them] there are (if they are lucky) books which give them ... permission to become the sort of writers they have it in themselves to be. This is what Grass's great novel said to me in its drumbeats: Go for broke. Always try and do too much. Dispense with safety nets. Take a deep breath before you begin talking. Aim for the stars. Keep grinning. Be bloody minded. Argue with the world.[1]

This was four years after the publication and great triumph of his own *Midnight's Children*, a novel which demonstrates the daring that Rushdie claims Grass inspired in him, and which in its own right has inspired a generation of Indian writers. *Midnight's Children* is now a central text in the study of the postcolonial phenomenon in writing in English, and has engaged the attention of scholars and critics, as well as the general student of literature.

Midnight's Children was published in 1981, and before the end of that year had made its author famous and won him the Booker Prize. It was received with enthusiasm by most of its reviewers, who recognised its originality and dynamism even when its detailed ambitions were not yet clear to all its readers. Rushdie himself has described how Western readers take his writing to be fantasy, and South Asian readers take it to be history.[2] Perhaps it is both, and like other great books, much else besides: politics, social history, farce, filmic extravaganza, uncouth comedy, and a tragedy of loveless families.

The discussion that follows will be organised in four parts: the novel's structure, its methods of narration and their sources, its form, and its engagement with India's recent history.

I

The novel is divided into three parts. The first part covers the period 1915–47, and is told over eight chapters. It recounts the lives of the grandparents' generation, and establishes the trail of loss and disillusion that begins with Aadam Aziz's loss of faith and his discovery of the God-shaped hole in his chest: 'can't you see there's a hole in the middle of me the size of a melon?'[3] The loss is associated with Abroad, a metaphorical and physical location of unsettling knowledge whose outcome is division and doubt, 'that middle place' of unbelief. Before travelling, the world is a Paradise, a condition which 'diaspora' transforms into loss of both innocence and belonging: 'Now, returning, he saw through travelled eyes ... and felt sad, to be at home and feel so utterly enclosed' (MC, p. 11). It is a theme which is developed and made complex in *The Satanic Verses* (1988), but here the novel opens with this sense of loss, and through the figure of Dr Aziz inaugurates the narrative of India's modernity as ambivalence and doubt. Aadam Aziz knew that the 'orientalist' narrative his German friends had constructed about him was 'an invention of their ancestors' and was untrue, yet he was stranded in unbelief: 'unable to worship a God in whose existence he could not wholly disbelieve' (MC, p. 12). The antithesis of Aadam Aziz's doubt is Tai the boatman, 'a quirky, enduring familiar spirit of the valley' (MC, p. 15) whose conviction of the continuity of existence is almost nihilistic. It recognises neither time nor 'the inevitability of change' (MC, p. 15), and runs human history through the valley as if it were a personal spectacle. Tai refuses to wash because he deplores change, a characteristic fusion of the real and the metaphorical which is one of the methods of the novel.

The opening section also introduces the nose as an organ of note, and later of miracle. This is one of the intertexts with *Tristram Shandy*, as we shall see later, and in both novels it is a misleading indicator of aristocratic ancestry. It is Tai the boatman, who first draws attention to the mystic powers of the nose, and in particular, Aadam Aziz's great nose: 'A nose like that, little idiot, is a great gift. I say: trust it' (MC, p. 17). Later, we find that it is in the nose that Saleem Sinai's miraculous 'midnight' powers reside.

Padma, the listener in the novel, appears in this opening section too, a plump muscular 'goddess'. Where Scheherazade had the king, Shahariya, as her listener, Saleem has Padma: '[T]hick of waist, somewhat hairy of forearm', who spends her days stirring vats of pickle (MC, p. 24). The repeated references to *The Thousand and One Nights* both gesture towards a genre of narrative which informs this one, but also make play with the idea of narrative under pressure. Scheherazade tells her story to stay alive, and she tells her stories to an all-powerful King Shahariya who also needs to be saved from himself. Each night's story will beguile him from carrying out his despairing cruelties, until after a thousand and one nights he will rediscover his humanity and learn to love. Saleem's audience is Padma, the 'unofficial' listener. (This will be discussed in a little more detail later in this chapter.) To her Saleem entrusts the story, and in this respect she represents 'the people', the line of transmission of 'unofficial' stories.[4] It is worth noting here that 'the people' are often privileged as trustworthy and 'authentic' in Rushdie's early novels – in *Midnight's Children*, for example, the occupants of the magicians' quarter are one representation of 'the people', profanely squatting in the shadow of the Friday mosque and clinging to a vision of plurality and secularism despite the erosion of these founding principles by Indira Gandhi's ambition. Padma's 'earthiness' is one of the many narrative expectations that *Midnight's Children* overturns. In the aristocratic traditions of *A Thousand and One Nights*, protagonists are often kings and princesses, often menaced by besotted jinns, and even the most humble figures cannot be taken for granted, because they are capable of transformation into holy men or heiresses. Padma's 'nobility' lies in her uncomplicated directness, which is figured as a kind of integrity. Her tenderness, despite appearances, affirms this unselfconscious truthfulness.

In the domestic narrative of the novel, the central event of this first part is the extended courtship of Aziz and Naseem Ghani through the 'perforated sheet'. We witness the early days of their marriage, which establish the lines of their lifelong confrontation, and the transformation of Naseem Aziz into the Reverend Mother, a figure of melodramatic narrow-mindedness. The public narrative is that of approaching independence and the debate over partition. There is a dramatic account of the notorious Amristar massacre (MC, p. 36), where the British General Dyer ordered his soldiers (who were mostly Indian) to open fire on the civilian protesters. This account also includes the first film intertext 'we cut to a long-shot – nobody from Bombay should be without a basic film vocabulary' (MC, p. 33). It is an event which has a huge impact on Indians and the British in the decolonising process. Another dimension of the independence narrative is the debate over partition, and this is figured, at this stage in the novel, through Mian Abdullah, a Muslim who opposed the partition of India, and whose opposition persuaded many other Muslims who preferred nation to religion, including Aadam Aziz. Mian Abdullah is later recalled in the figure of Picture Singh, the Most Charming Man in the World, who presides over the magician's quarter at the time of Indira Gandhi's Emergency, and who also speaks for India's multiplicity against the drive to simplify it. One of Mian Abdullah's followers is Nadir Khan the poet, soft-bellied and timid, who falls in love with Mumtaz, the daughter of Aadam Aziz and the mother of Saleem. The domestic narrative merges with the public one, and this too is a characteristic conceit of the novel, taken at times to fantastic lengths.

In the figure of the poet, Rushdie plays with stereotypes. This poet is effete and (as it turns out) impotent, yet he remains Mumtaz's lifelong love. Until his impotence is discovered by the Reverend Mother, and he is expelled, he and Mumtaz live a contented child-like life under the floorboards, embracing and whispering, playing with the silver spittoon they had been given as a wedding present (MC, p. 45). It is the only love which endures in the novel, despite the obstacles, privileging the understatement of mutual undemanding affection over the havoc and the inevitable bitterness of passion. (Padma's devotion to Saleem, although a more robust besottedness appropriate to a muscular pickler, also hints at a selfless integrity.) Mumtaz is re-named Amina by Ahmed Sinai, her new husband and Saleem's 'father', and makes no objection. Hers is an act of compliance she has grown into as the youngest and the darkest daughter, whose marriage to Nadir Khan had brought humiliation on the family. His is an act of controlling patriarchy: 'this man who had re-named and so re-invented her, thus in a sense becoming her father as well as her new husband' (MC, p. 66). The contrast between the two marriages is striking, and Mumtaz/ Amina has to teach herself to love Ahmed Sinai in bits, as her own father had learned to love his wife through the perforated sheet. In both cases, the full figure is intolerable.

Ahmed Sinai has no sense of direction (MC, p. 73) but somehow he selects the move to Bombay, the city of miracle, although his choice is thoroughly material: 'Property is dirt cheap there now' (MC, p. 90). In good time, before the arrival of India's independence and of Saleem, who needs to be born there, Ahmed Sinai and his pregnant wife make the move to Bombay. Ahmed Sinai never quite stops thinking of Bombay as something he can make money out of, but in Saleem's narration (and in Rushdie's œuvre) Bombay – 'Our Bombay, Padma!' (MC, p. 93) – is both a metaphor for possible futures for India, and the site for memories of lost childhood and home. In later novels it also becomes a metaphor for India's *lost* futures, as it comes to signify the displacement of tolerance and plurality by a narrow and criminal sectarianism.

The second part of the novel spans 1947–65 and tells of the birth of Saleem Sinai and of India. Pakistan was born the previous day. In other words, the narrator of the novel is born in the ninth chapter, 116 pages after his narrative began, so he had been absent from everything he earlier described in such dramatic detail. In this respect too *Midnight's Children* recalls *Tristram Shandy* as well as *The Tin Drum*, where the narrator is born some considerable way into the events of the novel. At the heart of this section is the story of the Methwold children growing up and of the children of midnight learning of their telepathic abilities. The narrative of childhood is intimate and painful as Saleem suffers one farcical humiliation after another, culminating in the discovery of his miraculous powers while hiding in a washing basket full of dirty laundry. When the midnight's children are properly introduced, they signify a transforming potential of global magnitude:

> as though history, arriving at a point of the highest significance and promise, had chosen to sow, in that instant, the seeds of a future which would genuinely differ from anything the world had seen up to that time. (MC, p. 195)

There were 1,001 children but 420 die, another play on *One Thousand and One Nights*, of course, but 420 is also an intertextual reference to *Shree 420*, a film which has an important influence in Rushdie's work, and which in this instance would have been a joke with his Indian readers.[5] It is as if the moment of India's independence was a moment of promise for humanity, signified by the 'Midnight Children's Council' as a group capable of profound understanding of each other, but which corruption and cynicism could not allow to survive. Nehru's great ambition for post-independence India begins to disintegrate almost as soon as India is founded, in the partition violence and in the language marches. Throughout this period, Saleem's delusion that he is the cause of all major national events grows.

It is in this middle section of the novel that suspicions about Saleem's parentage become evident to his 'father': 'I should have known. Just look, where am I in that face. That nose, I should have …' (MC, p. 236). Ahmed Sinai thinks his wife had been unfaithful, but the reader has known for more than 100 pages before this that the babies were swopped at birth by the nurse, Mary Pereira. The scene of Ahmed Sinai's rage is described as a 'take' with soundtrack, and closes with a '(Fade out.)' (MC, p. 237), not only reiterating the filmic intertext but drawing attention to an ancient narrative ploy and a favourite of Indian popular cinema: swopped babies and mistaken identities. Finally, during this middle section, the Sinai family moves to Pakistan, and the move itself is a narrative of convoluted melodramas and lingering tragedies. There is a return to Bombay, during which Saleem's sinuses are drained and he loses his miracle powers:

> The operation whose ostensible purpose was the draining of my inflamed sinuses and the once-and-for-all clearing of my nasal passages had the effect of breaking whatever connection had been made in a washing-chest; of depriving me of nose-given telepathy; of banishing me from the possibility of midnight children. (MC, p. 304)

There is another move to Pakistan, and the section reaches a climax with the war between India and Pakistan in 1965, during which Saleem is 'brained (just as prophesied) by my mother's silver spittoon' (p. 343) and loses his memory as well as his home.

The third part, of seven chapters, covers the period 1970–8 and tells of the events in East Pakistan that led to the breakup of Pakistan and the formation of Bangladesh. By now, Saleem's nose has proved to have other miracle qualities; he can smell treachery, vengeance and mines. In this capacity, Saleem's nose is taken to East Pakistan, as 'a human dog' in a West Pakistani hit squad, but also to allow the narrative to witness the killings in the Bangladesh war. Saleem himself has no memory, no knowledge of himself, and, brutalised by unselfconsciousness, he has no feelings. But in a novel in which the miraculous is mundane, Saleem regains his memory in the Sundarbans and is magically returned to Bombay by Parvati-the-Witch, one of the children of midnight, accompanied by Picture Singh. In India, Mrs Indira Gandhi declares the Emergency, and among other things, brings to an end Nehru's promise of freedom, or at least the particular form of it that he celebrated in his 'tryst with history' speech on the night of independence. It also puts an end to Saleem's delusion of responsibility for India's history as he comes to grasp his impotence under the onslaught of Mrs Gandhi's sterner form of history-making and her desire for power. The novel ends with the defeat of Mrs Indira Gandhi and the hope that new myths will have to be made now that the Nehru one of an awakening tolerant India has proved too optimistic. Despite the suggestive optimism of its conclusion, Timothy Brennan, in a very apt phrase, rightly includes the novel in a genre which he calls 'the nationalism of mourning'.[6]

2

As we have observed, the narrative has an audience, the muscular, earthy Padma, whose name is also the name of a mythic lotus goddess. The lotus grows in mud or dung and represents the possibility of beauty and nobility arising out of impurity. The presence of Padma as listener enhances the mythic form of the story. She is familiar with the sensationalist realist form of mythic narrative and interrupts to speed the story in directions she anticipates and prefers. These interruptions refine the cultural context of the narrative's reception, but they also give Rushdie the opportunity to describe his method, to say what kind of narrative this is not: 'But here is Padma at my elbow, bullying me back into the world of linear narrative' (MC, p. 38). Saleem's narration repeatedly refuses a linear narrative, anticipating, delaying, at times unable to resist blurting out the significance of an event to a future outcome, at other times appearing to struggle with admissions. Part of this is to do with the retrospective nature of the narrative, so that the meaning and significance of what is narrated is already known to the narrator, and the drama is created as much by withholding as by revealing. Linear narrative in these circumstances will lie. It will suggest order where there is disorder, a simple meaning where only complex fragments are possible. A linear narrative is 'official' in this respect, in the sense that Bakhtin uses the word, whereas the non-linear and interrupted form of the narrative suggests 'heteroglossia', where a multiplicity of voices and meaning are brought into play, a characteristic of 'unofficial' discourse.[7]

The presence of a listener affirms the suggestive orality of the narrative, its repetitions, its accumulation of details, its anticipations. Here is a famous quotation of Rushdie's describing his method in the novel:

> It's not linear. An oral narrative does not go from the beginning to the middle to the end of the story. It goes in great *swoops*, it goes in *spirals* or in loops, it every so often reiterates something that happened earlier to remind you, and then takes you off again, sometimes summarises itself, it frequently digresses off into something that the storyteller appears just to have thought of, then it comes back to the main thrust of the narrative. Sometimes it steps sideways and tells you about another, related story which is like the story he has been telling you and then it goes back to the main story ... So it's a very bizarre and pyrotechnical shape.[8]

Rushdie emphasises orality in this description of his technique, but he might just as well have been speaking of what Bakhtin calls the 'carnivalesque',[9] where facts and fantasy mingle to subvert the language of authority, and hierarchies are overturned by allowing the impossible to happen, where an impotent poet can come to signify enduring love and an illiterate stirrer of pickle-vats can be 'the ideal reader'. Padma as listener is 'captivated, helpless as a mongoose frozen into immobility by the swaying, blinkless eyes of a hooded snake, paralysed – yes! – by love' (MC, p. 121). Saleem reads this to Padma who is wounded and runs away, feeling herself mocked by his discovery and flaunting of her love. But in her absence, he finds he loses the sense of his narrative: '[I]n her absence, my certainties are falling apart' (MC, p. 166). He can no longer tell the difference between the pickles, and if the pickles signify something about how the process of history is a combination of sources out of which a narrative is blended, then his uncertainty also signifies a loss of the intuitive grasp that enables Saleem to sense the true narrative from the false one. This is how Saleem describes her return:

> I am at my table again; once again Padma sits at my feet, urging me on. I am balanced once more – the base of my isosceles triangle is secure. I hover at the apex, above present and past, and feel fluency returning to my pen.
>
> (MC, p. 194)

Typical of confused intentions which crowd the narrative and an aspect of a perversity consistent with the carnivalesque, on her return Padma unintentionally poisons Saleem with the love potion that was to make him love her.

The use of the grotesque is a dimension of the 'carnivalesque', and signifies an aspect of the 'unofficial' in the way it dwells on the body and its unavoidable transformations. The moment of Saleem's discovery of his telepathic ability comes about in the grotesque form of 'mucus rising higher than mucus was ever intended to rise' (MC, p. 162) and making an electrical contact that brings to life the capacity to receive telepathically. This happens while he is in the washing-chest involuntarily watching his mother on the commode. The body of Saleem dictates how and who he is, and proceeds in its anarchic logic to confound linearity and logic. One of the novel's allegorical metaphors is accelerated decline, in which moments of disintegration or transformation of the body coincide with national crises (MC, pp. 254, 298). One such moment, the disintegration of the potential of India's Midnight's Children, coincides with the destruction of yet another myth of the nation: 'The gradual disintegration of the Midnight's Children's Conference – which finally fell apart on the day the Chinese armies came down over the Himalayas to humiliate the Indian fauj – was already well under way' (MC, p. 254). Equally, power is given a grotesque dimension to emphasise its materiality, from Shiva's deformed knees and his irresistible fecundity, to the Widow's centre parting and her black-and-white hair.

As we remarked earlier, the novel's method has a number of different sources. We have noted an intertextual relationship with *The Thousand and One Nights* in the figure of the listener, and that there are many references to the text and repeated play with the number 1,001 throughout the novel. As is well known, another important source for *Midnight's Children* is Laurence Sterne's *Tristram Shandy*, whose narrator is also obsessed with the degeneration of his body and his approaching death, and breaks into the narrative to give an account of his decay. The novel begins long before the narrator's birth, postponing the 'real' beginning with delays and asides. There is some doubt about the narrator's parentage. Both narrators have extraordinary noses, and both are undone by a Widow.[10] In *Tristram Shandy*, there is a pseudo-scientific discussion of the nose as signifier of aristocratic ancestry, and in *Midnight's Children*, the first comment that Amina Sinai makes to her husband about their baby, is to remark on his nose and its resemblance to Aadam Aziz's, affirming the ancestral link. His nose, though, is not descended from Aadam Aziz but from the Englishman Methwold, and thus the Raj has left its mark on India while seeming to confirm Indian ancestral origins. And yet this sly imperial mark does not prevent self-definition, does not make Saleem less Indian. When the story of the baby-swap became known, Saleem tells Padma: 'we all found that it *made no difference*! I was still their son: they remained my parents. In a kind of collective failure of imagination, we learned that we simply could not think our way out of our pasts' (MC, p. 118). The 'collective failure of imagination' signifies Rushdie's sense of a forgiving and inclusive idea of Indian self-recognition, an idea which is consistent with the novel's valorisation of plurality and tolerance.

What Rushdie appears to admire about Sterne, in so far as we can extrapolate this from his comments about eighteenth-century literature in general and *Tom Jones* in particular, is the order that lies behind the appearance of disorder:

> the thing that's very impressive about *Tom Jones* is the plot, that you have this enormous edifice which seems to be freewheeling, rambling – and actually everything is there for a purpose. It's the most extraordinary piece of organization which at the same time seems quite relaxed and not straitjacketed by its plot. I think that's why the book is so wonderful. So, yes, I would have thought the eighteenth-century novel has something to do with mine.[11]

In particular, he appears to admire the 'relaxed' organisation, which looks permissive, inclusive and 'freewheeling', while never losing control. In other words, in addition to some plot devices that allow us to draw comparisons between *Midnight's Children* and *Tristram Shandy*, we can see that the novels' methods also bear comparison.

As was observed earlier, another novel that is often mentioned as 'lying behind' Rushdie's is Günter Grass's *The Tin Drum*.[12] The narrator of *The Tin Drum*, Oskar, is physically deformed and has magic powers. His voice can shatter glass and when he plays his tin drum(s) he can revisit moments in history. He too has a listener in the novel, his keeper in the asylum, and he is impotent just as Saleem is. Both narrators are compelled to write about their 'becoming' and about the unacknowledged roles they played in the events of their times. Both narrators see themselves as responsible for the history and politics of their thirty-year lives – for Oskar it is the history of Germany, and Danzig in particular, in the second quarter of the twentieth century, and for Saleem it is the history of India from Independence to the end of the Emergency, with all the atrocities and horrors of those times. Both narrators are menaced by a Widow/Witch.

Finally, the third text that Rushdie mentions as 'lying behind' his is Gabriel García Márquez's *One Hundred Years of Solitude*.[13] I think Timothy Brennan is right in seeing that Márquez's influence on Rushdie's novel is on providing a theory of fantasy which is referred to colonialism, whereas *The Tin Drum* 'provides a model in the figure of a physically deformed and morally reprehensible hero with magical powers'.[14] What Rushdie takes from Márquez is to write the presence of the magical in the everyday, to make the 'real' and fantasy run into each other. As critics have commented, this is not a technique which is unique to Márquez, and indeed the form of Hindu myth does just this as does the Indian popular cinema. However, Márquez's use of fantasy links it to a critique of colonialism, and Rushdie's even more so.

3

Against the appearance of 'chaos' in the method of the novel is imposed a series of forms. Form, Saleem tells us, is a longing for correspondences even against the odds: 'As a people we are obsessed with correspondences ... It is a sort of national longing for form – or perhaps simply an expression of our deep belief that forms lie hidden within reality; that meaning reveals itself only in flashes' (MC, p. 300). The midnight motif, linking the birth of the children with the birth of the nation, for both a moment of miraculous potential, is a recurring form in the novel. All major events happen at midnight: India's independence, the 'pepperpots' coup in Pakistan, the war with China. Midnight is the time of the uncanny, associated with magic and the unreal. Rushdie makes extensive use of the midnight trope, both as a pastiche of 'traditional' storytelling, and also as a satire on how the brutal (a coup or a war) and the banal (a flag ceremony) can be mystified by this kind of staging.

The figure 'thirty' is also a formal element in the narrative. The story is told in thirty chapters, by a thirty-year-old narrator, who is also the age of post-independence post-partition India. There are thirty pickle jars, one for each year, one for each chapter, and a thirty-first which is unfilled, signifying the stories of the future (MC, p. 460). Indeed, the process of writing itself takes place in the pickling factory (MC, p. 458) and pickling is figured as the historical process (MC, p. 461).

Allegory is a prominent formal device in the novel. Allegory does not rule out metaphor, but allows an event to have a concrete and metaphorical meaning simultaneously. For example, Saleem is a mutiplicity in himself: Hindu mother, English father, brought up Muslim by a Catholic ayah, and in this respect he is also a metaphor for polyglot and multi-faith Bombay, itself an example to India. But Saleem is also cracking, just as India is disintegrating, first through partition and then through corruption and the betrayal of its hopes by Indira Gandhi's Declaration of Emergency and the cruelties it made legal. This disintegration is also suggestively linked to the dispersal of the family, itself an allegory of nation.

But to speak of allegory as a fusion of the concrete and the metaphorical may also be to simplify Rushdie's practice in *Midnight's Children*, for the 'real' here can also be magical. Food, for example, conceals emotion and takes on the personality of the cook. The food Reverend Mother made is described as 'curries and meatballs of intransigence', because she had become so domineeringly obstinate. Mary Pereira, the ayah who had switched the babies at birth and who was so tormented by this act that she had given up midwifery to nurse Saleem, made pickles that 'had a partially counteractive effect – since she had stirred into them the guilt of her heart' (MC, p. 139). The 'counteractive effect' was not enough to prevent Amina Sinai filling up with rage when she ate the Reverend Mother's food. Amina herself stirred her 'disappointments into a hot lime chutney which never failed to bring tears to the eyes' of anyone who ate it (MC, p. 175). Saleem could also feel Aunt Alia's vengefulness in her furniture, and food: 'while we lived in her Guru Mandir mansion, she fed us the birianis of dissension and the nargisi koftas of discord' (MC, p. 330).

There are other examples of this method by which metaphors become 'real', where the abstract mingles with the concrete. Ahmed Sinai's shock at the freezing of all his assets because he was a Muslim makes him blurt out: 'The bastards have shoved my balls in an ice-bucket' (MC, p. 135), and Amina Sinai 'began to feel them growing colder and colder' (MC, p. 136). She manages to conceive Jamila just before they turn into cubes of ice, and Ahmed Sinai turns into an unapproachable monster.

Another example is the episode in the Sundarbans, the great tidal jungle at the mouth of the Ganges – 'the jungle which is so thick that history has hardly ever found the way in' (MC, p. 359) – which signifies a descent into the Underworld. The episode describes events that can only be fantastical in a way which takes them for 'real':

> Rainwater poured off leaves all around them, and they turned their mouths up to the roof of the jungle and drank; but perhaps because the water came to them by way of sundri leaves and mangrove branches and nipa fronds, it acquired on its journey something of the insanity of the jungle, so that as they drank they fell deeper and deeper into the thraldom of that livid green world where the birds had voices like creaking wood and all the snakes were blind.
>
> (MC, p. 362)

The Sundarbans episode is a trope of the epic form, because it is through this descent that Saleem will regain his memory, and the Pakistani soldiers with him will see through the national myth that had obscured their sense of responsibility as human beings. None the less, its method of allowing fantasy to become 'real' is characteristic of the novel. If the Sundarbans episode is something of a set-piece in this respect, the pseudo-curse that Ahmed Sinai makes up to impress Methwold with his ancient ancestry is flexibly worked into the narrative to very useful effect. Ahmed Sinai came to believe in his own invention and for years practised the curse on the dog. He assumed it did not work because he had the phrasing wrong, and kept practising to get it right. An old servant of the family, Musa, robbed Ahmed Sinai but swore his innocence and 'called down upon himself the curse of leprosy if he should prove a liar' (MC, p. 280). Years later, Musa returns, having contracted leprosy and now come to seek forgiveness from Ahmed Sinai. Mary Pereira catches sight of the man 'whose body lacked fingers and toes and was littered with boils and holes' (MC, p. 279) and takes it to be the ghost of her lover Joe D'Costa. Mary had switched the babies Saleem and Shiva to win back D'Costa, who was a socialist, and to whom Mary had thought this metaphorical redistribution of wealth would appeal and would win her back his love. She assumes that the ghost of Joe D'Costa has come back to expose her and rushes in to confess her baby-switch to the family. So the pseudo-curse persuades the old servant Musa that his leprosy is the result of a curse, and his return to seek forgiveness precipitates another series of events which were nothing to do with him, but which were necessary to move on the story.

4

The most pronounced allegorical forms in the novel concern the representation of history. There are repeated references to Saleem being linked to history ('I had been mysteriously handcuffed to history' (MC, p. 9);

'*Why, alone of all the more-than-five-hundred-million, should I have to bear the burden of history?*' (MC, pp. 382–3 (emphasis in the original)). What befalls India befalls him, indeed he is responsible for it happening. By the end, as the heteroglossic and multiple Indian family is fragmented and at war, he too cracks (or will soon crack) into six hundred million fragments. The figure of Saleem is an allegory for India, but it is also a misunderstanding of the individual's centrality to the narrative of nation.

Saleem is repeatedly inclined to see himself as the central figure of existence: 'I was already beginning to take my place at the centre of the universe; and by the time I had finished, I would give meaning to it all' (MC, pp. 126–7). The explanation he gives to himself is that, after the portents and prophecies before and at the moment of his birth, he fears insignificance: 'I became afraid that everyone was wrong – that my much-trumpeted existence might turn out to be utterly useless, void, and without the shred of a purpose' (MC, p. 152). So when he first hears voices, the first sign of the telepathic connection with the other 'midnight's children', he thinks he hears an archangel, like the prophet, and that he is therefore the last prophet come to announce the end of the world. This is what had been prophesied for him, he thinks, and he promptly announces himself to his family, only to receive a great slap on his left ear for his blasphemy, which deafens him.

The language marches in Bombay in the 1950s constitute another example of this self-positioning. Saleem inadvertently lands among the Marathi language marchers as a result of a mishap with a bicycle. When invited to say something in Gujarati he can only offer a childish phrase he had overheard the school bully using in mockery of the Gujarati. When this is taken up as a marching chant, he takes responsibility for the violence that came out of the language marches: 'In this way I became directly responsible for triggering off the violence which ended with the partition of the state of Bombay' (MC, p. 191).

Lord Khusro's ascension to swami-hood is another example of Saleem's delusion of centrality. Saleem lends one of his childhood friends Cyrus a Superman comic. It is the first issue in which the magical power of Superman is explained by his miraculous origin elsewhere in the Galaxy and his subsequent implanting in Mrs Kent as if he were a normal human baby. Saleem believes this is the source of the fake-mythic story that Mrs Dubash (Cyrus's mother) tells about the miraculous birth of her own son, whom she re-names Lord Khusro of Khusrovand. Saleem sees himself as the source of all significant contemporary events: 'I saw the hoardings trumpeting the coming of Lord Khusro of Khusrovand Bhagwan; and found myself obliged, yet again, to accept responsibility for the events of my turbulent, fabulous world' (MC, p. 270). As his power to control his mind grows, Saleem 'becomes' the people whose mind he enters 'And finally I hit my highest point: I became Jawaharlal Nehru' (MC, p. 174). During this 'occupation', it is he, Saleem, who was making things happen.

There is something comic and light-hearted about Saleem's obsessive delusion of centrality. The paragraph which describes his responsibility for the death of Nehru is a good example of this,[15] but the obsessiveness also describes the isolation of the self and the failure of family and community. It also allows Rushdie to develop the parallels between Saleem and India. Saleem, like India and Bombay, is also an imperial bequest. The Methwold estate is a further elaboration of this, and of course Saleem himself is a concrete allegorisation of the impossibility of refusing history: English father, Hindu mother, brought up Muslim etc. The birth of India coincides exactly with the birth of Saleem (MC, p. 116) and as we have seen, in some respects Saleem is an allegory of India. But in addition to these symbolic duties, there are other senses in which Saleem acts as a means of revisiting the Bombay of the 1950s for the power and poignancy of those recollections in their own right. And he is also a means of describing the failure of Pakistan and the great tragedy of the Bangladesh War. But within the two frames of the birth of nation and the birth of his voice, on the one hand, and the Emergency on the other, the central stories are those of Saleem and India. The moment of birth is one of great potential but it is attended by bloodshed and war which also anticipate the failure of the nation. Saleem and India are both cracking from the moment of their birth.

As we have observed, Bombay is constructed as an image of India's multiplicity: its languages, religions, cultures, histories. In contrast to Bombay is Pakistan. In Pakistan, Saleem could not reach the midnight's children: 'so that, exiled once more from my home, I was also exiled from the gift which was my truest birthright' (MC, p. 284). Karachi is described as 'grotesque' (MC, p. 309), and possessing 'an ugliness which eclipsed even my own' (MC, p. 307) and smelled of 'acquiescence' where Bombay smelled of 'nonconformity' (MC, p. 308). Most of all, it was not Bombay (MC, p. 307). In Pakistan, also, Saleem describes himself as 'surrounded by the somehow barren certitudes of the land of the pure' (MC, p. 316), and is almost overpowered by its formless meaninglessness (MC, p. 317). As is consistent with the novel's method, Pakistan as dystopia is made into a family metaphor, and the nation is allegorised as family. Pakistan is like a betrayal of 'our Bombay roots' and the family Sinai is mysteriously punished for its desertion by an 'occult series of reprisals' (MC, p. 338) which finally kills off all members of the family who made the move.

But it is in East Pakistan, the future Bangladesh, where the true corruption of the human potential represented by the rhetoric of independence is evident. Saleem describes Pakistan as 'a country where the truth is what it is instructed to be' (MC, p. 326), whose rulers and ruling families are cynical and arrogant. The authoritarian nature of this ruling elite is represented by the military and their intervention in government. The episode of the 'pepperpot revolution' comically exposes both the greed and the malleability of the officer corps in advancing their narrow interests. The East Pakistan sections in the novel describe the climax of the 'wrong-doing' of the Pakistani military (MC, pp. 356–8). The 'wrong-doing' has reached through all levels of the military and the government, as a corrupt myth of nation distorts reality, and prompts ordinary soldiers to participate in mass killings and atrocities (MC, p. 357). The pursuit-flight south of Saleem's 'hit squad' (he is only the 'man-dog' tracker for the team but, arguably, is just as blindly guilty as the rest) is towards the Sundarbans, which, as we have already noted, is a location of overwhelming otherness. We might see the flight as an attempt to escape from this sense of 'wrong-doing' by deserting 'into the historyless anonymity of rainforests' (MC, p. 360).

It is worth noting the predominance of the grotesque in this section of the novel, from the electrified urinal (MC, p. 353) to the colourless leeches and pale pink scorpions (MC, p. 362). It is a landscape in which reality is shifting and unprevailing, a nightmare landscape without history, in which the soldiers are tormented in turn by guilt and nostalgia, and are forced to learn new responsibilities as adults, although this is not the end of their torment, which increases to such a pitch that in the end they fill their ears with mud and become deaf. It is also in the Sundarbans that 'a transluscent serpent' bit Saleem and restored his memory (MC, p. 365) – except his name, which would be given back to him by Parvati-the-Witch. The descent to the Underworld has taught them almost intolerable shame and humiliation, and offered the ones still living the seduction of resignation in the shape of the temple girls who represent the waste of their dreams (MC, p. 367). They are returned to land by 'a tidal wave' and end up in the field of 'strange crops' outside of Dacca, covered with dead Pakistani and Indian soldiers, being harvested by 'a scavenging peasant moving about' (MC, p. 371). Amongst them Saleem sees the barely living bodies of Eyeslice, Hairoil and Sonny, childhood friends whom the venality of politicians had brought to this field of the dead.

Picture Singh makes his first appearance in Dacca (MC, p. 378) and inaugurates the final section of the novel. He is a snake charmer – 'the Most Charming Man in the World' – in Dacca to entertain Indian troops after their successful campaign. Parvati-the-Witch is also there and recognises Saleem from the 'Midnight's Children Conference' days. It is she who gives Saleem his name back: 'Saleem! O my God Saleem, you

Saleem Sinai, is it you Saleem?' (MC, p. 379). It is Parvati who magically transports him from Dacca back to Bombay, to the magicians' ghetto where Picture Singh benignly rules by example and by a rhetoric of justice. The magicians' ghetto is a realisation in miniature of Nehru's dream of a plural secular community. In some respects, then, Picture Singh represents the myth of India that was about to be terminated by the Emergency. But he also plays match-maker between Saleem and Parvati. At this point Parvati is already pregnant with the child of Shiva, Saleem's grotesque double, who will be born Aadam Sinai, another child who has misplaced a father. Aadam Sinai is constructed as representative of a generation which will have to create 'new myths' that are more practical and more durable than the one the Emergency was about to put to an end. So, in a sense, Picture Singh is also midwife to the new myths. For the Emergency is both the death of the old India and the moment of a new birth (MC, p. 419). The birth of Aadam Sinai is told in a language which repeats the birth of Saleem – with the difference that nothing grand is prophesied for Aadam, and his arrival was not accompanied by celebrations. He does not speak, as a protest against the Emergency, 'rendered dumb by a surfeit of sound' (MC, p. 420).

The Widow, driven by 'occult tyrannies' (MC, p. 9), brings into being a new India, an India of 'midnight', a time of darkness now, rather that the noisy miraculous promise of 1947. The penultimate chapter of the novel, 'Midnight', describes the vengefulness of the Emergency and the capture of Saleem, who is forced to reveal the secret and the names of the midnight's children. The Widow, fearful of what promise the 'children' represent, excises everything out of them, including their reproductive capacities. Clearly this a metaphor for the effect of the Emergency and its cruelties, to 'drain' hope and possibility out of the myth of India. To hold on to power, Mrs Gandhi had to flatter and ally herself with the enemies of that hope, and destroy all that Nehru had promised for the new nation: tolerance and freedom. The final chapter of the novel quotes Aadam Sinai's first words, 'Abracadabra', after three years, one month and two weeks, the period of the Emergency. 'New myths' (MC, p. 457) will have to replace the one Nehru had offered his nation in 1947.

Midnight's Children runs history with the narrative of the self, with the ego's vulnerability and its delusions. In the end, Saleem has to see himself in the mirror of humility and understand his defeat and that of the dream of a nation. The novel achieves its ends by employing a multiplicity of narrative forms and sources; oral, mythic, novelistic and filmic. The result is a complex and dynamic text which challenges and debates processes of fictional as well as historical narratives.

NOTES

1 Salman Rushdie, 'Salman Rushdie on Günter Grass', *Granta* 15 (Spring 1985), pp. 179–85. The lines cited are on p. 180.

2 Peter Craven, Michael Heyward and Penny Hueston, 'Interview', *Scripsi* 3 (2–3) (1985): 'Rushdie: [T]here was a tendency' to discuss it [*Midnight's Children*] much more as a Fantasy novel, whereas in India it's discussed as a history book' (p. 113).

3 Salman Rushdie, *Midnight's Children* (London: Jonathan Cape, 1981), p. 22. All further references will be abbreviated to MC and will be cited in the text.

4 'Why I have chosen to expound on Padma's musculature: these days, it's to those muscles, much as to anything ... that I'm telling my story .... I am learning to use Padma's muscles as my guides. When she's bored, I can detect in her fibres the ripples of uninterest; when she's unconvinced, there is a tic which gets going in her cheek.' (MC p. 270)

5 For a more detailed discussion of this influence, see Mishra in this volume. The number ('associated with fraud') is also significant in *The Satanic Verses*.

6 Timothy Brennan, *Salman Rushdie and the Third World* (London: Macmillan, 1989), p. 100.

7 For a detailed discussion of 'heteroglossia' see Mikhail Bakhtin, 'Discourse in the Novel', *The Dialogic Imagination: Four Essays*, ed. Michael Holquist, trans. C. Emerson and M. Holquist (Austin: University of Texas Press, 1981).

8 Salman Rushdie, '*Midnight's Children* and *Shame*', *Kunapipi* 7.1 (1985), pp. 1–19; this citation p. 7.

9 M. Bakhtin, *Problems of Dostoevsky's Poetics* (1929), trans. R. W. Rostel (Ann Arbor: Ardis, 1973).

10 For an interesting discussion of Rushdie's interest in *Tristram Shandy*, see Clement Hawes, 'Leading History by the Nose', *Modern Fiction Studies* 39.1 (1993), pp. 147–68.

11 Una Chaudhuri, 'Imaginative Maps: Excerpts from a Conversation with Salman Rushdie' (Interview conducted, 1983), in *Salman Rushdie Interviews: A Sourcebook of His Ideas*, ed. Pradyuma S. Chauhan (Westport, Conn.; London: Greenwood Press, 2001), pp. 21–31.

12 Günter Grass, *The Tin Drum* (London: Penguin, 1965), first published in German 1959, first translation into English, 1961. Rushdie talks about his admiration for Grass's novel in the *Granta* piece quoted above (see note 1), and in the Chaudhuri interview (see note 11 above). 'Lying behind' is Rushdie's own phrase for what is often described as the relationship between the two novels.

13 Gabriel García Márquez, *One Hundred Years of Solitude* (London: Jonathan Cape, 1970), first published in Spanish in 1967.

14 Brennan, *Salman Rushdie*, p. 66.

15 'If I hadn't wanted to be a hero, Mr Zagallo would never have pulled out my hair. If my hair had remained intact, Glandy Keith and Fat Perce wouldn't have taunted me; Masha Miovic wouldn't have goaded me into losing my finger. And from my finger flowed blood which was neither-Alpha-nor-Omega, and sent me into exile; and in exile I was filled with the lust for revenge which led to the murder of Homi Catrack; and if Homi hadn't died, perhaps my uncle would not have strolled off a roof into the sea-breezes; and then my grandfather would not

have gone to Kashmir and been broken by the effort of climbing the Sankara Acharya hill. And my grandfather was the founder of my family, and my fate was linked by my birthday to that of the nation, and the father of the nation was Nehru. Nehru's death; can I avoid the conclusion that that, too, was all my fault?' (MC, pp. 278–9).

8

BRENDON NICHOLLS

Reading 'Pakistan' in
Salman Rushdie's *Shame*

The pressures of contemporary civilization and the flux of values lead to
the forceful imposition of simplistic explanations, upon which befud-
dled men can base concerted courses of action, always with the end in
view of getting out of the mess of modern day reality.[1]

Our thoughts have bodies ...[2]

I

Salman Rushdie's *Shame* is as much a contemplation of the migrant artist
as it is an engagement with the problems of narrating Pakistan[3] – a
nation superimposed upon an Indian geopolitical substrate and created-in-
division, comprising a sizeable (im)migrant population created by Partition's displacement of 12 million people across South Asia (and the deaths
of 1 million). If *Shame* speaks of the artist-figure – Omar Khayyam, who
provides the model for the novel's peripheral hero, Omar Khayyam Shakil –
with the consolatory sentiment that something can 'be gained' in the
translations of the migrant (*Shame*, p. 29), then the shifting nature of
reading practices should permit us to indulge in similarly beneficial transports. In effect, *Shame*'s insistence upon the primacy of translation
authorises the changeable character of our acts of interpretation. As
Rushdie's fiction is keenly aware, translation always addresses at least two
places, whether it involves a movement between a source language and a
target language, or the migrant's movement across borders and cultures. As
I hope to show, much of *Shame*'s imaginative work consists in a doubleness
of articulation that not only addresses post-Partition Pakistan and racism in
Britain in the early 1980s, but may also enable literary criticism as a
political act within its own place and time. Formulating this aphoristically,
we might say that in the moment of writing, there may not be only one
story in town.[4]

2

In *Shame*, Rushdie engages with some of the most significant tensions and concerns at work within formulations of postcolonial nationhood. Central to Rushdie's project is the sense that a national narrative founded upon repression inevitably exhibits a crisis of plausibility. As such, any cultural claim staked upon the homogeneity of the nation already authorises the alternatives, detours and embellishments that antagonise its intention. To put this another way, since the authoritarian state actively suppresses possibilities within its own puritanical narratives, it at some level unconsciously imagines-into-being the very same cultural contestants that it seems unable to avow. Appropriately enough, in *Shame*'s imagining of a heavily fictionalised Pakistan, Rushdie must seek an adequate literary form through which to convey collective experiences and to indicate the consensual silences that allow such collective experiences to operate. In Pakistan, he suggests, a fundamental silence surrounds the subordinate position occupied by women within the national corpus. This silence forms part of the larger patterns of repression that texture national political life.

In this essay I shall argue against the orthodox view of Rushdie's project which holds that *Shame* is less fully achieved in formal or imaginative terms than its counterpart, *Midnight's Children*.[5] *Shame*'s relative underachievement has become something of a critical commonplace.[6] But while the majority of Rushdie scholars are no doubt justified in their view that *Shame*'s form and structure are unadventurous or inhibited, we might rethink the conclusion that its limiting of possibilities amounts to formal underachievement when compared with *Midnight's Children*. Instead, I would suggest that *Shame* may be viewed as an extension of the critical project begun in the earlier book. In my view, 'literary failure' forms an important part of *Shame*'s political strategy. If *Midnight's Children* implies that India's official history is outweighed by its capacity for story, then *Shame* suggests of Pakistan that a delight in extremity is the only workable extremism. In short, *Shame* uses the conditions and contradictions within Pakistan's historical experience – and the reductive political logic of the Bhutto and Zia regimes – as an apparatus upon which to base exaggeration.

This means that *Shame* exhibits a particular kind of formal response to the imagining of community. In the post-Independence years, the postcolonial novel frequently undertakes a writing of national identity that can be read in terms of a modernist quest for form. For instance, the multiperspectival focalisation of Ngugi wa Thiong'o's *A Grain of Wheat* (1967) emulates the piecemeal structure of disclosure or confession necessary for the Kenyan community to come to terms with the history of mutual betrayals and collective traumas that it has suffered during the *Mau Mau* insurgency. Likewise, Ken Saro-Wiwa's novel, *Sozaboy* (1986), invents 'Rotten English' as an analogue for the complete disorder of Nigeria's Biafran War and as a way of relating the semi-educated consciousness of the hero, Mene.[7] Rushdie's project in *Shame* is slightly different, because as a migrant writer, the dispersals and displacements of the mobile subject are incommensurate in places with a located or rooted national identity. Self-evidently, *Shame*'s emphasis upon mobile and dispersed identities accords with its focus upon the historical experience of the *mohajir* community and the influence it has exerted upon Pakistani nationhood. The *mohajirs* (or *muhajirs*)[8] were Indian Muslims displaced by partition to Pakistan, who initially 'formed an urban and commercial elite' and 'enjoyed a certain prestige due to the fact that they had played a leading role in the making of Pakistan and had often suffered severe hardships for migrating to the new state'.[9] As Raza tells us, 'in Urdu, the term *mohajir* refers explicitly to an emigrant or refugee whose decision to leave the homeland is directly related to the preservation of his/her faith'. As such, the *mohajirs* initially embodied 'an exalted form of migration',[10] implying substantial sacrifices made on behalf of their religious ideals. Thus, in *Shame*, Raza Hyder's *gatta*, or bruise of devotion, is a residual mark not only of his faith but, by extension, a marker of his *mohajir* status. In larger cultural terms, *Shame* suggests that the *mohajirs* are an incompletely assimilated community within Pakistan who evidence the unassimilable dimensions of trauma and loss that Partition created.[11]

If trauma is by definition made up of those aspects of our experience that memory is unable to claim,[12] then a national narrative animated by a traumatic history must surely result in a failure of resolution. In other words, the unrepresentable or unreclaimable elements of traumatic national memory must emerge as disruptions or flaws in narrative design. Moreover, in *Shame*, the tangential relation of the migrant writer to the nation, and especially a nation that is itself composed of a sizeable *mohajir* constituency, makes formal resolutions of national identity very difficult to accomplish. Therefore, instead of embarking upon a modernist quest for form, *Shame* undertakes a shifting postmodern quest for figure in order to find metaphors proportionate to the extremity of historical experience on the South Asian subcontinent and beyond.[13] Indeed, as Hima Raza suggests, the displacement that operates within metaphors (where, for instance, a nation might be made analogous to a bird) correlates with the multiple displacements at work within the diasporic subject.[14] Diasporic subjectivity has reference points in the world that are multiple, fluctuating and unstable, and this fluidity approximates the substitutional mechanisms at work within metaphor. Likewise, substitutional mechanisms are arguably at work in the imposition of the *mohajir* language, Urdu, as the lingua franca of Pakistan. Thus, Rushdie's writing of the *mohajir* diaspora is unavoidably figurative.

Shame's shifting postmodern quest for figure allows Rushdie to write a changeable national narrative whose 'history' responds situationally to the political circumstances of the present. To put this more simply, *Shame*'s writing of the national past is revisionist. The past is shaped retroactively, taking on the political character of the present. As part of this strategy, Rushdie writes a provisional, partial history appropriate to the impoverished politics of post-Partition Pakistan. It is for this reason that Rushdie's account of Pakistani history must omit what one critic terms the 'positive sense of nationhood that inspired millions of Muslims to fight for independence from the British and then migrate from India to Pakistan'.[15] In other words, the epic Pakistani history that we might expect *Shame* to gesture towards is unavailable because, in the novel's analysis, Pakistan is a belated, contrived invention and because the recent present of *de facto* one-party rule under Zulfikar Ali Bhutto and military dictatorship under Zia ul-Haq exhibits none of the magnificence or grandeur that an epic history might accumulate. Thus, to read *Shame* is, quite appropriately, to succumb to a necessary logic of disappointment after the dazzling inventiveness and the explosive virtuosity of *Midnight's Children*. If Pakistan is a nation that has been 'insufficiently imagined' (*Shame*, p. 87), then Rushdie's response has been to write a novel that is, perhaps deceptively, 'insufficiently imaginative'.

As I have suggested, these fictional strategies arise out of the complications of writing Pakistan. What are these complications? What is it about Pakistan's circumstances that makes Rushdie describe it as 'insufficiently imagined'? As an imaginative construct, Pakistan is fraught with theoretical difficulty. Pakistan formally came into existence with the partition of British India in 1947, based on the Muslim League's demand for a separate Muslim nation. As *Shame* informs us, Pakistan's establishment approximates a palimpsest that 'obscures what lies beneath. To build Pakistan it was necessary to cover up Indian history, to deny that Indian centuries lay just beneath the surface of Pakistani Standard Time. The past was rewritten' (*Shame*, p. 87). This belated nation was divided into an East Wing (later to become Bangladesh) and a West Wing, separated from one another by the Indian landmass. Indeed, *Shame* addresses the formal problem of a nation with an excluded centre by describing Pakistan as 'that fantastic bird of a place, two Wings without a body, sundered by the landmass of its greatest foe, joined by nothing but God' (*Shame*, p. 178), metaphorically linking the disembodied geography of Pakistan to the highly provisional and insubstantial coherence offered by God. The secession of Bangladesh, described in *Shame* (pp. 179–80), means that Pakistan has undergone subsequent rewritings of its own horizons. Omar Khayyam Shakil, *Shame*'s 'peripheral hero', is marginalised from the narrative's political action in a manner that repeats and intensifies Pakistan's establishment on the subcontinent's geopolitical sidelines. The legacy of Partition and of Bangladesh's secession means that the Pakistan Rushdie inherits is always destined to be complex.

However, the name 'Pakistan' contains even more complicated dimensions. As *Shame* indicates, Pakistan's nomenclature is derived from outside the subcontinent, divesting it of an archaeological embedment within its own political territory:

> It is well known that the term 'Pakistan', an acronym, was originally thought up in England by a group of Muslim intellectuals. P for the Punjabis, A for the Afghans, K for the Kashmiris, S for Sind and the 'tan', they say, for Baluchistan. (No mention of the East Wing, you notice; Bangladesh never got its name from the title, and so, eventually it took the hint and seceded from the secessionists. Imagine what such a double-secession does to people!)
>
> (*Shame*, p. 87)

Hence, Pakistan's name – its supposed guarantee of political singularity – is imported from without like its *mohajir* constituency, scrambled from within by its anagrammatic ensemble of ethnic divisions and sustained in the face of two abiding moments of separation (Partition and secession). Of course, Rushdie's account is ever so slightly fictionalised, as Goonetilleke demonstrates:

> In fact, the name was coined by Chaudri Rahmat Ali, a Muslim graduate student, in 1933 (the date is significant – this was in the era of simple Indian nationalism), at Cambridge, England (he died there) – along the lines indicated by Rushdie's narrator. Though the fiction and fact do not tally completely, the two accounts are agreed that the name was invented in England – remote from the aspirations and experience of the people of Pakistan.[16]

Understood as a nominal fiction of coherence, as a unit of historical presence, as a figure of territorial unity, as a metonym of a located political history or as a rhetoric of belonging, 'Pakistan' is destined to be a complicated proposition.[17] Given Rushdie's professed estrangement from 'Pakistan' as a space, as a project and as an ideal, it is unsurprising to find that nationhood is figured so problematically in *Shame*. Hence, *Shame* enters a more viable proposition: that the nation's historical, nominal and territorial untenability is a way of floating free of the past, of transcending national memory. In this respect, Pakistan's unorthodox viability consists in 'coming unstuck', or embracing the migrant's levity and cultural optimism (*Shame*, p. 87). Likewise, *Shame* patterns itself upon notable migrations within Islamic history more generally. In other words, Rushdie suggests that Pakistani national identity must become unfixed if it is to embrace its fluctuating historical precedents and its varying constituencies.

As a response to the endlessly shifting horizons of the nation, *Shame* cannot be easily superimposed upon or written into an official history of Pakistan, even if the glaring discontinuities and departures within such an official history could be overlooked. Instead, informed by the precedents of Partition, exile and migration, the novel works within a rubric of dispersal and fragmentation. As a result, its characters, action and patterning are juxtaposed with the sediments of the past. They exhibit a kind of nearness to history, but escape becoming entangled within the formulas of 'historical narrative'. This strategy of proximate placement enables *Shame* to inhabit the dispersals of history as bases for narrative hyperbole. For example, Raza Hyder's name 'incorporates a submerged allusion to the cruel "raja" Hyder (Ali) of Mysore (1761–82)',[18] but also suggests the British Raj.[19] The surname 'Harappa' glosses the archaeological site of the 'Harappan civilization that borders Bhutto's family estate in the Sind province'[20] and is a 'subtle reference to Bhutto's reign of terror'.[21] 'Iskander' alludes to 'Alexander the Great', a figure both powerful and profligate who 'invaded the part of India that is now Pakistan in 326 BC', but it also refers to 'the real-life ex-major-general Iskander Mirza' as a way of casting aspersions on Bhutto's democratic credentials.[22] Even Barbar 'is a pathetic version of the Mughal Emperor Babur ("the Great") [and] Pinkie Aurangzeb, Iskander's mistress [...] takes her name from the last great Mughal monarch and a fanatical anti-sensualist'.[23] All of these names obliquely suggest the archaeological sediments of once-absolute power, whose fragmented legacy is unearthed or re-articulated in the present as ironic decline. There is here an unmistakable hint that any autocracy – civilian or military, secular or Islamised – might heed such cautions from history and exercise restraint in the interests of longevity.

3

Many critics have noticed that female characters are crucial to *Shame*'s narrative architecture.[24] Self-evidently, this is a consequence of filtering a national history through the Harappa and Hyder family dynasties. Since the ruling elite of Pakistan has been comprised of a relatively small class of people, Rushdie elected to write about 'the private life of the master race', 'a kind of domestic story about kitchen tyranny'.[25] Given this domestic focus, it becomes necessary to look upon the domestic as a conflicted space. The narrator claims that 'the women seem to have taken over; they marched in from the peripheries of the story to demand the inclusion of their own tragedies, histories and comedies' (*Shame*, p. 173). In a reference to Bilquìs and Rani as circumstance, and Sufiya as consequence, the narrator continues:

> Repression is a seamless garment; a society which is authoritarian in its social and sexual codes, which crushes its women beneath the intolerable burdens of honour and propriety, breeds repressions of other kinds as well.
>
> . . .
>
> *If you hold down one thing you hold down the adjoining.* In the end though, it all blows up in your face.   (*Shame*, p. 173; original italics)

The women in *Shame*, especially a character like Rani Harappa, are always powerful, if not necessarily empowered figures. The narratives contained in Rani's eighteen shawls may not necessarily be heeded by her daughter, Arjumand Harappa (the 'virgin ironpants'), but they do at least attempt to address her directly with another perspective; admonishing the daughter, '*how selective, Arjumand, your ears*' (*Shame*, p. 193). The shawls articulate a suppressed memory of Iskander Harappa's infidelities, violent conduct and abuses of political power. For instance, one of the shawls depicts the abortive military campaign against East Pakistan in terms of puerile destructiveness. It shows 'Harappa and Shaggy Dog like cruel boys slitting the throat of an emerald chicken and plucking the feathers from its east wing' (*Shame*, p. 193). As garments that embroider history with memory, Rani's shawls are perhaps the best indication of the seamlessness of oppression. They are patiently worked expressions of how chauvinism and political suppression converge.

But while gender is a multiform site of political critique in *Shame*, I think it is important to highlight the novel's submerged association of rape with the law. Many of the principal female characters in *Shame* are subject to acts of real or implicit or potential sexual violation. Most obviously, we might consider Omar Khayyam Shakil's rape of Farah Zoroaster and others under hypnosis, which supplies his belated alibis of consent: ' "You will do anything that I ask you to do, but I will ask you to do nothing that you will be unwilling to do." ' (*Shame*, p. 52). Equally, the bomb that explodes in the Empire Talkies 'during a particularly suggestive love scene' denudes Bilquìs of all but her 'dupatta of modesty': an item of clothing that fails to completely repudiate the act of violation, even though it is symbolically crucial in preserving Bilquìs's dignity. In a moment that coincides with the political violence and demographic upheaval of Partition, Bilquìs is left like her fellow migrants 'stripped of history, to stand naked amidst the scorn of strangers' (*Shame*, p. 63). Arguably, the language of denuding amidst hostile strangers gestures uncomfortably towards the scene of rape: a form of sexual violence that ran to 'unaccountable numbers' during Partition.[26] Beyond Bilquìs, Naveed Talvar (Good News Hyder) views her own succession of pregnancies in terms of culturally licensed forms of sexual imposition: 'no matter how hard you tried to be the most proper of ladies the men would come and stuff you full of alien unwanted life' (*Shame*, p. 207). Both Arjumand and Rani Harrapa narrowly avert rape during their period of house arrest, Rani by a kind of patient acceptance of Captain Ijazz's presence and Arjumand by stylising her sexual desirability (*Shame*, pp. 188–90). Furthermore, even though the precise intricacies of Omar Khayyam Shakil's conception at Chunni, Munni and Bunnee's party are obscured, this moment is at the very least shadowed by a suggestive and problematic discourse of sexual imposition. In phraseology that uncomfortably mimics the 'music that acquired a fatally demonic quality when *forced* out of the virtuosi's *outraged instruments*', we are informed that 'it began to be *bruited* in the bazaars of Q. that one of the three nose-in-air girls *had been put*, on that wild night, into the family way' (*Shame*, p. 16, my emphasis). In this instance, the language of forcing sits suspiciously alongside the elision of the Shakil sisters' sexual agency, and both moments are placed within an associative auditory relation – the 'forced' musical instruments at the party are 'outraged' and the bazaar rumours are 'bruited' (a word that, etymologically, derives from the French *bruire*, 'roar').[27] But most significantly, perhaps, Sufiya Zinobia's first experience of shame and her first symptomatic blush occur after her father, Raza Hyder, disputes the fact that Bilquìs has borne him a girl. We are told that 'Raza tore away the swaddling cloth; having penetrated to the baby within, he jabbed at its nether zones: "There! I ask you, sir, what is that?"' (*Shame*, p. 90). Raza's denuding of his daughter is a symbolic act of violation rendered in a language of sexualised aggression. Even Omar makes the:

> mistake of commanding [Sufiya] to lie down on the bed, without explaining that he had no intention of forcing her to, of demanding his marital, so of course she misunderstood his purpose and at once the thing began, the yellow fire burning from her eyes, and she leapt from the bed and came at him with her hands stuck out like hooks. (*Shame*, pp. 235–6)

Sufiya's attack on Omar is based upon the assumption of culturally licensed sexual prerogatives that he might exercise via demand, rather than request. The unspoken issue of sexual consent is crucial in Sufiya's monstrous reaction.

Shame's real or implicit acts of sexual violation have a bearing on how we might read the novel's gendering of political critique. A few points should be made here. Firstly, the novel hints that sexual violation occasionally produces female subjectivity in Pakistan/Peccavistan, and it is telling that the prime perpetrator of rape in the novel is its otherwise ineffectual and shabby 'hero', Omar Khayyam. Omar is disreputable not only for the atrocious liberties he takes during hypnosis, but also for the mechanics of his alibi. The alibi is notable for its belated transferral of blame onto the victim as a way of disavowing Omar's own profligacy: ' "She was willing," he told himself. "Then where's the blame." ' (*Shame*, p. 52). The point here is not simply that Omar's alibi is a version of the age-old subterfuge ('She was asking for it'). Rather, Omar's alibi stages a far larger narrative of masculine self-justification that has unmistakable political coordinates: those of the *Hudood* Ordinances. The *Hudood* Ordinances were first introduced 'in 1979 by General Zia-ul-Haq, the self-proclaimed president of Pakistan, as a first step in his Islamization policies' aimed at securing his fragile military power base through 'alliances with right-wing religious parties'.[28] The legal interpretation of rape within the second of the ordinances, the *Zina* Ordinance, means that the rape victim's testimony may amount to *prima facie* evidence of her indulgence in illicit fornication, as might any pregnancy resulting from the rape, while the perpetrator's denials, or even the complete failure to mount a legal defence, might mean that he avoids incrimination altogether. Compounding the difficulty in prosecuting the rapist are discrepancies in the weighting of evidence. Women's testimony carries only half the weight of a man's. Furthermore, the eyewitness evidence of four Muslim males is required before the more serious and well-defined punishment for *Zina* (*Hadd*) can be implemented. This punishment is the stoning to death of married Muslims, or the meting out of a hundred lashes in public for unmarried Muslims and non-Muslims.[29]

Zia-ul-Haq's introduction of the *Zina* Ordinance – which recasts rape as adultery or fornication – is implicitly given an anxious psychosexual motivation in *Shame* via Raza Hyder's discovery of Bilquìs's reputed infidelity with the cinema manager, Sindbad Mengal (*Shame*, pp. 102–3). Furthermore, read against Zia's *Zina* Ordinance, Omar Khayyam may be the exemplary sexual subject of the Pakistani legal system and its manipulations of Sharia'h Law. Like many other perpetrators of rape in Pakistan, Omar violates in the assurance that his alibi is politically guaranteed and in the assurance that his victim is dispossessed not only of her honour but also of her story.

In these terms, then, we might reconceptualise Sufiya Zinobia and the larger gender-political silences that she may inhabit. Self-evidently, the mentally disabled Sufiya is a muted woman. 'Raped' by Hyder (a symbolic counterpart to Shakil/Jekyll),[30] Sufiya becomes a subject without a narrative. Unable to voice the shame that she absorbs from all of the other characters, Sufiya erupts into acts of violence. Hence, it is precisely because of her unfulfilled potential, precisely because of her unrealised capacity for narrative, that Sufiya Zinobia acquires her dangerous energies. As the embodiment of others' shame, Sufiya expresses social ills in a psychosomatic manner – her adult body expresses what her childlike mind is unable to fathom. Sufiya acts out what she is unable to say. She responds bodily to her infantile violation – and her father's subsequent adulterous liaison with Pinkie Aurangzeb – with acts of traumatic repetition: 'pulling off' 218 turkey-necks, raping and beheading 4 youths,[31] and forcing a fatal climactic embrace of Omar while he is standing 'beside the bed and [waiting] for her like a bridegroom upon his wedding night' (*Shame*, pp. 138–9, 224, 286).

If we read Sufiya as the embodiment of a suppressed narrative of sexual violation, Omar Khayyam's failure to consummate their marriage is doubly intelligible. It is impossible for Omar to situate Sufiya within a larger cultural structure of 'female shame' because she already embodies or epitomises that structure. Her own raping of four youths is an act of adultery, which may also – let us not forget – traumatically repeat the covert scene of her own infantile rape. Sufiya's surname, Zinobia, may reference the ordinance on '*Zina*' ('illicit sex')[32] and this reading is reinforced by the fact that Sufiya is a character inspired by a Pakistani father's murder of his daughter in London's East End for dishonouring her family by 'making love to a white boy' (*Shame*, p. 115). No matter which context she inhabits, Sufiya's acting out of shame amounts to the politically and sexually inexpressible.

4

In Rushdie's fiction, situation is politics. It assembles circumstantial evidence from culture and history and asks what other possibilities it might contain. In this sense, Rushdie's mode of critique is something like dream-formation: it operates through displacement, condensation, juxtaposition, distortion, misrecognition, duplication and duplicity. And by occupying an oblique position in relation to the histories it addresses, Rushdie's fiction refuses to submit to any culture's narratives of legitimacy. How might this form of critique work in *Shame*? As is well known, *Shame* was banned in

Pakistan, despite the novel's disclaimer that it was about the fictional country 'Peccavistan'. In this example, *Shame*'s transpositional footwork lures the Pakistani censor into a structure of irrationality. By claiming to legislate over 'Peccavistan', the Pakistani censor must unavoidably reveal and recognise the irrational basis of its own authority. To put this another way, by claiming to legislate over a fiction, the censor lets slip that the law is fictitiously constituted. Rushdie anticipates this moment in his deployment of the name 'Peccavistan' – a Latin pun that translates 'Peccavi' or 'I have sinned' into 'I have Sind'. Relying upon an apocryphal moment of colonial wit, *Shame* ensures that to claim this space ('I have Sind') is irrevocably to undermine the legal foundations of its possession ('I have sinned'). Furthermore, by claiming a relation between Peccavistan and Pakistan, as the censor does, one confers a priority upon transgression of the law ('I have sinned') that threatens to unwrite the purity of principle upon which the law itself claims to be constituted. This is an entirely apt subterfuge, given that the received translation of 'Pakistan' as 'the land of the pure' is immediately contested by the anagrammatic contaminants that first produced its name.

This subtle form of critique may explain why the figure of the artist in *Shame*, Omar Khayyam Shakil, is also a rapist. I have tried to demonstrate that Omar Khayyam's retroactive alibi for rape operates within a larger framework of legality: the *Zina* Ordinance. Leading on from this, I would like to suggest that the *narrative* mechanisms of Omar Khayyam's hypnotic alibis ('"You will do anything that I ask you to do, but I will ask you to do nothing that you will be unwilling to do."') and of the *Zina* Ordinance's legalisation of rape are exactly those employed by Rushdie at the level of political critique. If Omar and Pakistani law retroactively legalise the crime of violation in ways that criminalise the victim and deprive her of response, then I would suggest that Rushdie's provision of a retroactive history adjusted to the impoverished politics of the present functions in similar ways. As a retroactive, revisionist reading of Pakistan or Peccavistan, *Shame* offers its political opponents critique in the form of travesty or violation. Like Omar Khayyam or the *Zina* Ordinance, the novel deprives its cultural opponent of response by evacuating all bases of authority from which that opponent might appeal.

5

D. R. C. A. Goonetilleke has argued compellingly that 'Sufiya is innocent and good and, like Stevie in Conrad's *The Secret Agent*, she is able to preserve these qualities in a corrupt world because she is an idiot.'[33] But the allusion to Conrad's novel contains a more profound possibility yet. As a repository of the multiple versions of shame transacted in national and international theatres, Sufiya becomes something like a vehicle for affective coherence, an instrument who concentrates insurrectionary energies that are no less lethal for being misplaced. Omar Khayyam's medical diagnosis of Sufiya makes this explicit in its translation of the language of psychic defence and immune function into the language of political warfare: 'even a broken mind is capable of marshalling macrophages and polymorphs; even a stunted intelligence can lead a palace revolution, a suicidal rebellion of the janissaries of the human body against the castle itself' (*Shame*, p. 143). In Rushdie's novel, the body politic's immunity to shame results in its own destruction. As a national condition, shame turns the best defences of political culture into vulnerabilities in a way that is both even-handed and double-edged.

Doubleness of articulation is a theme with which I began this chapter. In the moment of writing, there may not be only one story in town. Rushdie's fiction reminds us that, although Pakistan formally gained its independence in 1947, the Imperial powers have remained invested in South Asian geopolitical turmoil – most notably in the West's support of the Afghan rebellion against Soviet occupation during the 1980s and in its consequent support for Zia's Islamisation policies (*Shame*, p. 29). Closer to home, the racist persecution of Britain's South Asian communities, and especially against British South Asian Muslim constituencies, has been an ongoing and at times officially sanctioned injustice. Like Omar Khayyam, the West also lives by its own hypnotic alibis and countless others suffer by them. In this theatre, migrants have a privileged kind of purchase with their 'stereoscopic vision'.[34] Sufiya Zinobia's name may not only reference the '*Zina*' Law but also the contemporary metropolitan injustice of 'xenophobia'. The scene of this xenophobia is, for the early Rushdie, somewhat close to home, in 'Proper London' (*Shame*, p. 117), the same London that provides the haunting setting of Anna Muhammad's dead body, 'its throat slit like a halal chicken' (*Shame*, p. 116). Sufiya Zinobia's origins, then, are also in a racist attack upon an 'Asian' girl by white youths on a late-night underground train and in the dream of retributive violence that this incident inspires, foreshadowing who knows what explosions? Thus, Sufiya Zinobia, like Conrad's Stevie, can be received in terms of a 'suicidal rebellion': a homegrown conflagration mapping extremities on both sides of a geopolitical meridian. If Sufiya Zinobia also lurks incandescent within the metropolis, a repository for collective shame in London or Karachi, who knows what headless chickens may come home to roost?

NOTES

1 Peter Brigg, 'Salman Rushdie's Novels: The Disorder in Fantastic Order', *Reading Rushdie: Perspectives on the Fiction of Salman Rushdie*, ed. D. M. Fletcher (Amsterdam: Rodopi, 1994), p. 174. I am very grateful to Ananya Jahanara Kabir for her careful reading of this chapter, and for her constructive criticisms and insightful suggestions.

2 W. H. Auden, 'Spain' in *Selected Poems* (1937), ed. Edward Mendelson (London: Faber, 1979), p. 53.

3 Salman Rushdie, *Shame* (London: Cape, 1983). All references will be to this edition and will be given in the text.

4 Rushdie, at least, is well aware of this. He writes, 'every story one chooses to tell is a kind of censorship, it prevents the telling of other tales ...' (*Shame*, p. 71). Some of these tales may reside in the future. In my view, reading *Shame* must also entail reckoning with its providential character.

5 Andrew Teverson has argued against this critical orthodoxy and mapped out the politicising dimensions of the novel's satirical intent. Andrew Teverson, 'Salman Rushdie and Aijaz Ahmad: Satire, Ideology and *Shame*', *The Journal of Commonwealth Literature* 39.2 (2004), pp. 45–60.

6 Damian Grant states that 'Rushdie's critics have tended to line up against the novel, treating it as the weak twin or dark shadow of *Midnight's Children*' (Damian Grant, *Salman Rushdie* (Plymouth: Northcote House, 1999), p. 57) before adding that 'one of the recurrent problems in *Shame* is the instability of its fictional discourse' (p. 58). Catherine Cundy writes: 'The blend of fairy-tale and hard-hitting social realism which characterises both *Midnight's Children* and *The Satanic Verses* is handled less deftly in *Shame*. It neither creates the psychological "reality" of *The Satanic Verses*, nor does it have the characteristic exuberance of *Midnight's Children*' (Catherine Cundy, *Salman Rushdie* (Manchester: Manchester University Press, 1996), p. 44). Timothy Brennan suggests that '[*Shame*'s] comic tyrants were so bitterly drawn that they induced only horror, and the comic relief Rushdie promised came primarily in the form of hopeless mockery on the verbal level, a willy-nilly distancing in a "postmodern" mood of automatic, and humourless, parody' (Timothy Brennan, *Salman Rushdie and the Third World: Myths of the Nation* (Basingstoke: Macmillan, 1989), p. 119). Roger Y. Clark argues that 'In *Shame* Rushdie also throws a cosmos at his readers, yet it is neither so complex, nor so studded with hidden meaning [as *Midnight's Children*]' (Roger Y. Clark, *Stranger Gods: Salman Rushdie's Other Worlds* (Montreal and Kingston: McGill University Press, 2001), p. 100). Sara Suleri identifies an evasion of the political in *Shame*, which results in 'the strangely shrugging course of Rushdie's narrative, which implies that because it can not possibly do justice to its history, it can at least do violence to itself' (Sara Suleri, *The Rhetoric of English India* (Chicago: University of Chicago Press, 1992), p. 174). Sabrina Hassumani notes that '*Shame* has not received the critical acclaim enjoyed by *Midnight's Children* or even *The Satanic Verses* because most scholars believe that in this novel, Rushdie is guilty of the very oppression he hopes to expose' (Sabrina Hassumani, *Salman Rushdie: A Postmodern Reading of his Major Works* (Madison: Fairleigh Dickinson University Press, 2002), p. 48). In interview,

Rushdie himself has said that *Shame* entails a 'closure of possibilities' instead of 'multiple possibilities' (John Haffenden, *Novelists in Interview* (London: Methuen, 1985), p. 253).

7 Ngugi wa Thiong'o, *A Grain of Wheat* (London: Heinemann, 1967). Ken Saro-Wiwa, *Sozaboy* (Port Harcourt: Saros International Publishers, 1986).

8 I follow Rushdie's orthography, *mohajir*, throughout.

9 Christopher Jaffrelot (ed.), *Pakistan: Nationalism without a Nation* (London: Zed Books, 2002), p. 16.

10 Hima Raza, 'Unravelling *Sharam* as a Metaphor for *Mohajir* Identity in Salman Rushdie's *Shame*', *SOAS Literary Review* 4 (Spring, 2005), pp. 1–24. Quotations are from pp. 1 and 3 respectively.

11 The political power-shifts in Pakistan have recently led to a feeling of marginalisation among the *mohajir* community. Jaffrelot tells us that 'to begin with, the Mohajirs identified themselves with the new State of Pakistan which was largely their creation. But the more they *felt* threatened, the more they projected themselves as an oppressed minority with a distinct identity.' Jaffrelot (ed.), *Pakistan: Nationalism without a Nation*, p. 32.

12 See Cathy Caruth, *Unclaimed Experience: Trauma, Narrative and History* (Baltimore: Johns Hopkins University Press, 1996), p. 1.

13 By this I mean that Rushdie formulates history and nation in terms of variation: the erstwhile modernist quest for form gives way to the figurative transformations that are possible within a series of critical metaphors. In *Shame*, one of these critical metaphors resides in the imagery of slaughtered birds, which figures the death of Anahita Muhammad in terms of halal practices, the triumph of Zia's inflexible Islamisation policies over the more interpretively tolerant tradition of Sufi mysticism, and the partition of Pakistan into an 'East Wing' and a 'West Wing'.

14 Raza, 'Unravelling *Sharam*', pp. 1–24; p. 7.

15 Sabrina Hassumani, *Salman Rushdie: A Postmodern Reading of his Major Works* (Madison: Fairleigh Dickinson University Press, 2002), p. 49.

16 D. R. C. A. Goonetilleke, *Salman Rushdie* (Basingstoke: Macmillan, 1998), p. 48.

17 Even Pakistan's political character suggests a national identity alienated from itself by its continuing investments outside of its political territory. As Jaffrelot observes: 'Pakistan, as a state, relies more upon anti-Indian nationalism than on national integration. To put this in a nutshell, this is a case of *nationalism without a nation.*' Jaffrelot (ed.), *Pakistan: Nationalism without a Nation*, p. 42.

18 Goonetilleke, *Salman Rushdie*, p. 60.

19 Timothy Brennan, *Salman Rushdie and the Third World: Myths of the Nation* (Basingstoke: Macmillan, 1989), p. 120.

20 Goonetilleke, *Salman Rushdie*, p. 61.

21 Brennan, *Salman Rushdie and the Third World: Myths of the Nation*, p. 119.

22 *Ibid.*, p. 120.

23 *Ibid.*, p. 121.

24 See, for example, Aijaz Ahmad, *In Theory: Classes, Nations, Literatures* (London: Verso, 1992), pp. 145–51.

25 Rushdie quoted in John Haffenden, *Novelists in Interview* (London: Methuen, 1985), p. 254.

26 Gyanendra Pandey, *Remembering Partition: Violence, Nationalism and History in India* (Cambridge: Cambridge University Press, 2001), p. 2.

27 See J. A. H. Murray, H. Bradley, W. A. Craigie and C. T. Onions (eds.), *The Oxford English Dictionary: Being a Corrected Reissue with an Introduction, Supplement, and Bibliography of A New English Dictionary on Historical Principles, Founded Mainly on the Materials Collected by the Philological Society* (Oxford: Clarendon Press, 1933).

28 Khan adopts a different spelling, Hadood: Shahnaz Khan, 'Zina and the Moral Regulation of Pakistani Women', *Feminist Review* 75 (2003), pp. 75–100. Quotations are from pp. 76 and 89 respectively.

29 Sara Suleri offers an extremely incisive account of the Zina Ordinance and details these *hadd* punishments in 'Woman Skin Deep: Feminism and the Postcolonial Condition', *Colonial Discourse and Postcolonial Theory: A Reader*, eds. Patrick Williams and Laura Chrisman (Hemel Hempstead, Hertfordshire: Harvester Wheatsheaf, 1993), pp. 245–56.

30 Sufiya's production within exogamous kinship structures means that she transforms 'from Miss Hyder to Mrs Shakil' in a movement approximating Stevenson's Dr Jekyll and Mr Hyde, as pointed out by M. Keith Booker, 'Beauty as the Beast: Dualism as Despotism in the Fiction of Salman Rushdie', *Reading Rushdie: Perspectives on the Fiction of Salman Rushdie*, ed. D. M. Fletcher (Amsterdam: Rodopi, 1994), p. 239 and by Joel Kuortti, *Fictions to Live In: Narration as an Argument for Fiction in Salman Rushdie's Novels* (Frankfurt: Peter Lang, 1998), p. 97. In my view, the structure of Sufiya's 'personality' is a complex of the social contradictions expressed by Omar's profligacy and Raza's piety.

31 Aijaz Ahmad reads the incident with the youths as rape, but objects that Rushdie has 'fashioned a caricature of what female resistance to cruelties might be; the woman herself becomes, in this version, a rapist'. Ahmad, *In Theory*, p. 149.

32 *Ibid.*, p. 146: 'Sufiya Zinobia' is also a pun 'on the word "Sufi" and on the name of Zainub, the granddaughter of the Prophet of Islam who is quite central to several of the popular strands derived from Sufic Islam.'

33 Goonetilleke, *Salman Rushdie*, p. 57.

34 See Rushdie's 'Imaginary Homelands', in *Imaginary Homelands* (London: Granta, 1991), p. 19.

9

JOEL KUORTTI

The Satanic Verses: 'To be born again, first you have to die'

The publication of Salman Rushdie's fourth novel *The Satanic Verses* in September 1988 released an unforeseen process of reaction and protest against and for the novel and its author.[1] The protests against the book concentrated on the issue of alleged blasphemy against Islam while those defending it argued for freedom of expression. The protest culminated in the *fatwa*, or a legal statement, by Ayatollah Khomeini on Rushdie, condemning him to death for intentionally opposing Islam:

> I inform all zealous Muslims of the world that the author of the book entitled *The Satanic Verses* – which has been compiled, printed, and published in opposition to Islam, the Prophet, and the Qur'an – and all those involved in its publication who were aware of its contents, are sentenced to death.[2]

Consequently, Rushdie was forced to live in hiding for fear of assassination. In the process, the novel itself attained the status of being talked about while it remained notoriously unread. The novel will be discussed here as a text: first its structure, characterisation and stylistic features, then the wide range of themes it discusses and its intertextual reaches. The discussion will close by considering the ethical issues Rushdie's novel raises.

Despite its often misrepresented reputation, *The Satanic Verses* is a complex, ambitious and rewarding novel which explores questions of identity and belonging. The novel's two main characters, Gibreel Farishta and Saladin Chamcha, are travelling in a jumbo jet which is blown up by terrorists over the English Channel. When they begin their fall – literally and metaphorically – they go through a process of transformation in which they become adversaries.

I

The novel is composed of two main storylines and is divided into nine chapters which take place in different settings. The storylines are presented in interchanging sequences in which the narration is not straightforwardly linear but flashes back and forth as the story evolves. In the first sequence every other chapter, beginning with the first one, is set in the present of the novel – late 1980s – in the United Kingdom (mostly London), Argentina or India. The four other chapters, beginning with the second, make up the other storyline sequence and take place in the Arabian Peninsula, in the imaginary towns of Jahilia and Yathrib – modelled on Mecca and Medina – as well as in the imaginary village of Titlipur, India and in London in the mytho-historical Islamic past in the seventh century as well as in the present. The main storylines are followed throughout their settings, with other stories embedded within them. The five chapters comprising the first setting are further divided in parts that focus on different characters.

It is important for the reading of the novel to perceive its embedded structure as a whole. For it was, indeed, the fragmentary, decontextualised readings of the novel that caused much of the controversy around it. The main connecting component between the two settings is Gibreel Farishta. The implication is that the first setting is the actual world while the second setting takes place in Gibreel's dreams or 'vision', as we can see in the beginning of Chapter 2, 'Mahound', where the opening lines frame the narrative: 'Gibreel ... submits to the inevitable, ... slides heavy-lidded towards visions of his angeling' (SV, p. 91; my ellipses). The dreams or 'visions' combine fragments of Islamic history and the present, and the themes are similar in both sequences. Gibreel suffers from insomnia – rather, he fears sleep – and, as it later turns out, he suffers from paranoid schizophrenia as well, causing him to see himself as an angel (SV, p. 429). As his condition worsens, he begins to hear his own 'satanic verses' which fuel his jealousy and lead ultimately to his death.

The other main character is Saladin Chamcha. He embodies several antagonistic views of the world from those represented by Gibreel, especially so in their approaches to identity: fixed (Gibreel) and fluid (Saladin). The antagonism and interconnectedness of the two characters is expressed in the beginning where their names are run together (SV, p. 5). Their destinies are bound together and form the novel's primary backbone and tension.

Gibreel – born Ismail Najbuddin – is an actor in Bollywood movies who specialises in playing deities in 'theologicals' (SV, pp. 16–17).[3] He had taken the stage name *farishta*, 'angel', modelled on the appellation used for him by his mother. This identification is emblematic, for when his schizophrenia sets in he imagines that he is Archangel Gabriel – in Urdu 'Gibreel Farishta' – and he dreams revelations of the Prophet of Islam. Later, as his condition deteriorates in London, he proclaims fire and brimstone with his trumpet which he names '*Azraeel*' (SV, p. 448; emphasis original).[4]

Saladin Chamcha, too, is an actor. Born Salahuddin Chamchawala he had since his youth had an obsession with England. Like Gibreel, Saladin struggles with identity and shortens his stage name in order to assimilate to England. But if Gibreel's name is grandiose, Saladin's is mundane: the Urdu word *chamcha* is a spoon and colloquially also 'a yes-man, a sycophant'.[5] Saladin first makes a career in England in radio voiceovers: 'he was the Man of Thousand Voices and a Voice'. While Gibreel plays celestial roles Saladin plays earthly ones, successfully impersonating carpets, baked beans and even the President of the United States – finally becoming a star of *The Aliens Show* in children's television (SV, pp. 60–3).

The character gallery of the novel is rich, complex and allegorically suggestive; it comprises some hundred major and minor identified figures. In this context, it is not necessary to outline characters other than Gibreel and Saladin. Although most of the female characters in both sequences of the novel are secondary to the male characters – being wives or mistresses – many of them are significant both to the development of the plot and to the themes. Furthermore, it is not only human characters that have a role in the novel but places too. As in Rushdie's other novels, Bombay (Mumbai) and London have a special role. As metropolitan cities, they underline the themes of multiplicity and hybridity.[6] In *The Satanic Verses*, it is especially London that takes this place, Saladin's beloved 'Ellowen Deeowen' and Gibreel's labyrinthine *Geographer's London, A–Z* which he wants to redeem. Other places like Jahilia or Titlipur appear to be more allegorical, drawing from different sources.

There is one more 'character' that needs to be mentioned, one whose appearance in the narrative is as sporadic as it is intrusive: it is the narrative voice, the first-person narrator. The narrator shows up in the text explicitly to comment on things ('I mustn't interfere', SV, p. 4), to put questions ('Who am I? Who else is there?', SV, p. 4), give directions to the reader ('Slow down', SV, p. 5) or to comment on his own metanarrative position ('I know the truth, obviously', SV, p. 10; 'Don't ask me to clear things up one way or the other', SV, p. 408). This metafictional function of the narrative is used sparingly but always gives an ironic representation of authorial presence.[7] At one point, this 'author's' narrative voice, this 'Supreme Being', appears to Gibreel:

> [He] was not abstract in the least. He saw, sitting on the bed, a man of about the same age as himself, of medium height, fairly heavily built, with salt-and-pepper beard cropped close to the line of the jaw … the apparition was balding, seemed to suffer from dandruff and wore glasses.
>
> (SV, p. 318)

The resemblance with pictures of Rushdie from that time is striking. It works towards undermining any simple, simplistic mimetic readings by foregrounding the process of production.

The style and language of *The Satanic Verses* can be difficult at times. There are several reasons for this. First of all, Rushdie uses different registers and genres in his writing. The 'high' literary and linguistic forms are combined with the 'low' ones, the ornamental with the blunt, the artistic with the mundane, the erudite with the obscene. Through the use of postmodern and deconstructivist devices and strategies such as portmanteau words and *historiographic metafiction*,[8] Rushdie manages to create a heteroglossic, multi-voiced narrative which – explicitly as well as implicitly – plays ironically with the readers' expectations.[9] In addition, Rushdie uses multiple languages in his fiction. These can be just words from languages other than English (often from Hindi or Urdu), or they can be longer phrases. They are not always glossed in the text and this requires that the readers be aware of – or at least open to – the complexity of such a polyglot text. All in all, the structural characteristics of the novel present the reader with a multivocal and multifocal narrative that resists mastery. The evocation of such multiplicity is also a risky matter, as Homi K. Bhabha has commented on *The Satanic Verses* affair, for 'there is always the threat of mis-translation, confusion and fear'.[10]

2

The Satanic Verses is a deeply thematic novel.[11] Its themes are not isolated entities but overlap, interact, counterbalance each other throughout the narrative. Here the discussion is restricted to the themes of migration, hybridity and blasphemy.

The foremost theme running through Rushdie's works, particularly *The Satanic Verses*, is the issue of migration and migrancy. Rushdie affirms this: 'If *The Satanic Verses* is anything, it is a migrant's-eye view of the world.'[12] Other writers like Naipaul, Sam Selvon, George Lamming in *The Emigrants* (1954) and G. V. Desani in *All about H. Hatterr* (1948) had already been writing the migrant experience. But Rushdie's *The Satanic Verses* was by the time of its publication the fullest and most ambitious attempt at voicing migrant issues – and despite the alleged failures, Rushdie has been among the first to attempt raising migrant women's concerns. The term *migrant* itself has been made familiar by Rushdie when he connects it in *Shame* (1983) with the international phenomenon of mass movements of people: 'All *migrants* leave their pasts behind ... , because it is the fate of migrants to be stripped of history, to stand amidst the scorn of *strangers* upon whom they see the rich clothing, the brocades of continuity and the eyebrows of belonging.'[13]

As they enter England in the opening scene both Saladin and Gibreel begin processes of transformation. This is another weighty theme in Rushdie's writing, allegorised here by the changes in Gibreel's and Saladin's breath: 'One man's breath was sweetened, while another's, by equal and opposite mystery, was soured' (SV, p. 133). This binarism of good and bad breath mirrors other oppositions between the men. Gibreel represents the fixed view of identity and consequently regards himself as the purveyor of truth; Saladin vouches for a fluid identity and, as a result, is treated as the embodiment of evil. Gibreel acquires angelic looks, complete with a halo; Saladin turns into a devilish creature, with hoofs and horns. Gibreel is received well in the UK; Saladin is treated in a violently racist manner. Gibreel reaches the upper echelons of London's cultural spheres; Saladin ends up with the marginalised, invisible East London community of migrants in the Shaandaar Café which functions as a community housing establishment. The opposition between the two men, however, is not necessarily decisive – they could be seen as different sides of the same character, as 'doubles'. Rushdie acknowledges this kind of doubling and connects it with his own migrant experiences as simultaneously 'belonging and not belonging'.[14]

The novel is especially explicit in its critique of the way migrants are treated in the UK. In this it reflects Rushdie's extra-literary activities in the 1970s and early 1980s when he was involved in community work and race relations. He wrote in 1982:

> I want to suggest that racism is not a side-issue in contemporary Britain; that it's not a peripheral minority affair. I believe that Britain is undergoing a critical phase of its post-colonial period, and this crisis is not simply economic or political. It's *a crisis of the whole culture*, of the society's entire sense of itself.[15]

What Rushdie points to in his emphasis on 'a crisis of the whole culture' is the importance of the postcolonial moment for a refiguration of both 'home' and 'abroad'. Colonialism has always carried its double within but when in the postcolonial period the colonised other is emerging from its imposed invisibility it poses a crisis for the colonial culture.

After being rescued from the fall – through authorial intervention (SV, p. 133) – Saladin faces a humiliating process: the police, who have received an anonymous report of suspected illegal entry, arrest him. They are described as thrilled by the chase, and they are even physically agitated, appearing 'like pointer dogs' (SV, p. 139). The moment they see him, they raise their hands, pointing theatrically at him. The 'pointing finger' (SV, p. 141) is a recurring figure from *Midnight's Children* where it indicates the imperial moment of description beyond doubt or disapproval.[16]

When the police finally get their hands on Saladin, they cannot believe their luck; they giggle, they laugh and cry for joy, make fun of Saladin, and it is implied that they use violence. The ultimate shock to Saladin – and proof for the police – is to realise that he is growing 'two new, goaty, unarguable horns' (SV, p. 141). Later on when Saladin is recovering in a 'mysterious institution' for immigrants, he gets an explanation why he and the other immigrants around him have turned into nightmarish creatures of the night: 'They describe us ... That's all. They have the power of description, and we succumb to the pictures they construct' (SV, pp. 167–8). This is a powerful image of the power of the pointing finger, the imperial move to subordinate, and Saladin's experience of police brutality is a part of that systematic structure of racialist policy in which migrants have to live.

Saladin's ideological and physical transformation into the image of the ultimate Other – the Devil – is at the same time a very real torment for him. He loses all his humanity in the hands of the immigration officers, is humiliated, stripped naked, defiled by being made to eat his own excrement, called names – 'Packy billy', 'animal', and he is not even sure if he has lost his voice when the officers mimic his vain attempts at reasoning with them with a goatish 'Maa-aa-aa' (SV, pp. 157–64). In the process, Saladin begins to think he is having a nightmare; this could not take place in his idealised England. But the pains are too real to be dismissed – it *is* England, 'a universe of fear' (SV, pp. 158–9). When it finally turns out that Saladin is 'a British Citizen first class' the officers quickly beat him unconscious to cover up their mistake (SV, p. 164).

It is after the beating that Saladin wakes up in the institution for immigrants. He is surrounded by creatures that the imperial descriptive act has turned into manticores, snakes and other transformed, disfigured beings. On Saladin's arrival, the creatures are planning to break out of the sanatorium, as the manticore explains to him: 'before they turn us into anything worse' (SV, p. 168). Saladin is uncertain about joining in the escape plan as he cannot yet understand the transformation. After all, he had lived in England for years and nothing like this had ever happened. He enters a state where he cannot tell whether he is awake or asleep. In this state, he experiences a strange dream: 'he found himself dreaming of the Queen, of making tender love to the Monarch. She was the body of Britain ... and he had chosen her' (SV, p. 169). This image of a sexual act with the Queen is another forceful counter-imperialist moment when Saladin is acting out the worst fears of colonialists: the native violating a white woman (SV, p. 169). That it is the Queen, the body of Britain, is the ultimate transgression. After this dream/un-dream Saladin is ready to join the escape.

The inmates, together with the 'prisoners' of the nearby Detention Centre, flee their captivity in different directions 'without hope, but also without shame' (SV, p. 171). This hopeless but courageous breakout is the migrants' realisation of resistance, done in the name of re-humanising those who had been demonised by the colonial centre. Saladin flees towards the East, London, and the Shaandaar Café. This, too, is a reversal of the colonial process: to go East to get to London. It also denotes the specific location that plays a decisive part in the novel: East London, named as Brickhall after the actual Southall and Brick Lane where many migrants live.

In the Shaandaar, Saladin acquires a special role. As he grows bigger as well as more devilish, his reputation grows among people of the '*tinted persuasion*' (SV, p. 286), the same people Saladin feels to be disadvantaged because of their skin colour: 'I feel sorry for you ... Every morning you have to look at yourself in the mirror and see, staring back, the darkness: the stain, the proof that you're the lowest of the low' (SV, p. 255). The image of the Devil Saladin embodies picks up explicit anti-racist meanings, as is explained to Saladin: 'people can really identify with you. It's an image white society has rejected for so long that we can really take it, ... occupy it, inhabit it, reclaim it and make it our own' (SV, p. 287). This counter-descriptive move is a recurrent theme in Rushdie's writing – like in reclaiming the English language. In *The Satanic Verses* it is especially manifest. Saladin's nightmarish transformation is reclaimed by the community as an image of resistance, of identity not described by others. Ironically enough, this 'Satanist revival' is also turned into merchandise: there are badges and rubber devil-horns (SV, p. 286).

The symbolic resistance erupts as violence, too, in the last London chapter. It is triggered by the death of a black activist, Sylvester Roberts aka Dr Uhuru Simba in custody (SV, p. 449). Another instance of implicit police brutality and systematic provocation, it fuels racial violence that ends with the burning of both the Brickhall community relations council building and the Shaandaar Café where 'faceless persons stand at windows waving piteously for help, being unable (no mouths) to scream' (SV, p. 463).[17] The invisible, faceless tenants without voice are a clear manifestation of the novel's underlying criticism of the persistent racist attitudes towards migrants – and at the same time criticism of the exploitation *within* the migrant community of each other.

3

Rushdie does not only talk about migrants in the sociological sense. For him, migrancy is a dynamic possibility. In *Shame*, he celebrates it as a 'conquest of the force of gravity' – the achievement of the ancient impossible dream, of flying away (*Shame*, p. 85). Gibreel and Saladin manage in this, too, 'pitting levity against gravity' (SV, p. 3). The foremost form in which this positive dimension of migrancy is talked about in Rushdie's writings is *hybridity*. Migrants go through a process of transformation which is both real and metaphorical. The migrant experiences the transforming hybridity in his/her actual life, and migrancy also serves as a metaphor for the human condition of always being in such a process whether one accepts it or not. As Rushdie has commented, '*The Satanic Verses* celebrates hybridity, impurity, intermingling, the transformation that comes of new and unexpected combinations of human beings, cultures, ideas, politics, movies, songs. ... It is a love-song to our mongrel selves.'[18]

It is, ironically, through the character of Saladin that the text deals with issues of identity from the point of view of hybridity: whether one's identity is pure or impure, single or multiple, whole or fragmented. During the fall, Saladin realises a change is taking place: he was 'becoming metamorphic, hybrid' (SV, p. 7). Earlier he had tried to achieve a pure, single, authentic identity of an Englishman. This idealised image is shattered in the hands of the Immigration but the process had started earlier on in Bombay before he had boarded the plane, as is revealed later (SV, p. 34). When he comes to decide that a pure self is impossible, and comes to appreciate the optimism of the eclecticism and hybridity of Indian art which is a fusion of many traditions, he chooses inconstancy and mutability over constancy and continuity (SV, p. 288). In his hybridity he is the opposite of Gibreel who is untranslated, continuous, non-hybrid.

Interestingly enough, hybridity as a term does not feature in the second, Islamic sequence. In that, another textual device is used: blasphemy, although it appears in most of the other contexts of the story as well. Of all the issues that have been seen as problematic in the reception of the novel, this has been the most difficult one. Here I will not take issue with the novel itself about whether it is blasphemous or not but instead look at how blasphemy is treated as a theme.[19]

As a child, prompted by his mother's (possibly inaccurate) stories about the Prophet, Gibreel begins to dream 'blasphemous thoughts', fantasies of being in the Prophet's position (SV, p. 22). This is the first instance where the term blasphemy occurs in the text. The next involves Saladin, whose attempt at forming his identity as an Englishman the narrator describes as follows: 'according to one way of seeing things; he's unnatural, a blasphemer, an abomination of abominations' (SV, p. 49). This implicitly religious attitude to identity as given is contrasted with the 'heroism' of the migrant's socio-political necessity: 'Our own false descriptions to counter the falsehood invented about us' (SV, p. 49). The resonances with previous assertions about language and identity are clear: blasphemy is used as a positive device for identity politics, as a device for self-construction.

If the 'Devilish Saladin' is taken as a symbol of resistance by the migrant community, similarly blasphemy – containing 'the linkage between the term *black* and the sin *blasphemy*' (SV, p. 288; emphases original) – is remade into an oppositional principle. A major instance of claiming such an oppositional stance is the choice of the name 'Mahound' for the Prophet in the second sequence. The text assures us:

> To turn insults into strengths, whigs, tories, Blacks all chose to wear with pride the names they were given in scorn; likewise, our mountain-climbing, prophet-motivated solitary is to be the medieval baby-frightener, the Devil's synonym: Mahound. (SV, p. 93)

The name Mahound, used by Dante and other writers to denote their perception of the diabolic nature of the Islamic prophet, carries with it a history of Christian enmity against Islam. The narrative builds on this in its attempt at giving a fictional interpretation of Islamic history. That such an attempt is difficult is recognised by the text, too, when it refers to the protests against a film version of the life of the Prophet Muhammad, *The Message*: 'But would it not be seen as blasphemous, a crime against ...' (SV, p. 272).[20] That the sentence is left unfinished is significant as it stresses the religious void in the centre of the narrative, that the story is an attempt at retelling the history of Islam from a secular point of view, 'a secular man's reckoning with the religious spirit'.[21]

Even more explicitly the appropriation of blasphemy as an interpretive device occurs when Mahound discovers that his scribe, Salman Farsi, is adulterating his recitations. Mahound sentences him to death and Salman begins the *qalmah*, in vain, for Mahound does not relent: 'Your blasphemy, Salman, can't be forgiven. Did you think I wouldn't work it out? To set your words against the Words of God' (SV, p. 374). In a way, *The Satanic Verses* is just that, setting secular words against the absolute words of revelation. The narrative is to a great extent a wrestling match between different verses, satanic and otherwise. It contrasts various types of fundamentalism – Sikh terrorism, Christian Creationist fundamentalism, Hindu communalism, Muslim chauvinism – with a liberal humanist worldview. The Islamic history is used as one of the settings in which these fundamentalisms are criticised.

The architecture of *The Satanic Verses* is complex. Not only is it structurally and thematically varied with a lot of characters, but it is also richly intertextual. For this complexity, it requires a lot of cultural, intercultural and historical knowledge from its readership.[22] While it is not exactly a *livre à clef*, that is, a work of fiction that draws its material from actual persons disguised behind fictitious names, it certainly reveals a prism of aspects when looked at in its intertextual variety.

The intertextual features are there already in the title. The reference to 'the satanic verses' is problematic. The verses appear throughout the novel: in the form of revelation, poetry, fables or punishment. For a novel exploring the terrain between fact and fiction, the incident of the satanic verses is a productive source. It refers to a disputed incident in the history of Islam, mostly denounced by Muslim historians and theologians. Rushdie makes explicit use of the incident in the second chapter, but already in Chapter 1 Gibreel studies 'the incident of the Satanic verses in the early career of the Prophet' (SV, p. 24). The 'satanic verses' are, transliterated from Arabic, *tilk al-gharaniq al-'ula wa inna shafa'ata-hunna la-turtaja*, and translate into English as 'these are exalted females whose intercession is to be desired' (SV, p. 340).[23] As Rushdie's novel too records, these verses are said to have been added to the fifty-third sura of the Qur'ān entitled *Surat-annajm*, The Star, in order to acknowledge the validity of the goddesses Al-Lat, Al-Manat and 'Uzza. The tradition goes on to say that the verses were later withdrawn and denounced as 'satanic'.

The historicity of the event is disputed by early Muslim historians such as Ibn Ishaq, al-Waqidi, al-Zuhri, Ibn Sa'd, al-Tabari and Ibrahi. Ibn Hisham, Ibn Ishaq's editor, omits the passage but it is preserved as a quotation from al-Tabari in Guillaume's translation of Ibn Ishaq.[24] Most non-Muslim and some Muslim commentators on the Qur'ān have accepted this story of Muhammad's momentary acceptance of the verses. The prevailing Muslim view of the 'Gharaniq' incident is that it is a fabrication created by the unbelievers of Mecca in the early days of Islam, and Haikal comments, afterwards the 'story arrested the attention of the western Orientalists who took it as true and repeated it *ad nauseam*'.[25]

Whatever one thinks of this incident or its representations, Rushdie's novel has indeed stirred deep emotions and values. Srinivas Aravamudan has noted that regardless of the truth value or origin of the incident, the satire of the novel 'uses it to attack all names, all capital letters'.[26] Related to these ethical issues, one of the predominant aspects of the novel is the importance of storytelling. The whole oppositional setting of different 'verses' – pitting against one another the secular and the religious, the plural and the singular, constancy and inconstancy, sand and water – speaks volumes about the centrality of fiction in human existence as is expressed in the Jahilian poet Baal's comment: 'A poet's work ... to name the unnameable, to point at frauds, to take sides, start arguments, shape the world and stop it from going to sleep' (SV, p. 97). This stance reflects both an appreciation of the heteroglossic world of literature and specifically – as becomes even more pronounced in Rushdie's next novel *Haroun and the Sea of Stories* – the storytelling traditions recorded in *A Thousand and One Nights* and the *Katha-Sarit-Sagara*, 'The Oceans of the Streams of Story' (SV, p. 342).

If the ethical fault line of *The Satanic Verses*, its meaningful borderline, is fiction's importance, the overriding marker of that line is the theme of love, or failure of love. Love is approached from many angles in the relationships and thoughts of the characters and it is arguably the most recurring topic in the novel. There are many kinds of love: love between men and women, love between parents and children, religious love, love of the arts: 'the myriad forms of love' (SV, p. 443). But whatever the form, there is always a critical attitude towards it: the unequal aspects of marital love (SV, pp. 20 and 175), the suffocating aspects of maternal love (SV, p. 39), the clichéd tackiness of Romantic love (SV, p. 487), or the fearfulness of religious love (SV, pp. 213–14 and 483).

The novel makes an allusive gesture towards C. S. Lewis's book *Four Loves*, when it talks about 'a fourth and final love' (SV, p. 400).[27] Here, however, the fourth love beside affection, friendship and eros is not agape (the love of God), but 'the love of a dream' (SV, p. 400). Saladin dreams of being loved, adored in his childhood by his father. Towards the end of the novel, then, love acquires a redeeming quality. It happens first when Saladin understands that perhaps 'love was more durable than hate' and he loses his hostility towards Gibreel (SV, p. 407). Later on Gibreel, who is chasing Saladin, finally finds him injured in the burning Shaandaar Café. In a state of forgiveness this haunted schizophrenic saves him 'so that on a night when the city is at war, a night heavy with enmity and rage, there is this small redeeming victory for love' (SV, p. 468). The most redemptive moment of love happens between Saladin and his father Changez when the latter is about to die. Saladin ponders: 'To fall in love with one's father after the long angry decades was a serene and beautiful feeling' (SV, p. 523). For Saladin it is also a moment of coming to terms with his different selves. Even if he does not become a singular self in the process, he is ready for the final scene of letting the old die in order for the new to be born.

But before that there is yet one episode. Despite the mutual redemptive moments, the enmity between Gibreel and Saladin resurfaces. It is indicated that although they had both been freed of their devils, although 'love had shown that it could exert a humanizing power as great as that of hatred, it is not a final solution, it is not a complete cure but a temporary denouement' (SV, p. 540). This is its human scale. Perhaps the 'small redeeming victory for love' (SV, p. 468) is not so small after all. As a story about the importance of stories it can show the dangers of intolerance and the capacity of love.

NOTES

1 Salman Rushdie, *The Satanic Verses* (London: Viking, 1988). All references will be to this edition and will be cited in the text as SV.
2 'The *fatwa*' was first read as an announcement on Radio Teheran on 14 Feb. 1989; see Lisa Appignanesi and Sara Maitland (eds.), *The Rushdie File* (London: Fourth Estate, 1989), p. 84. The details of the 'Satanic Verses affair' are discussed in Joel Kuortti, *Place of the Sacred: The Rhetoric of the* Satanic Verses *Affair* (Frankfurt am Main: Peter Lang, 1997).
3 Rushdie comments that these 'theologicals' are actually called 'mythologicals' and that they are not a Bombay cinema form, but South Indian: 'Salman Rushdie Talks to the London Consortium about *The Satanic Verses*', interview with Colin MacCabe et al., (1996) in *Salman Rushdie Interviews: A Sourcebook of His Ideas*, ed. Pradyumna S. Chauhan (Westport, Conn. and London: Greenwood, 2001), p. 214.
4 Azraeel is the major Islamic angel of death and destruction.
5 Rushdie, 'The Empire Writes Back with a Vengeance', *Times* (3 July 1982), p. 8; furthermore, Saladin ironically alludes to the famous twelfth-century Muslim hero who conquered Jerusalem from the Crusaders in 1187 CE.
6 In his essay 'In Good Faith' (1990), Rushdie defines his own attitude further: 'To be a Bombayite (and afterwards a Londoner) was also to fall in love with the metropolis. The city as reality and as a metaphor is at the heart of all my work', in *Imaginary Homelands: Essays and Criticism 1981–1991* (London: Granta/Penguin, 1991), p. 404.
7 See Joel Kuortti, *Fictions to Live In: Narration as an Argument for Fiction in Salman Rushdie's Novels* (Frankfurt am Main: Peter Lang, 1998), esp. Chapter 4.
8 See Linda Hutcheon, '"The Pastime of Past Time": Fiction, History, Historiographic Metafiction', *Genre* 20 (1987), p. 285.
9 For more detailed discussion see: Hans Seminck, *A Novel Visible but Unseen: A Thematic Analysis of Salman Rushdie's* The Satanic Verses, *Studia Germanica Gandensia* 33 (Gent: Seminarie voor Duitse Taalkunde, 1993), pp. 70–3; Margareta Petersson adds to the postmodern and postcolonial approaches to hybridity the alchemical and the carnivalesque, *Unending Metamorphoses: Myth, Satire and Religion in Salman Rushdie's Novels* (Lund: Lund University Press, 1996), see pp. 284–99; Philip Engblom discusses *The Satanic Verses* as 'a modern Menippean satire', 'A Multitude of Voices: Carnivalization and Dialogicality in

the Novels of Salman Rushdie', in D. M. Fletcher (ed.), *Reading Rushdie: Perspectives on the Fiction of Salman Rushdie*, Cross/Cultures, 16 (Amsterdam and Atlanta: Rodopi, 1994), p. 301; Timothy Brennan acknowledges the metafictionality of Rushdie's writing but suggests that it is rather an example of 'Third-World cosmopolitans'' revisionist take on postmodernism, *Salman Rushdie and the Third World: Myths of the Nation* (London: Macmillan, 1989), pp. 85 and 141–2.

10 Homi K. Bhabha, 'Beyond Fundamentalism and Liberalism', *New Statesman and Society* 2.39 (1989), p. 35; repr. in Appignanesi and Maitland, *The Rushdie File*.

11 For Rushdie's views, see especially 'In Good Faith', in *Imaginary Homelands*, pp. 450–5, and his interview with Colin MacCabe in Chauhan (ed.), *Salman Rushdie Interviews*, pp. 213–29. See also Ameena Meer, 'Salman Rushdie' (1989), in Michael R. Reder (ed.), *Conversations with Rushdie* (Jackson: University Press of Mississippi, 2000), pp. 61–74, and Sean French, 'Falling towards England,' *Observer* (25 September 1988), p. 43. For critical consideration of the themes, see Catherine Cundy, *Salman Rushdie* (Manchester: Manchester University Press, 1996), pp. 1–11 and 65–6; Seminck, *Novel Visible*, passim; and Margaret Reynolds and Jonathan Noakes, *Salman Rushdie: The Essential Guide*, Vintage Living Texts series (London: Vintage, 2003), passim.

12 Rushdie, 'In Good Faith', in *Imaginary Homelands* (1991), p. 394.

13 Salman Rushdie, *Shame* (London: Jonathan Cape, 1983), pp. 63–4 (emphases and ellipsis added).

14 Rushdie interview with McCabe in Chauhan (ed.), *Salman Rushdie Interviews*, p. 219.

15 Rushdie, 'The New Empire within Britain', *New Society* 62.1047 (9 December 1982); repr. in *Imaginary Homelands*, p. 129 (emphasis added).

16 Salman Rushdie, *Midnight's Children* (London: Jonathan Cape, 1981), pp. 122 and 237.

17 In 1984, Rushdie wrote about a fire in such an establishment in 'Council Housing that Kills'. He comments on the resistance of people to their treatment: 'The Mice have Started Biting Back', *Guardian* (3 December 1984), p. 12; repr. as 'An Unimportant Fire', in *Imaginary Homelands*, p. 142.

18 Rushdie, 'In Good Faith', in *Imaginary Homelands*, p. 394.

19 For the blasphemy debate, see especially Kuortti, *Place of the Sacred*; see also Shabbir Akhtar, *Be Careful with Muhammad!* (London: Bellew, 1989), David Lawton, *Blasphemy* (New York: Harvester/Wheatsheaf, 1993) and Richard Webster, *A Brief History of Blasphemy: Liberalism, Censorship, and* The Satanic Verses (Southwold, Suffolk: The Orwell Press, 1990).

20 'A reverent but inept 1976 film, originally released as *Al-Risalah* (English, *Mohammed, the Messenger of God*) depicting the life of Muhammad, fiercely attacked by devout Muslims, who object to any pictorial depiction of the Prophet. As Rushdie notes, the film avoided ever actually putting the Prophet on the screen. This passage clearly reflects Rushdie's consciousness that the story he was about to tell would strike some as blasphemous', Paul Brians, 'Notes on Salman Rushdie *The Satanic Verses* (1988)', available at www.wsu.edu/~brians/anglophone/satanic_verses/ (1996).

21 Rushdie, 'In Good Faith', in *Imaginary Homelands*, p. 396.

22 Although it is not possible to discuss it in detail here, the single richest intertextual framework for *The Satanic Verses* is cinema. Not only are the references and allusions to different films, actors, actresses and directors abundant, the book also uses cinematic techniques and vocabulary as textual devices. Furthermore, Rushdie has on many occasions discussed the influence of cinema on him: 'movies had more impact on me than novels in a kind of formational way', 'Goodfellas', interview with David Cronenberg (1995) in Chauhan (2003), p. 168; see also Vijay Mishra's contribution to this volume, his *Bollywood Cinema: Temples of Desire* (New York and London: Routledge, 2002), and Rachel Dwyer's *All You Need Is Money, All You Want Is Love: Sex and Romance in India* (London: Cassell, 2000). The eclecticism of film is in line with the novel's emphasis on hybridity. Besides the influence of film, another source for reference and allusion Rushdie uses is literature, drawing from a rich variety of literary sources; see Brians, 'Notes on Salman Rushdie', for an overview of the intertextual connections of the novel.

23 The transliteration is here without the diacritics. The translation used in the novel is closest to the one in William Muir, *The Life of Mohammad from Original Sources* (1861), rev. edn 1923, ed. T[homas] H[unter] Weir (New York: AMS Press, 1975), p. 81. A different translation is in M. M. Ahsan, 'The "Satanic" Verses and the Orientalists', *Impact International* 18.20 (20 October 1988), pp. 17–18; repr. in M. M. Ahsan and A. R. Kidwai (eds.), *Sacrilege versus Civility: Muslim Perspectives on* The Satanic Verses *Affair* (Leicester: Islamic Foundation, 1991), p. 132: 'These are the high-soaring ones (deities) whose intercession is to be hoped for!' There are variant transliterations in Muhammad Husayn Haikal, *The Life of Muhammad* (1935), 8th edn, trans. Isma'il Ragi A. al Faruqi (N.p.: North American Trust Publications, 1976), p. 111. An intriguing contribution to the discussion of *The Satanic Verses* is Jaakko Hämeen-Anttila's article, in which he discussed the historical validity of the verses in the light of stylistic and textual evidence, 'Qur. 53:19, the Prophetic Experience and the "Satanic Verses" – A Reconsideration', *Acta Orientalia* 58 (1997), pp. 24–34.

24 Ibn Ishaq, *The Life of Muhammad: A Translation of Ishaq's Sirat rasul Allah*, ed. 'Abdu'l-Malik Ibn Hisham, trans. A[lfred] Guillaume (Karachi: Oxford University Press, 1990), pp. 165–6; see also Muir, *The Life of Mohammad*, pp. lxxix–lxxx.

25 Haikal, *The Life of Muhammad*, p. 105.

26 Srinivas Aravamudan, ' "Being God's Postman Is No Fun, Yaar": Salman Rushdie's *The Satanic Verses*', *Diacritics* 19.2 (Summer 1989), p. 12.

27 C. S. Lewis, *Four Loves* (London: Geoffrey Bles, 1960).

10

DEEPIKA BAHRI

The shorter fiction

Salman Rushdie's shorter fiction, the novella *Haroun and the Sea of Stories* (1990) and the short story collection *East, West* (1994), is distinguished by old-fashioned qualities associated with storytelling: the ability of a good story to give counsel and comfort and the potential for remaining meaningful well beyond the season in which the tale was first told. Almost any reading of these works, Rushdie's first publications after the *fatwa* of 1989, is likely to seem overly determined by the fateful event, but in the final analysis, these are books that outlast this immediate context to pose and answer enduring questions about home and the world, the power of speech and language, and the promise of stories. These themes are not new, even if the context imbues them with unprecedented urgency. The challenge and danger of writing fiction about issues that matter – language, religion, politics, history, identity, tyranny, migrations – have been familiar to the author since his turn to subcontinental material in *Midnight's Children* and continue to be relevant in works that follow.

Conceived in a commitment made to his son Zafar to write a book for children, *Haroun and the Sea of Stories*, published a scant year after the *fatwa*, is a book that keeps its word. 'There's no more absolute thing', Rushdie explained, 'than a promise to your child. You can't break it.'[1] Looking back on the dismal months following the Ayatollah Khomeini's *fatwa* and his confinement, Rushdie admits to feelings of doubt: 'I spent an awful lot of time thinking I would never write again, not because I couldn't but because I didn't want to.'[2] In the first summer of his enforced protective custody, however, Rushdie had begun to write a book set in the country of Alifbay (*alif* and *be* are the first two letters of the Arabic alphabet), a story of the struggle between Gup, where free speech *and* babble flourish, and Chup, reputed to be a 'place of shadows, of books that wear padlocks and tongues torn out; of secret conspiracies and poison rings'.[3] Inviting an allegorical reading, *Haroun and the Sea of Stories* tells a timeless story about language, returning to problems raised in *The Satanic Verses*: 'how to bend it shape it, how to let it be our freedom, how to repossess its poisoned wells, how to master the river of words of time of blood', and how to reclaim what has been 'irredeemably polluted by history'.[4]

Rushdie's shortest novel asks the question, 'is not the Power of Speech the greatest Power of all?' (*Haroun*, p. 119). Language is at the heart of the human enterprise, the tool that must be left free, even when it is trivialised and abused. To lose it is to suffer that 'unthinkable thing' (*Haroun*, p. 26), a fate that befalls Rashid Khalifa when his wife, Soraya, runs away with a Mr Sen, a doubter who wonders, 'What's the use of stories that aren't even true?' (*Haroun*, p. 20). Rashid's son Haroun keeps faith with the power of stories, travelling to the Moon Kahani to battle the forces that threaten the wellsprings of the ocean of stories, and to reconnect his father with his inspiration.

The lands of Gup, where debates can continue for weeks and months, even years, 'on account of the Guppee fondness for conversation' (*Haroun*, p. 88), are in imminent danger of siege by the grand panjandrum, Khattam-Shud, who governs the lands of Chup:

> Arch-Enemy of all Stories, even of Language itself. He is the Prince of Silence and the Foe of Speech. And because everything ends, because dreams end, stories end, life ends, at the finish of everything we use his name.
>
> (*Haroun*, p. 39)

Khattam-Shud, the Cultmaster of Bezaban, retains the power of speech he denies to his followers, the Chup-wallahs, and threatens the story-sea, upon which the Guppees draw. Tired, borrowed stories now circulate in the polluted sea, plugging the precious wellsprings. The forces that threaten free speech and creativity, even when they take the shape of Prince Bolo's empty prattle and Princess Batcheat's tuneless songs, must be fought. While they expose the squandering to which a very precious commodity is subject, the majesty and power of silence are evident in the person of Mudra, who speaks the unconventional but ancient indigenous language of silent *Abhinaya*. Haroun muses that 'the dance of the Shadow Warrior showed him that silence had its own grace and beauty (just as speech could be graceless and ugly); and that Action could be as noble as Words' (p. 125). Mudra becomes a valuable ally in the fight against the forces of Chup.

The Guppees eventually prove themselves worthy opponents in pitched battle: 'All those arguments and debates, all that openness, had created powerful bonds of fellowship between them' (p. 185). The Chupwalas 'turned out to be a disunited rabble', for 'their habits of secrecy had made them suspicious and distrustful of one other' (p. 185). Peace eventually breaks out in this hopeful saga, and Rashid is awarded the highest tribute possible, the 'Order of the Open Mouth' (p. 192). When he returns to his own world, now refortified with the powers of story-telling, his tale awakens its audience to injustice and the need for political action. Inspired by his message, they chase the corrupt politicos away, and are now free to elect leaders 'they actually liked' (p. 207). Fully aware that happy endings are rare, Rushdie nevertheless provides one because it is the prospect of happy endings that keeps struggles alive. Rushdie had written in *The Satanic Verses*: 'Language is courage ... the ability to conceive a thought, to speak it, and by doing so to make it true' (p. 281). The crowning lesson in the novella that follows *The Satanic Verses* is the reminder that to surrender a language is to rob the past of its capacity to instruct and the future of its promise of a better world (*Haroun*, p. 119).

For his next publication, Rushdie, an expansive writer at the best of times, continued to work in a smaller frame. The stories in *East, West* are divided into three sections, organised around a cartographic and civilisational rubric, four each in 'East' and 'West' and three in the last, 'East, West'. The stories in the first two sections are located in their nominal geographic locales and those in the final section move between the two. The stories none the less confound the translation of arbitrary boundaries into schematic difference. Each of these 'worlds' is in transition, each riven by conflicting and complex desires, each defying easy understanding. Together they sound notes familiar in much of Rushdie's later work: the crisis of the self in the fray of modernity, the dangers of state power, the lure and perils of migration, and above all, the need for stories and the danger of choosing the wrong ones.

'Good Advice is Rarer than Rubies' introduces us to big-eyed Miss Rehana, betrothed as a nine-year-old to Mustafa, then thirty and living in Bradford. Rehana is one of many 'Tuesday women' who arrive at the British Consulate on the allotted day in anxious quest of visas to join their husbands or fiancés already in England. Instead of perpetrating his usual scam, the fraudulent 'advice expert' Muhammad Ali who preys on the women finds himself charmed into offering Rehana a fake British passport. Rehana rejects the illegal proposition, walks through the consular gates, fails to secure a visa, and reveals to the old man the circumstances of her betrothal to a man she can no longer remember. In the end, Rehana will remain in Lahore with her job as a nanny to three good boys who would have missed her. Her smile as she is leaving on the evening bus, the author tells us, is 'the happiest thing ... [Ali] had ever seen in his long, hot, hard, unloving life'.[5] Rehana has not been turned down, but has contrived to be rejected by giving deliberately erroneous responses to the consular official's intimate questions.

The story draws attention to the plight of third world women in the East, complete with the horrors of child marriage and/or abandonment by partners who have left for the supposedly more desirable West, but Rehana's gentle refusal requires us to pause at the question of gender and ask if a movement West will set her free? Rehana who now roams bare-faced, big-eyed and independent might well find herself veiled and in service of an ageing master in Bradford, in a stridently Muslim immigrant enclave. Does the third world move with the woman, or indeed would Rehana find in the West the third world she may so far have escaped? In the very first story of the collection, Rushdie effectively undoes crude platitudes about women in the East, in the West, and in the diaspora by initiating discussion under the destabilising sign of woman, in what is one of few works to openly broach the question of gender.

The next two stories return to themes and events earlier portrayed in *Midnight's Children*: 'The Free Radio' returns to the Emergency rule of Indira Gandhi, with a focus on the topic of the mass sterilisation of mostly poor young men. Health agencies strove to meet sterilisation quotas by using the 'free radio scheme' which promised the aforesaid radio in exchange for voluntary vasectomy 'in the national interest' (p. 26). The star character of this story, Ramani, a good-looking young Rickshaw-puller, is 'an innocent' who succumbs to the dubious governmental scheme discreetly implemented in a mobile white van where 'things were done to [men]' (p. 24). The elderly narrator of the story relates how Ramani falls for and marries an attractive older widow with five children after undergoing a vasectomy, takes to riding his rickshaw while cupping an imaginary radio to his ear, is thrashed and thrown out into the dirt when he re-enters the van in pursuit of his promised prize, and finally leaves for Bombay in search of a new fantasy, that of becoming a film star. The coincidence of Ramani being sterilised for love of a widow, when Mrs Gandhi was referred to as 'the Widow' in *Midnight's Children*, is characteristically intertextual play with his own œuvre that Rushdie veterans will relish.

At the heart of this story is the power of fictions. Ramani attempts to supplement an ordinary life with the magic of imaginary radios or fantasies of Bollywood stardom. There is also the fiction of 'national interest', of seductively named groups such as the new 'Youth Movement' who turn out to be the state's hired goons, of the drama of the 'State of Emergency'. The narrative of national development and the importance of individual sacrifice for the nation may be one of the most effective and persuasive stories of all time, judging by their widespread use and appeal, second only to that other powerful narrative spotlighted in the next story: religion. 'The Prophet's Hair' returns to another historical moment referred to in *Midnight's*

Children, the theft and restoration of the prophet's hair from the Hazratbal mosque in Kashmir. News of the theft set off rioting in locations as far away as Calcutta in 1963–4. The relic reappeared as mysteriously as it had vanished shortly after the disclosure of its theft. In *Midnight's Children* Saleem would have us believe that his grandfather, Aadam Aziz, crazed by his son's suicide, had stolen away to Kashmir, there to spirit away the sacred relic as his revenge upon God (pp. 332–3). Dying five days before the announcement of its 'recovery', Aadam Aziz was not at hand to speak during the authentication process. Beginning to wonder, '[I]f ... [the authenticators] were wrong ...', the narrator leaves us with the irresolution of ellipses. Rushdie's short story chooses to take a stance of distance from the historical moment, resorting to the overtly fictional gesture of situating it '[e]arly in the year 19–', to spin an elaborately contrived response to the question left unanswered in *Midnight's Children*.

Hashim, a wealthy moneylender, decides to add the accidentally discovered relic to his collection 'purely as a secular object of great rarity and blinding beauty' instead of restoring it and peace to a region devastated by riots in the wake of its theft (*East, West*, p. 44). Hashim rationalises the misappropriation in the name of closer adherence to the Prophet's injunctions against relic-worship on the one hand and his purely secular interest in it as 'a man of the world, of this world' on the other (p. 44). In the presence of the relic, however, Hashim turns into a purist, intolerant domestic tyrant, burning all books but the Qur'ān, requiring regular prayer, rigid discipline, and chaste behaviour by the household women. In desperation, his family arranges for a thief, Sheikh Sín, to relieve them of the hair and the tyranny. The thief is killed but not before a visit to his blind wife whose sight is miraculously restored. Sheikh Sín's four sons, crippled by the father to ensure their successful begging careers, also find their limbs restored to wholeness, their earning powers thus 'reduced by 75 percent', (p. 58) and their future consequently ruined. The tragi-comic chronicle of disasters befalling those who come into contact with the relic, whether they were of reverent, secular or indifferent disposition toward it, underscores the power of symbols. These ideas are developed more fully in *The Moor's Last Sigh* where the rise of Hindu Fundamentalism under the banner of Ram Rajya is examined.

By the end of this cluster of stories one has learned that good counsel in our times is rare, miracles are not what they're cracked up to be, and radios aren't free, but dreams and fictions are. The characters in these stories have been living in the grip of powerful fictions, fictions about the West, salvation and miracles, governmental largesse, the benevolence of the state or the dreamworlds spun by Bollywood. Stories are powerful and they matter, but our future may depend on which ones we choose.

These themes and preoccupations are not abandoned with the turn to the West in the section that follows. If anything, they reach an apotheostic intensity in the invocation of iconic representations of Western culture: 'Yorick' with its metonymic reference to Hamlet and thus Shakespeare as the best known and most exported English cultural symbol; 'At the Auction of the Ruby Slippers' and its nostalgic recall of a magical American culture whose influence continues to grow in ever new forms; and 'Christopher Columbus and Queen Isabella Consummate their Relationship' which returns us to a curious moment in the history of European empire-making and the iconic historic figure of Columbus.

'Yorick' retells a version of Hamlet from the perspective of a 'multi-coloured' descendant of Yorick (p. 63). The second story foretells a future dystopia in hock to a retail society in which everything is for sale, and the final story reveals the sexual politics that underlie the desire for empire and conquest. Irreverence is a hallmark of each of the stories. The investment of objects, figures and historical personae with undue reverence functions multiply in these stories and the collection as a whole: as the engine of religious zealotry, as the schematic on which civilisation, difference and hierarchy are based, as a device for stirring feelings of nationalism, and as the signature mark of a commodity culture. Having questioned the conjoint agendas of nationalism and development, and cast some doubt on the authenticity of sacred relics, Rushdie goes on to tackle the aura surrounding three major Western cultural icons.

'Yorick' is a rambunctious retelling in which the author tries to out-Sterne Sterne, marrying a foul-breathed Ophelia to a superannuated Yorick who is done-in by the spoiled child-prince Hamlet's ear-poison 'SPEECH' which will drive Ophelia, 'accused and spurned by Yorick' to death by grief. It will also result in Yorick's one-way trip to the execution block from whence an 'unknown hand' will retrieve and bury the head such that the prince many years later will be confronted by his 'grinning bony guilt' (p. 80). The narrator's version, which is conceded to be different from 'Master CHACKPAW's', is offered as an alternative that might co-exist without requiring difficult choices (p. 81). The narrator's purpose has been 'to explicate, annotate, hyphenate, palatinate & permanganate' (p. 64) the history associated with Shakespeare's 'morbid prince' by taking a fragment from the famous play and floating Yorick's saga into the most delightful torrent of fustian. The empire writes back, speaking in many voices, bombastic and excessive, laced with the ironies of imperial influence and colonial education. If the action of the first story in the 'East' section takes place in the shadow of the British flag, the first one in 'West' is ceded to a multicoloured voice that exhumes a decayed relic, Yorick's skull, to retell its tale anew.

In a story flamboyantly celebrating the capacity of language to make sense *and* nonsense, speech as poison and gossip as a venene without antidote assume a central role. The excessive and nonsensical tone of the narrator, the descendant of a fool, no less, now in multicoloured motley, belies the harsh truth: Words can kill. For all that the story is a 'COCK AND BULL', the 'humble AUTHOR', playing the fool, has overlaid the Bard's narrative with a coded lesson of his own (p. 83), a fiction to rival more malicious fictions in circulation in a world that is ending. In *The Moor's Last Sigh*, which follows soon after these stories, the Moor might well be the multicoloured descendant on the run, short of breath, like Sterne and Tristram who both suffered from pulmonary tuberculosis, but determined to leave behind his tale.

The time is no less out of joint in the dystopic future depicted in 'At the Auction of the Ruby Slippers'. The collusion of state and capital, a theme that also reappears in *The Moor's Last Sigh*, finds pithy articulation in the short story. 'The cult of the ruby slippers is at its height' with the auction of Dorothy's ruby slippers, which lie behind bullet-proof glass, threatening to generate births as well as deaths, calling for the presence of obstetricians as well as helmeted SWAT teams (p. 87). Feelings, illnesses, remedies, problems and their solutions are all supersized: the cuspidors into which people may expectorate or vomit are 'extra-large', the psychiatrists in attendance at the auction house are not only many but of 'varying disciplines' (p. 87), and needs are 'numberless' (p. 93). Excess has become the norm and 'everything is for sale', mountains, monuments, spouses, pedigrees, selves, and on special occasions, souls (p. 98).

The story plays with MGM's historic 1970 auction of film memorabilia and recalls Bollywood dream factories, which generate even more successful fictions. While many are drawn by the talismanic power of the magical slippers, fundamentalists promise to burn them because of their fetish status, but the marketplace morality in operation has room for them: 'what price tolerance if the intolerant are not tolerated also?' (p. 92). Anyone who can pay – stars, collectors, tramps, exiles, poets, bandits or fundamentalists – is welcome in this marketplace world because 'anyone's cash is as good as anyone else's' (p. 93). Among the motley group, moreover, are entirely imaginary beings, characters from novels and paintings, who have successfully penetrated the real world. The blurring of the fictional and real, the constant movement of items on the auction block, and the air of impending disaster as societal unrest couples with the presence of the might of the state conjure up a world of ceaseless and nightmarish change in a state of perpetual storm, recalling Marx and Engels's poetic description of a world under the rule of capital: 'All that is solid melts into air, all that is holy is profaned, and man is at last compelled to face with sober senses his real condition of life and his relations with his kind.'[6] Not so much timeless as historyless, this condition speeds up time and compresses space, leaving the individual in a state of vertiginous uncertainty.

The futuristic society of Rushdie's story sparks uncomfortable moments of self-recognition for the present: in the descriptions of state control, violence, economic disparity, star worship, and covert references to environmental ruination which has made 'most of us ... sick' (p. 87). Thick with references to items of high and low art in the culture industry, the story lists numerous objects revered by a fetishised museum culture and its tendency to equate value with price.

The narrator wishes to buy the slippers to win back his lover, Gale, who would cry 'Home, boy! Home, baby, yes – you've come home', 'at the moment of penetration' (p. 95). The ex-girlfriend (Dorothy's surname is also 'Gale') who is also a cousin suggests that the narrator's relation is with a perfidious and powerful postmodern storm that sweeps everything up, leaving the individual quivering for more and longing for home. Like the marooned astronaut longing to come home to earth where no one seems at home, everyone is out of place. The ruby slippers promise to take the wearer home, however '[s]cattered, damaged [and] various a concept' home might now have become (p. 93). The narrator explains: 'We revere the ruby slippers because of their powers of reverse metamorphosis, their affirmation of a lost state of normalcy in which we have almost ceased to believe' (p. 92).

In its own bid to 'reverse metamorphosis', 'Christopher Columbus and Queen Isabella Consummate their Relationship' returns us to a past before Marx and before empire, evoking another time and place to which Rushdie will return in the novel *The Moor's Last Sigh* to compare the rise of Hindu fundamentalism to a historical juncture marked by religious despotism. Little is known of the historic Columbus who embarked early on a seafaring life. Shipwrecked in Portugal, he travelled widely with Portuguese voyagers and adventurers which fired his imagination to conceive a dream, 'The Enterprise of the Indies'. When King John II of Portugal rejected his request for finance, he approached Ferdinand and Isabella. Consumed by the Moorish wars and fearful of threatening the hard-won recent peace with Portugal, the Queen prevaricated for several years, finally sending word that Columbus should hasten to Santa Fé, there to sign a contract some four months after the fall of Granada. In Rushdie's story, Columbus, 'a foreigner', is first 'seen' in the story in a posture of dignified supplication. He is, in effect, courting the queen. Her favour is tied to his 'hopes of cash, and of three tall ships ... sailing across the ocean blue' (p. 107). Rushdie translates his courtly attentions to the Queen into a literal wooing with 'coarse epistles ... tuneless serenades'.

In casting him as a foreigner and an outsider, the story places the much maligned Columbus in a position aligned with some of the more wretched of the earth who 'are often poor and consequently willing to perform divers necessary but dirty jobs' (p. 108). It is sobering to see contemporary history's favourite anti-hero repositioned thus, obliging us to reorient our notions of East and West, hero and villain, then and now. In that place and that time, Columbus is not so much a Western hero (it remains for him to be made thus and then undone) as an attendant awaiting his turn as his resources dwindle, his body ages, and his odds diminish. As the migrant waits, Isabella's internal ruminations on foreigners, rendered in italic typeface, veer between rationalising their presence and resenting their pretensions to equality. Whereas '[t]hey lend the place a certain cosmopolitan tone' and function as 'a warning against complacency', they also tend to 'forget their place (having left it behind)' and 'begin to think of themselves as our equals' (p. 108). Torn by contradiction, yet tempted by his ambition, his foreignness, the Queen toys with Columbus, teasing him with attentions that are followed by banishment.

A series of equations between sexual, economic and imperial desire knots a variety of human impulses into a complicated motivational matrix. We are asked to consider that 'the loss of money and patronage ... is as bitter as unrequited love' (p. 115). Columbus says of Isabella: 'no conquest satisfies her, no peak of ecstasy is high enough' (p. 114). As Columbus waits, 'running out of possible patrons, sales talk, flirtatiousness, hair, steam', Isabella flourishes, increasing her dominion and her power. This waxing and waning is prefaced thus by the narrator: '[t]he sexual appetites of the male decline; those of the female continue, with the advancing years, to grow' (p. 111). The marriage of Columbus's desire for money, ships, patronage and position to Isabella's desire for greater power and more possessions marks a signal moment in the birth of a new history. The author likens this consummation of intersecting desires to the yoking together of 'bonds far harder to dissolve than those of any mortal love, the harsh and deifying ties of history' (p. 117).

Columbus's and Isabella's desires spring from deep within their consciousness, operating at the level of dreams which finally communicate with each other when flirtations and courtly seductions have failed: '*Columbus dreams her seeing* ... visions of her own' and dreams her remembering him as the crucial realisation of the mutuality of their needs dawns upon her (p. 116). When she understands that it is the unknown that sustains desire, Isabella is able to see that 'her need for him is as great as his for her'

(p. 116). Thus are the pioneer and the patron united in a sexualised relationship of co-dependence. Like a proud lover, Columbus fantasises that he will refuse her when she calls. He dissembles and resists the heralds' bribes and cajoling. Opening his mouth to refuse, he answers, 'Yes. I'll come' (p. 119). Columbus has answered nothing less than the call of history. He could not have known that the desire for the unknown, conceived in his mind as 'The Enterprise of the Indies' (and translating crudely but accurately into the quest for cheaper spices) would lead him to the New World. In 1498 another voyager, Vasco da Gama, would arrive on the coast of Malabar (with the assistance of a pilot native to Gujrat), to discover India, an event which will inaugurate the narrative of *The Moor's Last Sigh*.

The final group of stories, written expressly for the collection, is titled 'East, West', and begins with the promisingly and deceptively titled 'The Harmony of the Spheres', a tale of perfidy featuring Eliot Crane, schizophrenic expert on matters occult, his wife Lucy Evans, his friend 'Khan' from their Cambridge days, and Khan's wife Mala. As youngsters in Bombay, Lucy and Khan had exchanged kisses, an experience the narrator is 'anxious to repeat' (p. 131). Opposites in so many ways, as Khan labours to elaborate, Crane and Khan are unlikely but very close friends. Mala even hints at their homoerotic relationship, suggesting that 'Maybe you should go to bed together and we-all can go home and get some rest' (p. 139). Crane has been working on 'The Harmony of the Spheres', a study of occultist groups in Europe in the nineteenth and twentieth centuries while Khan 'was trying to be a writer' (p. 140). Khan learns from Crane that in the occult realm, the spheres have already been harmonising, unlike in the visible world driven by history and its binary logic.

> But in Eliot's enormous, generously shared mental storehouse of the varieties of 'forbidden knowledge' I thought I'd found another way of making a bridge between here-and-there, between my two othernesses, my double unbelonging. In that world of magic and power there seemed to exist the kind of fusion of worldviews, European Amerindian Oriental Levantine, in which I desperately wanted to believe. With his help, I hoped, I might make a 'forbidden self'. (p. 141)

Khan hopes that it is Eliot, whose name recalls that other Westerner who attempted a similar fusion of disparate worlds, who will show him an alternative to 'the apparent world, all cynicism and napalm', one 'wholly without kindness or wisdom' (p. 141).

After Eliot's suicide, Khan goes through his papers to discover neither a life of the Welsh nationalist Owen Glendower he was supposed to be working on nor a manuscript on the occult but rather pages full of 'inchoate rants' and obscenities, most disturbingly in fantasies about sex with Mala and hate-filled fantasies about his friends. 'Since then', the narrator confides, 'there has been no intercourse between the spiritual world and mine' (p. 144). Even when we find, in the story's surprising if somewhat formulaic punch-line delivered by Mala, '[t]hose weren't fantasies', the more poignant and heart-breaking lessons have already come through: the longing of the self for the other will break our hearts. The apparent world is what there is and it is 'without kindness or wisdom' (p. 146).

The next story, 'Chekov and Zulu', again features two close friends and a failed reconciliation. Bearing the 'cosmonaut aliases' of Chekov and Zulu [sic] from the *Star Trek* series since their Doon School days, the two work in the Indian secret service, remaining close friends and debating colonialism and its chief culprits. While Chekov rants against colonial theft of 'our treasures' (p. 156), Zulu urges nuance, restraint and forgiveness because to him '[t]he colonial period is a closed book' (p. 157). Chekov's nationalism and uninflected stance of postcolonial resentment humorously recalls his *Star Trek* namesake's brash pronouncements and ethnic pride. Different in their outlook and lifestyle, they nonetheless profess to be 'blood brothers', (p. 157) until they fall out over the collusion of the state government with anti-Sikh rioters.

Zulu's disappearance from Birmingham on 4 November 1984, shortly after the assassination of Indian Prime Minister Indira Gandhi at the hands of her Sikh bodyguards, gives Chekov many moments of doubt as to his Sikh friend's reliability as a government agent infiltrating the separatist Khalistani movement. Zulu, however, remains faithful to his task, returning with useful intelligence but determined to quit the service in protest against state-supported terrorism in the 1984 riots. While Zulu flourishes in private enterprise upon his return to Bombay, Chekov, who cannot renounce careerism for friendship, succumbs along with Indira Gandhi's son, Rajiv, in a terrorist attack by a homegrown Tamil revolutionist. Chekov and Zulu, men with a mission in service of the nation, find it impossible to have a common purpose when the abstract ideal of nation confronts the fissures of ethnic identity and the challenges of reckoning with the might of state power. Personal relationships, it would seem from the two stories, are not only personal after all, whether in the East or in the West.

The title of the last story in the collection, 'The Courter', refers to the chivalrous East European porter who serves as apartment hall porter in an expensive building in London. He is thus named by the narrator's Indian nanny, Mary, whose habitual peppering of her conversations with the adverb 'certainly', has earned her the sobriquet of 'Certainly-Mary'. Her difficulties with English produce a more apt description for the courtly porter after all: 'English was hard for Certainly-Mary ... The letter p was a particular problem, often turning into an f or a c. ... As the elevator lifted her away, she called ... "Thank you, courter!"' (p. 176). The misnomer intrigues the East European: '"Courter," he repeated to the mirror ... People called him many things ... But this name, this courter, this he would try to be' (p. 177). The gentle courtship of this unlikely couple and their transformation of chess into a private language of romance takes place against a backdrop of racism on the public stage and a coming of age on the familial one where the pubescent narrator is undergoing predictable growing pains.

Much of the story is concerned with language, its loss, its seductions, its misprision and its substitutes. The English of the immigrant subcontinental family, however upper class and snobbish, is foreign to the locals, humiliating the former and unintentionally offending the latter when the narrator's father innocently asks a shopgirl for 'nipples' for his newborn. Shocked to learn that 'here they call them teats', the family denounces the word choice as 'shameless' (p. 184). Meanwhile, on the American side of the pond, neither 'teats' nor 'nipples' will do when a perfectly good euphemism, 'pacifier', can suffice. Wilde's remark that the Americans and the English have everything in common except the language strikes one as both witty and insightful in having lighted upon the significance of the stamp of place on the consensual usage of words even within the same language. Certainly-Mary's verbal tics further privatise what we take to be a public and shared medium of communication. To understand her one would need not only to know English but to know Mary as a user of English with particular habits and limitations. Over time, the courter is charmed by her lingual lapses and her habitual use of the word 'certainly'. Humbled by a stroke which has impaired his faculties and clouded his once sharp brain, the former Chess Grandmaster is now reduced to being a porter and covering for a Maharajah with a taste for prostitutes and violent sex. For one so adversely and irreversibly changed by circumstances, Mary's practice of liberally larding her language with the definitive qualifier 'certainly' offers reassurance, if only verbal. Mecir's own loss of both certainty and language (and indeed a name which no one seems able to pronounce) have none the less left him with one means of communication: chess, a game he teaches Mary, perhaps in exchange for the grace she has offered him.

The courter comes to a poor end protecting Mary and her mistress from revenge-seeking goons who mistake them for the Maharajah's women, while Mary chooses to return to Bombay, because England 'was breaking her heart' (p. 209). The narrator too admits to having 'ropes around my neck ... pulling me this way and that, East and West', but he refuses to choose (p. 211). 'I buck, I snort, I whinny', he says, recalling Forster's horses at the end of *A Passage to India*, when Mr Fielding asks Dr Aziz why they could not be friends *now*:

> But the horses didn't want it – they swerved apart; the earth didn't want it, sending up rocks through which riders must pass single file; the temples, the tank, the jail, the palace, the birds, the carrion, the Guest House ... they didn't want it, they said in their hundred voices, 'No, not yet,' and the sky said, 'No, not there.'[7]

There is but a comma between East and West, a pause, an interval, a difference in pitch, something cut off that longs for reconciliation but cannot yet have it. Home, reconciliation, friendship, redemption turn out to be fictions, albeit necessary ones. The world, as it is, is breaking our hearts, forcing us to choose. The spheres are everywhere divided, in the East or West, or indeed within ourselves. In *The Moor's Last Sigh* Rushdie will remind us of 'that most profound of our needs, to our need for flowing together, for putting an end to frontiers'.[8] Till such reconciliation is possible, the narrator will fall asleep with the hope that he will awaken 'into a better time' (p. 434). In the shorter fiction as in the more magisterial novel to follow, the author keeps the faith with the promise of stories to recall us to the *promesse du bonheur*.

NOTES

1 Martin Amis, 'Rendezvous with Rushdie', *Vanity Fair* (December 1990), pp. 160–3; this citation on p. 163.
2 James Fenton, 'Keeping up with Salman Rushdie', *The New York Review of Books* (28 March 1991), pp. 26–34; p. 33.
3 Salman Rushdie, *Haroun and the Sea of Stories* (London: Granta, 1990), p. 102. Further references are to this edition and will be cited in the text.
4 Salman Rushdie, *The Satanic Verses* (London: Viking, 1988), pp. 281, 297.
5 Salman Rushdie, *East, West* (London: Jonathan Cape), 1994, p. 16. Further references will be cited in the text.
6 Karl Marx and Friedrich Engels, 'Manifesto of the Communist Party', in *The Marx–Engels Reader*, ed. Robert C. Tucker (New York: Norton, 1978), pp. 469–500; p. 476.
7 E. M. Forster, *A Passage to India* (New York: Harcourt, 1924), p. 362.
8 Salman Rushdie, *The Moor's Last Sigh* (London: Cape, 1995), p. 434.

MINOLI SALGADO

The politics of the palimpsest in *The Moor's Last Sigh*

The Moor's Last Sigh, Rushdie's first major publication after *The Satanic Verses*, was written in the shadow of the *fatwa* and in the wake of Rushdie's political exile from his former homeland.[1] The novel appears to replicate the author's predicament by foregrounding a sense of banishment and impending death, opening and closing the eponymous Moor's narrative with his premature death in exile. Exile and death thus frame the rich narrative collage that constitutes this saga of the Catholic–Jewish Da-Gama-Zogoiby family, containing the events in a foreclosed temporal register that offers both cultural and historical density to the text. The Moor's retrospective narration 're-covers' – simultaneously reclaims and layers – four generations of family history drawing intricate connections between fiction and history by drawing on the trope of the palimpsest – a writing surface upon which the original traces have been overwritten. This trope – which I explore in depth later – is central to the model of historiography as re-covery in the text and reflects the contingency of historical narration, its production within a specific historical moment. Indeed, this novel is one of Rushdie's most 'readerly' texts in that its prime concern, as Stephen Baker has pointed out, is 'the rediscovery of a creative, historical dimension in the reading process itself'.[2] It is appropriate therefore to begin by applying these terms to our own reading of the text: to reflect upon its own moment of production as part of our engagement with a 'palimpsestic', or multilayered, reading of the novel.

I

Rushdie's post-*fatwa* political exile and the upsurge of communal violence in India are key events that shape the novel's moment of production. Both events reveal that religious boundaries are perhaps the least negotiable of social boundaries, a fact highlighted by Samuel Huntingdon in his influential essay, 'The Clash of Civilisations':

> Even more than ethnicity, religion discriminates sharply and exclusively among people. A person can be half-French and half-Arab and simultaneously, a citizen of two countries. It is more difficult to be half-Catholic and half-Muslim.[3]

On 6 December 1992, the seventeenth-century Babri Masjid mosque in Ayodha was destroyed by Hindu militants, inflaming a long-standing religious dispute over the claim that the site was sanctioned as the birthplace of Rama, a Hindu deity. This event is written into the fictional trajectory of the Moor's life, creating the conditions for his exile (MLS, pp. 363–5). Over 1,000 people were killed in the Hindu–Muslim riots that followed the destruction of the mosque, and Bal Thackeray, the founder of the Hindu nationalist Shiv Sena party upon whom the character of Raman Fielding is based, was alleged to have incited them.

This exclusionary context informs the heightened sense of dislocation in the novel such that the India of *The Moor's Last Sigh* is in fact 'doubly lost to its author',[4] as the barriers of exile come to be reinforced by the unhomely transformation of Bombay – Rushdie's birthplace and Thackeray's stronghold – into a cauldron of religious bigotry and intolerance. The fact that Thackeray has never held political office but nevertheless retains tight political control in the state, informs Rushdie's reading of India itself as a palimpsest in which a fictional veneer of spuriously objective official facts hides incompatible contradictory social truths. What is more, in a text that celebrates the democratising impulses underpinning social, cultural and political pluralism – what Rushdie has described as 'hybridity, impurity, intermingling ... [that which] rejoices in mongrelization and fears the absolutism of the Pure'[5] – it is fitting that Rushdie's presentation of the palimpsest is correspondingly plural and diverse. His palimpsest is at once a metaphor for the multilayered and multicultural social reality of India, a historical paradigm that makes active agents of his readers, a literary device that informs the intertextuality of the novel in which multiple texts are invoked, and a model of visual art that plays a central role in a narrative that focuses on painting and visual representation. Through presenting the palimpsest as an object, a theoretical paradigm, and a transformative process, Rushdie is able to embrace his own contradictory position as an exilic observer of events and one who is critically engaged in exposing injustice.

Indeed *The Moor's Last Sigh* brings to crisis fundamental tensions in Rushdie's aesthetic and political preoccupations. The desire to write a national allegory from an exilic perspective and the qualified promotion of secularism are contained in a further paradox: the desire to satirise the present while simultaneously presenting the 'ideal' of a multicultural past. As Timothy Brennan has succinctly observed, 'exile and nationalism are conflicting poles of feeling',[6] but Rushdie's insistence on writing the nation from the margins of belonging and on promoting what Rustom Bharucha has called a 'very privileged reading of the Nehruvian legacy of secularism'[7] while simultaneously calling it into question, reveal ideological tensions and divergent impulses that appear to be self-effacing. Furthermore, they are impulses that are themselves framed within the seemingly antithetical drives of satire and utopianism. Rushdie's self-conscious layering of Indian and Spanish history in the novel is contained within a specific reading of history: a presentation of the past with the ironic utopianism of a postlapsarian perspective. The exiled imagination is clearly in evidence in Rushdie's nostalgic restitution of a 'golden age' of India's hybrid past written from a utopian temporal and cultural perspective marked by the era's demise. The 'Moor' Moraes's preternatural and premature death in the fictional Spanish town of Benengeli revives the 'last sigh' of Boabdil, the last Moorish monarch of Granada whose abdication marked not only the end of Muslim rule in Spain but 'the annihilation of Europe's most highly articulated syncretic civilisation'.[8] These emphatic temporal markings that draw into alignment the hidden hybrid histories of India and Spain reveal that Rushdie's idealism is not only conscious and overt, but weighted with the revisionist political charge of satire, so that the seemingly anti-thetical drives of satire and utopianism converge. It is an idealism that is utopian in its bearings and directed by the satiric impulse to revise the political order.

For satire and utopianism are, as Fredric Jameson reminds us, homo-logically linked, emerging as they do from related impulses: 'each is always secretly active within the other's sphere of influence'.[9] 'All satire', he claims, after Robert C. Elliott, 'necessarily carries a utopian frame of reference within itself; all utopias, no matter how serene or disembodied, are driven secretly by the satirist's rage at a fallen reality.'[10] Rushdie's 'rage' at the demise of the secular ideals that frame his vision of postcolonial India's identity bears similarities with the political drive underpinning much of *Midnight's Children*,[11] but also marks an important shift. Whereas the earlier novel presents the threat to the secular 'children' of Indian independence from within the framework of a revisionist national allegory, *The Moor's Last Sigh* presents the erosion of secular ideals from a framework that challenges the very possibility of a nationally bounded vision. Here Nehruvian secularism is examined as both a dynamic belief and a fixed ideal. As a dynamic belief it informs the changing representational styles of the secular artist Aurora, the Moor's mother, as she explores her relationship to the nation on canvas, and as a fixed ideal it takes the form of a treasured family pet, Jawaharlal, who not only shares the former Prime Minister's name but also, it seems, the fate of the political principles that Nehru stood for. The bulldog is taxidermised after his death, taken out of the country and 'consigned to a broom cupboard in a foreign land' (MLS, p. 407) after 'he had lost most of one ear and there were a couple of missing teeth' (MLS, p. 395). Following a corresponding logic, most of Aurora's paintings are destroyed and the Moor's exile is partly driven by his search for the ones that remain. Nehruvian secularism is not dead but preserved as a damaged ideal that brings hope and comfort to the banished narrator, suggesting that Rushdie is all too aware of the limited agency of political idealism to effect social change. Thus, as I will show shortly, one of the significant shifts in Rushdie's rationale between the writing of *Midnight's Children* and *The Moor's Last Sigh* is in the status accorded to individual agency, a shift that is directly registered in his use of the palimpsest.

Unsurprisingly, given the furore generated by its literary precursor, *The Moor's Last Sigh* is also in dialogue with *The Satanic Verses*.[12] Fictional characters from both *Midnight's Children* and *The Satanic Verses* reappear to critique Rushdie's earlier political stance. Aadam Sinai, the progeny of the principal child of midnight whose strength inspires hope that the anti-democratic forces that have set out to exterminate his forebears will not be successful, and Zeeny Vakil, the art critic who champions multiculturalism in *The Satanic Verses* by writing a book that claims that 'the entire national culture [was] based on the principle of borrowing whatever clothes seemed to fit, Aryan, Mughal, British, take-the-best-and-leave-the-rest' (SV, p. 52), meet fates that delineate Rushdie's perspective on the political trajectory of secularism in India. Sinai reappears as an agent of destruction and Vakil is murdered, suggesting that there is now little hope for effective resistance to religious nationalism.[13]

In revisiting his earlier work, a practice that marks Rushdie's œuvre as a whole, the author is using intertextual self-referencing to engage in a practice of self-critique that suggests the processual, open-ended nature of his literary enterprise. There are several other intertexts in the novel – fictional and historical – which serve a similar purpose. These include *Othello*, *The Merchant of Venice*, *The Tempest*, *Don Quixote*, *Tristram Shandy*, *The Thousand and One Nights*, the nationalist film *Mother India*, R. K. Narayan's *Waiting for the Mahatma*, Carlos Fuentes's *Terra Nostra*, Juan Rualfo's *Pedro Paramo*, short stories such as Saadat Hasan Manto's 'Toba Tek Singh' and Rudyard Kipling's 'On the City Wall', as well as a host of real historical figures – what Umberto Eco referred to as 'transworld identities'[14] – from the political, literary and aesthetic fields.[15] The self-reflexive use of this vast array of literary and extra-literary references, this juxtaposition and negotiation of a multiplicity of different discourses and realms, works to promote an open-ended differential discourse whose form is contingent on its intersection with the reading process. This, it appears, is Rushdie's main aim in *The Moor's Last Sigh* – the creation of an open dialogue that works to address the needs of the present. The time of writing and the time of reading intersect to generate and re-generate debates on the key issues of his time: the role of religion in secular society, the appeal of national allegiance, and the politics of exclusion. In the essay 'Is Nothing Sacred', Rushdie made a claim that seems to be a guiding principle in *The Moor's Last Sigh*:

> Can art be the third principle that mediates between the material and spiritual worlds; might it by 'swallowing' both worlds, offer us something new – something that might even be called a secular definition of transcendence?
> I believe it can. I believe it must. And I believe that, at its best, it does.[16]

I will now show that it is through a radical, performative engagement with the palimpsest – a central trope in postcolonial literature – that Rushdie comes to mediate the material world of secular, rationalist politics and the spiritual world of art and aesthetic endeavour in a way that promotes 'a secular definition of transcendence'.[17] I will begin with a reflection on the place of the palimpsest in postcolonial inscriptions of time, and move on to show how in *The Moor's Last Sigh*, Rushdie presents a performative model of the palimpsest – one inscribed in the reading process itself – that effectively destabilises the very discourse of pluralism that seems so central to his political aesthetic.

2

The palimpsest has been defined as 'a parchment or other writing-material which has been written on twice, the original writing having been erased or rubbed out to make space for the second'.[18] It informs Freud's formulation of memory in his essay 'A Note upon the "Mystic Writing Pad"'' when he describes a toy writing instrument consisting of a waxed pad and celluloid paper which allows writing to be inscribed and magically erased while the writing surface bears the traces of the original inscription. The mystic writing pad is, according to Freud, like memory, as it 'provides not only a receptive surface that can be used over and over again, like a slate, but also permanent traces of what has been written'.[19] This model of memory as a slab that can be inscribed, erased and reinscribed while carrying traces of the original inscription, has parallels with models of history found in much postcolonial writing. It is a model that is inherently *paradoxical*, built on the contradiction of simultaneous erasure and retention, violation and restoration, and rests on a specific reading of the past as both manufactured and man-made, the product of contestatory power relations.

A postcolonial text is multiply marked by this process of erasure, inscription and partial emergence of suppressed discourse. To mark a text as postcolonial is of course to acknowledge the doubleness of inscription and its effects. The very term 'postcolonial' contains within it a double time that marks both a break from the past – that which happens after colonial rule – and connection to it – a writing back, to, or against the grain of colonial history and its effects.[20] Thus a postcolonial text by its very definition occupies a liminal historical space of national emergence: one that looks back towards the violence of colonial inscription and the partial erasure of a precolonial past, as well as gesturing towards the more recent violence of nationalist reinscription and the erasure of the colonial past. It is an ambivalent space, both fluid and historically determined, locked in a dynamic that serves a hegemonic reading of history as domination in the very process of attempting to deconstruct it. Thus the postcolonial palimpsest – the inscription of history as a palimpsest in postcolonial literature – marks a qualified subversion as it is effective only as a means of countering a prescribed past, marking both the erasure and retention of this dominant narrative.

Rushdie's representation of history in his novels begins with an engagement with this oppositional model of the postcolonial palimpsest in his earlier work and moves on to the more radical use of the palimpsest as a trope for historical deconstruction and cultural regeneration in *The Moor's Last Sigh*. The desire to subvert the dominant narrative and write against the grain of official discourse is clear in his first historical novel, *Midnight's Children*. Here monumental time and mythical time are connected and made subject to scrutiny by the enforced links made by the unreliable narrator, Saleem, who rewrites the Indian past from an overtly subjective position. His connections between national and familial events foreground the selectivity of the historian and serve to deconstruct the national narrative:

> If I hadn't wanted to be a hero, Mr Zagallo would never have pulled out my hair. If my hair had remained intact, Glandy Keith and Fat Perce wouldn't have taunted me; Masha Miovic wouldn't have goaded me into losing my finger. And from my finger flowed blood which was neither-Alpha-nor-Omega, and sent me into exile; and in exile I was filled with the lust for revenge which led to the murder of Homi Catrack; and if Homi hadn't died, perhaps my uncle would not have strolled off a roof into the sea-breezes; and then my

grandfather would not have gone to Kashmir and been broken by the effort of climbing the Sankara Acharya hill. And my grandfather was the founder of my family, and my fate was linked by my birthday to that of the nation, and the father of the nation was Nehru. Nehru's death; can I avoid the conclusion that that, too, was all my fault? (MC, pp. 278–9)

Rushdie is asserting here both the absurdity of enforced correspondence, the illogicality and artifice underpinning the historical enterprise, and at the same time asserting the individual's need for meaning, order, coherence, logic. In the process, the teleological projection of history as a goal-directed enterprise is radically reinforced. Causality gives way to casualty – and I use the word here to capture both the minor accident and the major tragedy – but is wedded to a model of the world that reinforces the tyranny of linear time in which Saleem is 'handcuffed to history' (MC, p. 9).[21]

Rushdie's emphasis on the tyranny of linear history and on our impulse to manufacture 'meaning' from otherwise random events, presents the discourse of history as an oppressive force that directs and determines the construction of the past. It follows the historiographic logic characteristic of many postcolonial writers who write back to the colonial or postcolonial past and are thereby locked in a dynamic that serves the dominant order. This approach subscribes to the model of history found in the postcolonial palimpsest described earlier – a writing back to a prescribed past, marking both the erasure and retention of this dominant narrative. Is it possible, however, that in the liminal spaces afforded by the 'double time' of post-coloniality there might be room to escape from the prescriptions of the past? Is it possible to use the trope of the palimpsest to present not merely erasure and reinscription upon the slate of a prescribed past but to challenge the very linearity that such layering suggests?

Rushdie suggests it is – but only at a price. In *The Moor's Last Sigh* he radically revises his teleological model of history found in *Midnight's Children* and offers a dramatic and far-reaching challenge to the logic of cause and effect. In this novel Rushdie explores the full implications of the postcolonial palimpsest, the struggle for inscription of competing discourses – colonial, postcolonial and postnational. In drawing richly upon the palimpsest as trope, metaphor and artefact, Rushdie serves to create a new model of the postcolonial palimpsest, one that has the potential to subvert the linear logic of layered time. This change in representation of course has ideological implications. Rushdie's use of the palimpsest in the novel is – as I will also show – constitutive of his apparent *volte face* in critiquing post-modernism, a critical manoeuvre he has acknowledged in an interview after the novel's publication: 'I've always been on the side of mongrelism. [. . .]

But I was interested to try to suggest [in *The Moor's Last Sigh* that] there's a flip side to pluralism; the down side can be confusion, formlessness, chaos, a lack of vision or singleness of purpose. There are some very strong, mono-lithic, brutal views around, and sometimes those who have a clearer view get further.'[22] It is therefore imperative to analyse the siting/citing of the palimpsest in the novel if we are to identify Rushdie's paradoxical political stance as both an apologist for and critic of cultural hybridity and pluralism.

The palimpsestic layering of histories in the novel calls upon a cross-referential reading of the text that is simultaneously dependent on the multiple intertexts in the novel. As has been shown, the novel presents the reader with a rich and ever-expanding set of intertextual connections. Fictional characters are layered into historical events and 'transworld identities' such as Nehru, Gandhiji, Vallabhbhai Patel and Indira Gandhi, and a host of well-known writers and artistes of the 1940s and 1950s such as Manto, Premchand, Mulk Raj Anand, Ismat Chughtai and Nargis. Characters from the novel are simultaneously written into and shown to emerge out of other fictions, and visual art and written discourse are brought into palimpsestic alignment – each writing into and over one another – as the novel parallels the development of the artist with the evolution of the nation. Aurora, the Moor's mother, is the artist who spends her life trying to represent the changes in personal relationships and national development, documenting the changes in the country as it moves from a history of cultural hybridity to a present of communalism. The novel itself gains its name from multiple associations that are historical, fictional, metafictional and extra-literary: the historical Sultan Boabdil's last sigh as he relinquished power and the Alhambra palace, the real Spanish place named after the event, Othello's sighs, the two fictional paintings in the novel that are so named, and of course Moraes's own impending death.

History, fiction and art are thus interlayered in an intertextual, multi-cultural narrative accretion that brings to crisis the politics of representa-tion. For this accretion of stories does not simply present a pluralist discourse that serves to promote the cultural hybridity from which the Moor's story is constituted, it serves to reveal the impossibility of finding a causal connection between events. This lack of logical connection works simultaneously to promote a notion of enforced historical determinism, which is a central feature of *Midnight's Children*, and relativity which is reflected in a corresponding lack of individual agency. Hence, in contrast to Saleem who inscribes himself into a national past and alters it in so doing, reflecting an assertion of individual will, the Moor is clearly shown to have no agency at all. He is, as Laura Moss points out, not responsible for history but subject to its processes.[23] His accelerated ageing is symptomatic of his powerlessness in the face of historical determinism. In a passage that merits comparison with the earlier one cited from *Midnight's Children*, Rushdie reveals how the experience of temporal acceleration is one which means that the Moor's 'inside and outside have always been out of sync.' (MLS, p. 162) so that his life comes to be determined by metaphors from the past that have little correspondence to his will:

> Ten years later the Moor [painting] found his next incarnation in me; and the time came when Aurora Zogoiby, following in V. Miranda's footsteps, also made a picture which she called *The Moor's Last Sigh* ... I have lingered on these old tales of Vasco because the telling of my own story obliges me to face again, and reconquer, my fear. How am I to explain the wild, stomach-dropping-away, white-knuckled scariness of living an over-accelerated life, of being forced, against my will, to live out the literal truth of the metaphors so often applied to my mother and her circle? In the fast lane, on the fast track, ahead of my time, a jet-setter right down to my genes, I burned – having no option – the candle at both ends ... how to communicate the growing pains in my knees that often made it impossible for me to run?   (MLS, p. 161)

The Moor's life is not only scripted for him by a predetermined past but subject to compression through the experience of accelerated time. Such temporal acceleration finds its visual counterpart in the palimpsest – a layered representation not only constitutive of linearity, but of temporal compression and simultaneity. The paintings referred to in the cited passage are both visual presentations of compression. The first, Miranda's painting, is indeed a palimpsest, painted over the picture of Aurora with an exposed breast, and Aurora's painting of the same name metaphorically relates the Moor's expulsion through Boabdil's expulsion from Granada (MLS, p. 218). Thus Rushdie exposes the potential of the palimpsest as a model not only for historical revisionism – the ability to write back to and over hegemonic history – but as a paradigm for temporal compression and synchronicity that subverts the very possibility for ordering history into a logic of cause and consequence.

Rushdie's use of the palimpsest as a discursive paradigm – a model for literary and historical representation – is also central to his ethical revaluation of hybridity. The novel's narrator is of mixed Spanish, Arab, Catholic and Jewish descent but being born out of wedlock describes himself as 'neither ... Catholic, nor ... Jew. I was both and nothing: a jewholic-anonymous, a cathjew nut, a stewpot, a mongrel cur. I was – what's the word these days? – *atomised*. Yessir: a real Bombay mix' (MLS, p. 104). Here Rushdie takes the logic of palimpsestic discourse to its logical conclusion, accelerating the process of cultural fusion by truncating, splicing and indigenising the English language to create a new hybridised discourse. The multicultural historical layers that make up the Indian past are made evident in such disjunctive creolisation. The awkward register of this discourse has drawn vituperative criticism from an Indian reviewer and generated heated debate on the status of Rushdie's work,[24] but it serves a specific political purpose. It works to distance all readers, regardless of background, from identifying with the cultural register of the text, dislocating them from any easy identification, and by so doing makes us attentive to the way in which hybridity itself can be a product of discourse, subject to construction. Hybridity here is destabilising and non-assimilationist. It forms what Bakhtin refers to as 'intentional hybridity' which, as Robert Young puts it, 'enables a contestatory activity, a politicized setting of cultural differences against each other dialogically'.[25] Its interpellation of the reader insists on a corresponding respect for heterogeneity and difference.

Thus Rushdie's focus on the palimpsest as a form of historical compression not only works against any straightforward oppositional stance symptomatic of historical revisionism, but also works to spatialise history, releasing it from the teleological temporality of sequential time. In this novel temporal and spatial logic are not merely juxtaposed (as they are, for example in *The Satanic Verses*, in which early Islamic and contemporary British history are spliced together to create an *intellectual* rationale to promote a specific model of migration and immigration) but flattened into simultaneity, so that the past and present of India and Spain merge and the reading of the one is dependent on the other. It is an *aesthetic* rationalisation that brings to bear on his fiction a consideration of the negative side to cultural mergence. Hence Aurora's fantasy world of 'Palimpsestine', 'where worlds collide, flow in and out of another, and washofy away' (p. 226), operates as a metaphor for cultural fusion. Bombay – and by extension the whole of India[26] – is represented as a palimpsest in a passage reflecting on the corrupt business practices of Abraham, the Moor's father:

> The city itself, perhaps the whole country, was a palimpsest, Under World beneath Over World, black market beneath white; when the whole of life was like this, when an invisible reality moved phantomwise beneath a visible fiction, subverting all its meanings, how then could Abraham's career have been any different? How could any of us have escaped that deadly layering? How, trapped as we were in the hundred per cent fakery of the real, in the fancy-dress, weeping-Arab kitsch of the superficial could we have penetrated to the full, sensual truth of the lost mother [India] below? How could we have lived authentic lives? How could we have failed to be grotesque?
>
> (MLS, pp. 184–5)

Here the surface of the palimpsest is a fiction that obscures the reality below. It is a 'deadly layering'. But in condensing and accelerating time in the novel and presenting us with a multiplicity of realities, Rushdie has released the palimpsest from the bounds of a linear history into a simultaneity of simulacra that compete for authority. The tyranny that George Orwell describes in *Nineteen Eighty-Four* in which 'All history was a palimpsest, scraped clean and re-inscribed exactly as often as was necessary',[27] and which so many postcolonial writers contend with in their work, is here transformed into an open and emergent present and history itself is shown to have no ontological status. The passage plays upon the notion of surfaces, extrapolating from Abraham's exploits a world of subterfuge that challenges the certainty of the fictions that try to erase them.

Hence, we are told, land reclaimed from the sea could be built on by people who had been rendered 'invisible' (by being excluded from the national census) in order to construct buildings that did not officially exist:

> Abraham explained how invisible funds could find their way through a series of invisible bank accounts and end up, visible and clean as a whistle, in the account of a friend. He demonstrated how the continued invisibility of the dream-city across the water would benefit those friends who might have, or by chance acquire, a stake in what had until recently been invisible but had now risen up like a Bombay Venus from the sea. He showed how easy it would be to persuade those worthy officers whose job it was to monitor and control the number and height of new buildings in the Reclamation that they would be advantaged were they to lose the gift of sight ... so that great crowds of new edifices could actually remain invisible to public scrutiny, and soar into the sky as high as any one would wish. And, once again, hey presto, the invisible buildings would generate mountains of cash, they would become the most valuable real-estate on earth ... Suppose the invisible buildings could be built by an invisible work-force ... the million or more ghosts who had just been created by law ...
> (MLS, p. 186)

Rushdie's blending of fantasy and fiction, his play on the invisibility of 'real estate', marks a disjunctive temporal order in the construction of the palimpsest. The palimpsest here is not so much a layering of inscription in time, but an open field of representation which is organised spatially rather than temporally. In this novel the surface contaminates what it covers and operates in opposition to it. The process is not closed, inscribed in the past, but held in suspension in an open and unresolved present. Although set during the period of the Emergency in the 1970s, the corruption this passage registers is a feature of the corporate present from which Rushdie writes, offering us a collapsing of time-frames so that temporal layers blend with one another.

3

Rushdie clearly presents us with a performative model of the palimpsest that draws upon the discourses of the past to disarticulate the present from its prescriptive role. He is challenging the model of a culturally homogeneous history maintained by Hindu nationalists of the present day by celebrating the radical uncertainty and open-endedness of a hybridised Indian past. In doing so, he also alerts us to the inherent dangers of a dehistoricised vision: as in the cultural depthlessness of Uma whose multiculturalism is, as Alexandra Schultheis points out, a matter of style and not belief.[28] The transference of the Moor's affections from Aurora to Uma marks an allegiance to a false pluralism, one that has no historical basis and lacks cultural roots. What is more, Uma's assimilationism bears striking and profoundly disturbing similarities to the ideological underpinning of the Hindu nationalists themselves, the very political movement that Rushdie sets out to critique in the novel. As Jill Didur has pointed out in her incisive study of secularism in the novel, there is, embedded in Hindu nationalism, a notion of cultural assimilationism that effectively works to silence minority groups.[29] It promotes, she notes, 'a formal notion of equality that normalizes a majoritarian agenda'.[30]

Rushdie's critique of cultural hybridity therefore is directly connected to his awareness of the pitfalls of a historically vacuous multiculturalism embodied in Uma, 'the pluralist Uma, with her multiple selves, her highly inventive commitment to the infinite malleability of the real, her modernistically provisional sense of truth, who ... turned out to be the bad egg' (MLS, p. 272). It is also connected to its troubling correspondence with the historical and political revisionism found in religious fundamentalism, which also appropriates the discourse of pluralism for its own ends. For Fielding the fundamentalist, Rushdie shows us, is quick to defend Muslim culture, 'sing ghazals and recite Urdu poetry ... from memory' (MLS, p. 299) presenting us with an appropriation of minority culture that threatens to eradicate its agency.

In taking the logic of palimpsestic discourse to its logical conclusion, Rushdie reveals the urgent need to connect the cultural pluralism of secularist discourse to the social and historical context that generated it. It is a need that is movingly presented through Camoens, the Moor's grandfather, whose words of comfort to his dying wife seem to be extinguished by events even as he speaks:

> He would whisper to her about the *dawning of a new world, Belle, a free country, above religion because secular, above class because socialist, above*

caste because enlightened, above hatred because loving, above vengeance because forgiving, above tribe because unifying, above language because many-tongued, above colour because multi-coloured, above poverty because victorious over it, above ignorance because literate, above stupidity because brilliant, freedom, Belle, the freedom express, soon we will stand above that platform and cheer the coming of the train, and while he told her his dreams, she would fall asleep and be visited by spectres of desolation and war.
(MLS, p. 51; original emphasis)

Here Camoens's dream of a 'freedom express' is countered by the prophetic visions of his wife who sees instead 'spectres of desolation and war' reminiscent of the death trains that carried the mutilated corpses of those who migrated across the border between the emergent nations of India and Pakistan at the new countries' dawn. The utopian basis of Nehruvian secularism is powerfully projected in this 'whisper' reminiscent of the Moor's last sigh.

In this novel Rushdie reveals that he is all too aware of the idealism underpinning his vision of a secular India but holds on to these ideals nevertheless. He goes much further though. He brings to bear upon his utopian vision of India a satirist's rage and insight that compels his readers to demand a more robust model of secularity, one that neither simply celebrates nor conceals the contradictions of a multicultural past but, instead, confronts the disjunctive temporalities it brings to bear – its multiplicity of historical relations and time zones – in a way that requires us to attend not only to the connection between cultures but also to the differences between them. It is a view foregrounded by Didur when she refers to Homi Bhabha's notion of ' "subaltern secularity" ' which is based on the need to 'keep faith' with the 'recognition of difference'.[31] Didur points out that Bhabha's notion is – characteristically perhaps – kept suitably vague, but that it also 'raises the possibility that a *fully rational* understanding of cultural difference may not be possible or even desirable in debates around secularism' (original emphasis).[32] Rushdie's text, in its wholehearted investment in a palimpsestic reading of history, culture and discourse, does more than insist its readers find their own bearings between the text's multiple temporalities and spatialities. By positioning the text between two extreme political and cultural markers – that of historically revisionist, exclusionary fundamentalism on the one hand, and historically vacuous, inclusive multiculturalism on the other – it directs its readers to move towards a space that might come close to 'a secular definition of transcendence'.

NOTES

1 Salman Rushdie, *The Moor's Last Sigh* (London: Jonathan Cape, 1995). All subsequent references are from the Vintage edition and will be given in the text with the abbreviation MLS. Rushdie's political exile from India was exacerbated by the fact that this novel was banned in the country for the first few months after publication.

2 Stephen Baker, '"You Must Remember This": Salman Rushdie's *The Moor's Last Sigh*', *Journal of Commonwealth Literature* 35.1 (2000), pp. 43–54; p. 46.

3 S. Huntingdon, 'The Clash of Civilisations', *Sunday Times* (14 October 2001), p. 4. The essay was first published in *Foreign Affairs* (Summer 1993).

4 Maya Jaggi, 'Interview: The Last Laugh', *New Statesman and Society* (8 September 1995), pp. 20–1; p. 21.

5 Salman Rushdie, 'In Good Faith', in *Imaginary Homelands: Essays and Criticism 1981–1991* (London: Granta, 1991), pp. 393–414; p. 394.

6 Timothy Brennan, *Salman Rushdie and the Third World: Myths of the Nation* (London: Macmillan, 1989), p. 23.

7 Rustom Bharucha, *In the Name of the Secular: Contemporary Cultural Activism in India* (New Delhi: Oxford University Press, 1998), p. 4, cited in Jill Didur, 'Secularism Beyond the East/West Divide: Literary Reading, Ethics, and *The Moor's Last Sigh*', *Textual Practice* 18.4 (2004), pp. 541–62; p. 550.

8 Stephen Henighan, 'Coming to Benengeli: The Genesis of Salman Rushdie's Rewriting of Juan Rulfo in *The Moor's Last Sigh*', *Journal of Commonwealth Literature* 33.2 (1998), pp. 55–74; p. 63.

9 Fredric Jameson, 'Third World Literature in the Era of Multicapitalism', *Social Text* 15 (1986), pp. 65–88; p. 80.

10 *Ibid.*, p. 80.

11 Salman Rushdie, *Midnight's Children* (London: Jonathan Cape, 1981). All subsequent references are to Picador edition, 1982, and will be given in the text with the abbreviation MC.

12 Salman Rushdie, *The Satanic Verses* (London: Viking, 1988)). All subsequent references are to the Vintage edition, 1998, and will be given in the text with the abbreviation SV.

13 Baker, '"You Must Remember This"', p. 51.

14 Cited in Brian McHale, *Postmodernist Fiction* (London: Methuen, 1987), p. 57.

15 Some of these intertexts are studied in detail in Stephen Baker, '"You Must Remember This"', Stephen Henighan, 'Coming to Benengeli', and Paul Cantor, 'Tales of the Alhambra: Rushdie's Use of Spanish History in *The Moor's Last Sigh*', *Studies in the Novel* 29.3 (Fall 1997), pp. 323–41, Jonathan Greenberg, '"The Base Indian" or "the Base Judean"? *Othello* and the Metaphor of the Palimpsest in Salman Rushdie's *The Moor's Last Sigh*', *Modern Language Studies* 29.2 (1992), pp. 93–107, and Laura Moss, '"Forget those damnfool realists!" Salman Rushdie's Self-Parody as the Magic Realist's "Last Sigh"', *ARIEL* 29.4 (October 1998), pp. 121–39.

16 Rushdie, 'Is Nothing Sacred', in *Imaginary Homelands*, p. 420.

17 For a helpful critique on the palimpsest in relation to postcolonial debates see B. Ashcroft, G. Griffiths and H. Tiffin (eds.), *Key Concepts in Post-colonial Studies* (London: Routledge, 1998), pp. 174–6.

18 *The Oxford English Dictionary*, Vol. XI, prepared by J. A. Simpson and E. S. C. Weiner (Oxford: Clarendon Press, 1989), p. 95.

19 Sigmund Freud, 'A Note upon the "Mystic Writing Pad"', in *Collected Papers: Vol. V (Miscellaneous Papers, 1888–1938)*, ed. J. Stachey (New York: Basic Books, 1959), p. 178.

20 Homi Bhabha develops the idea of a postcolonial 'double time' in 'DissemiNation: Time, Narrative and the Margins of the Modern Nation' in *Nation and Narration*, ed. Homi Bhabha (London: Routledge, 1990), pp. 290–322.

21 Rushdie's construction of time and agency bears striking correspondences to the temporal dynamics found in chaos and complexity theory. This idea is explored in Minoli Salgado, 'Nonlinear Dynamics and the Diasporic Imagination' in *Diaspora and Multiculturalism: Common Traditions and New Developments*, ed. M. Fludernik (Amsterdam: Rodopi, 2003), pp. 183–98.

22 Jaggi, 'Interview', p. 21.

23 Moss, 'Rushdie's Self-Parody', p. 124.

24 See C. J. Wallia, 'The Rushdie Phenomenon: A Second Look', *IndiaStar: A Literary-Art Magazine*, http://www.indiastar.com/rsighs.htm. Wallia's 1996 book review focused on Rushdie's use of Indian English claiming that it was 'absurdly inauthentic' constituting a 'grotesque exoticizing ... for the amusement of his Western readers'.

25 R. J. C. Young, *Colonial Desire: Hybridity in Theory, Culture and Race* (London: Routledge, 1995), p. 22.

26 Ania Loomba has pointed out how Rushdie's 'presentation of "hybrid" Kerala is described in terms that are remarkably similar to his "hybrid" Bombay', suggesting that his representation of pluralism in India as a whole is dependent on a culturally specific reading of his native city. A. Loomba, '"Local-manufacture made-in-India Othello Fellows": Issues of Race, Hybridity and Location in Postcolonial Shakespeares', in *Post-colonial Shakespeares*, ed. A. Loomba and M. Orkin (London: Routledge, 1998), pp. 143–63; p. 153.

27 G. Orwell, *Nineteen Eighty-Four* (First published Martin Secker and Warburg, 1949; this edition London: Penguin, 1990), p. 42.

28 A. W. Schultheis, 'Postcolonial Lack and Aesthetic Promise in *The Moor's Last Sigh*', *Twentieth Century Literature* 47.4 (Winter 2001), pp. 569–95; p. 583.

29 Didur, 'Secularism', p. 546.

30 *Ibid.*, p. 547.

31 *Ibid.*, p. 548.

32 *Ibid.*, p. 548.

12

ANSHUMAN A. MONDAL

The Ground Beneath Her Feet and *Fury*: The reinvention of location

I

The Ground Beneath Her Feet (1999) and *Fury*, published two years later in 2001, warrant critical attention as a pair of texts not only because of their overt intertextual references, nor even because they are bound together by the density of their shared themes, concerns and attitudes, but also because they represent a profound ideological shift in Rushdie's writing. The shift began to emerge in his non-fiction from as early as 1992 but remained embryonic in his major fictional work until the publication of *The Ground Beneath Her Feet*.[1] It is signalled most obtrusively there by the relocation of Rushdie's imaginative geography away from the Indian subcontinent. *Fury* consolidates this departure; whilst the earlier novel had embedded substantial portions of the narrative in Bombay, this latter work barely touches upon Indian space at all, except for a few oblique references to the childhood of its protagonist, Professor Malik Solanka. Although India figures in the narrative as the site of a repressed but nevertheless significant trauma, the putative centre of this novel, as in *The Ground Beneath Her Feet*, is the West and specifically the United States.[2] In place of Bombay, which Rushdie had chronicled with almost Dickensian exhaustiveness, there is New York, 'the beating heart of the visible world'.[3] The reasons for this shift, and its effects on Rushdie's fiction, will be the object of this essay.

Accompanying the geographical relocation are two other themes that bind *The Ground Beneath Her Feet* and *Fury* together: globalisation, driven by the irresistible energies of consumer capitalism, and a global media and telecommunications network with its attendant culture of celebrity. It is not coincidental that these concerns intersect with the realignment of Rushdie's imaginative centre of gravity away from the global South to the North, from the economic and cultural margins to the centre, from the postcolonial stage to the hegemonic arena of the world's only current superpower. For globalisation is a process which is marked by the extension of footloose capital on a planetary scale but which is nevertheless thereby still anchored – if more loosely – to capital-intensive sectors of the global economy. The force of Rushdie's critique of globalisation, such as it is, depends on his recognition of this economic and political fact. At the same time, these novels oscillate towards an aestheticism that consistently undermines this critique. The relation of *The Ground Beneath Her Feet* and *Fury* to these issues is of utmost importance.

Triangulating between them are a set of familiar themes in Rushdie's fiction: the relationship between image, imagination and reality; the society of spectacle; epistemological questions over truth, perception and experience; ontological questions concerning being and the fragmentation of identity; and, pre-eminently, the effects of migration. *The Ground Beneath Her Feet* and *Fury* extend and complicate his earlier attitudes toward these ideas, constituting an ideological shift that is informed by personal factors germane to his own position within what might be termed the 'iconography of globalisation', as well as by more structural processes that have visibly transformed the world from the end of the 1980s.

2

In interviews prior to and following the publication of *The Ground Beneath Her Feet*, Rushdie elaborated on his desire to find an appropriate subject and form through which to examine and interrogate the accelerating social, cultural, economic and political changes that are now signified by the term 'globalisation'.[4] Rock music, he felt, was the perfect vehicle for such an ambition because it had 'become only the third globalised phenomenon in history after two World Wars'.[5] Its history is, in this sense, the history of globalisation, and it provides perhaps the original template of the globalised celebrity. Rock music stands, therefore, not only as a metaphor of the processes of globalisation but also as a metonym, representing it at its most visible and extreme.

This convergence of rock music and literature in *The Ground Beneath Her Feet* had an extra-textual analogue in Rushdie's much criticised, though much publicised, appearance on stage with the most successful rock band in the world, U2. And yet, as he appeared on that stage, he did so not as a *mere* writer but as perhaps the most famous, and infamous, writer in the world – the very embodiment, in the eyes of some, of the idea of 'the writer'. In other words, Rushdie's appearance on stage with global celebrities such as U2 is the consequence of his own status as a global celebrity. It is here that his personal trajectory intersects with that of the subject of his novel. For just as his characters Vina Apsara and Ormus Cama both ride on the crest of fame and yet find themselves engulfed by its machinery of representation, so too has 'Rushdie' become more signifier than signified, so much more – and so much less – than the man himself and the books he has authored. The 'Rushdie' who appeared on the stage at Wembley Stadium was a conflicted sign within various representations that had circulated around 'the Rushdie Affair'. For some, he symbolised the most cherished value of Western liberal democracy: freedom of expression, whilst for others he was the very embodiment of western anti-Islamism: a blasphemer and apostate.

It must be pointed out that Rushdie capitalised on his celebrity even if it was a consequence of the trauma of Ayatollah Khomeini's *fatwa*. Nevertheless, Rushdie's media presence offers an opportunity to locate his relation to the subject matter of his later novels more precisely because his authority to speak *on* celebrity and globalisation is bound up with his own status *as* a globalised celebrity.

The consequences of this are two-fold. On the one hand, Rushdie is in a better position than most to appreciate the duplicitous nature of celebrity, and the rapid reversals of fame and reputation that celebrities are prone to. This, however, is bound up within the larger contradictions and conflicts of globalisation itself. As many commentators have pointed out, the 'paradox' of globalisation is that tendencies towards diversification, heterogeneity and polarisation are enmeshed with processes that increasingly draw diverse places and peoples into the hegemonic and homogenising frame of a single economic system and its attendant cultural logic: postmodern consumer capitalism.[6] The effect, then, of the impersonal determinant on Rushdie's later work – globalisation – is to imprint paradox, contradiction and irreconcilability into the fabric of the texts as significant tropes both at the level of thematics and in terms of the novels' structural metaphors. In *The Ground Beneath Her Feet* the unstable earth, which results in ever more frequent earthquakes, signifies the seismic shift represented by globalisation and its paradoxical effects. The metaphor of constantly shifting tectonic plates colliding and readjusting, swallowing up and throwing up, represents the contemporary conjunction of contradictory social, political and economic forces – a multiplicity of forces that can result in both binarism and polarisation but also hybridisation, solidarity and new sites of identity.

In the time-line of the novel, these earthquakes occur more frequently, and with greater intensity, during the 1980s and early 1990s (the novel closes in 1995). The seismic historical events of the period are paradoxically literalised by metaphor, 'Did you see that fault that just ripped out the whole iron curtain? ... Oh, man, the things these quakes are throwing up. Poets for Presidents, the end of apartheid ...' (GF, p. 501). Moreover,

Rushdie is aware that the effects of globalisation are felt more intensely and cause more upheaval outside the 'West' in the economic peripheries of the global capitalist system:

> In the West ... [t]he scars left by the quakes are being transformed into regeneration zones, gardens, office blocks, cineplexes, airports, malls ... In the South, however, the devastation continues ... To many third-world observers it seems self-evident that earthquakes are the new hegemonic geopolitics.
>
> (GF, pp. 553–4)

As if to underscore the point, *Fury* opens with a paean to New York once the faults are covered over, once the scars are healed; New York in 'the first hot season of the third millennium' is enjoying 'a golden age ... The city boiled with money' (F, p. 1). And yet here too the effects of globalisation can be felt in the more nebulous realms of the affective – in psychology, in culture, in aesthetics – and this is registered in the novel's central paradoxical principle:

> Life is fury ... Fury – sexual, Oedipal, political, magical, brutal – drives us to our finest heights and coarsest depths. Out of *furia* comes creation, inspiration, originality, passion, but also violence, pain, pure unafraid destruction ... We raise each other to the heights of joy. We tear each other limb from fucking limb.
>
> (F, pp. 30–1)

Numerous other contradictions are dispersed in the texts as epiphenomena of globalisation. Malik Solanka muses on his situation as a '*sanyasi* in New York, a *sanyasi* with a duplex and a credit card ... a contradiction in terms' (F, p. 82). Sometimes, the paradox of globalisation throws up unexpected ironies: in *The Ground Beneath Her Feet*, the 'cosmopolitan, wholly secularized and Westernized' businessman Yul Singh is revealed to be 'a secret zealot ... one of the financial mainstays of the terrorist fringe of the Sikh nationalist movement' (GF, p. 407); and it is ironic that America's defeat at the hands of the Indochinese is merely the prelude to a much greater victory:

> They'd left a wooden horse standing at the gates, and when the Indochinese accepted the gift, the real warriors of America – the big corporations, the sports culture of baseball and basketball, and of course rock'n'roll – came swarming out of its belly and overran the place. (GF, p. 441)[7]

At other times, however, there is a melancholic anger at a world that seems to be falling apart at the seams. Ormus Cama sings, '*It's not supposed to be this way*' (GF, p. 184) and Malik Solanka, amidst the glittering splendour of *fin de siècle* New York, notes that 'Something was amiss with the world' (F, p. 7).

Inevitably, the shadow of the *fatwa* looms large over Rushdie's encounter with globalisation. Indeed, the climactic event in *The Ground Beneath Her Feet*, the swallowing of its heroine Vina Apsara by an earthquake, takes place on 14 February 1989 – the date Khomeini issued his edict. This trauma not only engendered a severe dislocation in Rushdie's personal life by forcing him into hiding but it also caused a dislocation in his political and ideological affiliations. Propelled by the 'Rushdie affair' into the glare of the media spotlight, in which the terms of the debate 'revolved around binary conceptions of censorship and free speech, sacredness and blasphemy, archaism and modernity, and human rights and tyranny',[8] Rushdie has increasingly come to see himself as many others in the West saw him, that is, as a figure of Western freedom. In the 1980s, all of Rushdie's major fictional works and the essays collected in *Imaginary Homelands* articulate a broadly left-liberal politics from a postcolonial perspective, challenging the hegemony of the 'West', dismantling its dominant and damaging representations, promoting multiculturalism and anti-racism, and contesting the binary model of centre and periphery, West and Rest. In contrast, most of the articles collected in *Step Across This Line: Collected Non-Fiction 1992–2002* are 'surprisingly indistinguishable, in their tone and argument, from many mainstream [US] media responses to the events of September 11'.[9] Actually, this is evident in many of the articles prior to September 11, 2001. In the 1999 essay entitled 'Globalization', first published in the *New York Times*, he writes,

> are there other universals besides international conglomerates and the interests of super-powers? And if by chance there were a universal value which might, for the sake of argument, be called 'freedom', whose enemies – tyranny, bigotry, intolerance, fanaticism – were the enemies of us all; and if this 'freedom' were discovered to exist in greater quantity in the countries of the West than anywhere else on earth; and if, in the world as it actually exists, rather than in some unattainable Utopia, the authority of the United States were the best current guarantor of that 'freedom'; then might it not follow that to oppose the spread of American culture would be to take up arms against the wrong foe?[10]

By invoking an absolute concept of freedom that can be understood universally, Rushdie deploys a binary rhetoric of freedom versus tyranny, good versus evil, 'US' and 'Them' that President George W. Bush would happily agree with. This is from the author of *The Satanic Verses*, which in his own words was a 'love song to our mongrel selves'.[11] In an ironic instance of the hyperreality that he elsewhere critiques, Rushdie's later 'writing self' seems to have merged with that simulacrum of him that had been deployed in polarised debates about the 'Rushdie affair'. Writing from within the celebrity glasshouse, his work now is as much written *from* the American centre as *about* it, as much a reinforcement of his own celebrity as an indictment of the culture that sustains it, as much an articulation of globalisation as a critique of it. The result is chronic ambivalence.

So even as Rai, the photographer, tells us that 'I saw the hand of Mighty America fall hard on the back yards of the world' (GF, p. 419); even as he acknowledges his love of America is based on a 'well-off, green carded life' in a 'dream America everyone carries round in his head' (p. 419) so too the text replays that dream not as mirage but as fact, reinscribing America's foundational myths – the melting pot; a shelter for the world's dispossessed and persecuted; the land of the free; manifest destiny; America *as* the world:

> I want to be in America, America where everyone's like me, because everyone comes from somewhere else. All those histories, persecutions, massacres, piracies, slaveries ... all that yearning, hope, greed, excess, the whole lot adding up to a fabulous noisy historyless self-inventing citizenry of jumbles and confusions; (GF, p. 252)

And yet, in between such panegyric, the text feels compelled – almost like a repressed thought that keeps slipping through – to mention the less salutary history of racial discrimination in America. On p. 291, for example, as Ormus and his manager discuss how to market him, they simultaneously acknowledge the importance of race even as they devise strategies to neutralise it.

Perhaps one might object in Rushdie's defence that these are conflicted and ambivalent characters, uprooted but needing to belong, and therefore comfortable in the ideological space afforded by such myths. And yet, as Nico Israel points out, such is Rushdie's propensity towards *parabasis*, in which the author-figure emerges either self-consciously or from behind the narrator or character, that it is difficult not to conclude that Rai, Ormus and Vina are on such occasions mouthpieces for Rushdie himself.[12] This seems to be the case in *Fury* too, as James Wood pointed out in his review of the novel.[13] Whilst fulminating about the degeneration of contemporary American culture, 'old world, dandyish, cane-twirling little Solly Solanka, in straw Panama hat and cream linen suit', demonstrates time and again a startling grasp of contemporary *Americana* even as he appears elsewhere to be thoroughly disoriented by 'the sheer immensity of his ignorance of the engulfing mêlée of ordinary American life' (F, pp. 134–5). Thus, when Solanka admits to being seduced by America, and that 'he was compromised by this seduction' (p. 87), we suspect it is true also of his author. The novel's frequent jeremiads against the debased nature of contemporary American reality therefore have something of a hollow feel because, as Wood rather witheringly puts it, 'It is one thing to write an allegory or an apologia about how America has compromised one's soul, but it is quite another to publish a novel that so emphatically re-enacts that compromise.'[14]

Ambivalence is also the key register in the novels' relation to celebrity. The ostensible attitude is one of concern, even outrage, and the dominant mode is satire. This is clearly more evident in *The Ground Beneath Her Feet*, a novel that has, at its centre, the paradigmatic figure of global celebrity: the rock/pop star. However, even in *Fury* the animating impulse at the narrative's core is also a celebrity, only this time it is not a human but a doll: Little Brain. Both novels concern themselves with the society of spectacle. Rémy Auxerre, a character who seems loosely modelled on Jean Baudrillard, states that the instantaneity of global mass communications creates a *'feedback loop* ... the initial purity of what happens is almost instantly replaced by its televisualization... This loop is now so tight that it's almost impossible to separate the sound from the echo, the event from the media response to it' (GF, pp. 484–5). In this scenario, reality is the effect produced by the circulation of repeated media signifiers that deliver not the thing or event itself but rather a simulacrum of it. As this effect is immediate, there is no space to distinguish the 'sound from the echo', the signified from the signifier, and so our sense of being is in this way enmeshed in a system of signs that blurs the boundary between reality and its representation. The point is made forcefully in *Fury* where a doll, 'not a thing in itself but a representation' (F, p. 73), becomes as real as any celebrity: 'She now endorsed products on television, opened supermarkets, gave after-dinner speeches, emceed gong-shows ... got her own talk show' (F, p. 99), and so on. That actual celebrities and dolls can be considered equivalent to each other underscores the collapse between reality and representation. In hyperreality only visibility signifies as such so that 'reality' increasingly becomes only that which is visible. Celebrities are just such signifiers, their visibility infiltrating the reality of the observer *as if* they shared the same experiential space.[15] In becoming an icon, the celebrity is transformed into a pure sign, the 'meaning' of which involves a tacit negotiation between observer and observed.[16] Vina and Ormus, by their very conspicuousness, 'entered that zone of celebrity in which everything except celebrity ceases to signify ... in a way they had ceased to be real ... they had become little more than signs of the times, lacking true autonomy, to be decoded according to one's inclination and need' (GF, pp. 425–6).

In such a context, Rushdie's aesthetics of excess is indeed appropriate to a culture in which media saturation fuels excessive consumption, in which enjoyment is reduced to entertainment, and culture constitutes nothing but the passing ephemera of superficial sensation. The incessant lists to be found in both novels, sometimes taking up more than a page at a time, breathlessly catalogue this phenomenal flurry of passing signifiers, fragments of a culture itself fragmented and graspable only in the shallow immediacy of the present. This depthless form reflects an obsession with surfaces where style is more important than substance, the dazzling multiplicity of which exhausts itself in the dull patina of mediocrity and disposability. While some reviewers found this a weakness (especially James Wood in his review of *Fury*), it could be argued in fact that it is a strength, a perfect coincidence of form and content.

Nevertheless, it could also be argued that this same aesthetics of excess generates a hyperbolic register that qualifies much of its critique by making visible an implicit admiration of celebrities, which seems to give some substance and stature to this apparently vacuous empire of signs. This is not merely because as a global celebrity himself, Rushdie's social circle includes quite a few of them. Nor is it because these novels are almost exclusively populated by characters with exceptional talents: VTO are the greatest rock group of all time, Ormus is 'genuinely ahead of his time', and an entire troupe of lesser characters are all invariably brilliant, extremely beautiful, massively successful, or part of the global elite in some form or other. The novels thus reinforce the idea that fame and privilege are a reflection of one's talent, that they are, in effect, deserved. This line of thinking rubs against the critique of celebrity outlined above in which celebrity is an effect of postmodern simulacra and instead articulates the old-fashioned liberal notion of meritocracy, another of the American myths that Rushdie recycles.

More problematic still is the hyperbole that surrounds Vina's death in the chapter 'Vina Divina'. If it is troubling to note that the death of a rock star can unite a planet that is otherwise shown to be bitterly divided and polarised; if it is surprising that 'Overnight, the meaning of Vina's death has become the most important subject on earth' (p. 482), at a time when the Cold War is ending, we can nevertheless accept this as part of the satiric comment of the novel on the rather bizarre manner in which celebrity has come to acquire an importance much greater than is warranted. But the novel goes further, and this time what is troubling is not so much its analysis of the world we live in but rather its representation of the potentiality of celebrity to effect social and political transformation. So, when we are told, 'in death she has indeed transcended all frontiers: of race, skin, religion, language, history, nation, class ... Inspissated women in sexually segregated societies cast off their veils, the soldiers of oppression lay down

Now, however, Rushdie advocates a 'thesis of the post-frontier' in which frontiers – like migrancy, 'home' and identity – are primarily abstract and metaphysical.[24] In 'Step Across This Line' he states, 'The first frontier was the water's edge ... In our deepest natures, we are frontier-crossing beings.'[25] What had been a political act now becomes an existential fact. If we all cross all sorts of frontiers all of the time because to do so is part of some general 'human condition', and not because of historical circumstance, political necessity or economic imperative then what makes boundary-crossing so special? It is not coincidental, then, that Rushdie's representative migrants in these novels are characters for whom crossing political frontiers is literally meaningless – all part of a day's work for a rock star on a global tour – because as members of a global elite they are freed from the constraints of other, often impoverished, migrants for whom the successful crossing of a state frontier is often an act of desperation, the difference between life and death.

Rushdie's discourse on migration has thus shifted from an earlier affiliation with postcolonial theories of transnationalism and diaspora, both of which complicate and dismantle nationalist perspectives on belonging, home and identity, to a species of cosmopolitanism. Transnationalism and diaspora are concerned with collectivities, with migrant flows across borders, and with the social, political and economic as well as cultural implications. Cosmopolitanism, on the other hand, has traditionally been more philosophical, a register which Rushdie now seems to adopt.[26] If examined critically, however, this cosmopolitanism, which ostensibly espouses a world without frontiers, can often be seen to be complicit with the very nationalism it supposedly opposes.[27] In the US, in particular, this duplicitous cosmopolitanism is, as Timothy Brennan has argued, an ideologically dominant position within intellectual circles. Far from rejecting American patriotism, cosmopolitanism is in fact an ambivalent expression of it.[28] Just as Rushdie's new concept of non-belonging articulates a binary rhetoric that excludes any third terms that might mediate between belonging (read: narrow chauvinism) and non-belonging (read: broad-minded global pluralism), so too does American cosmopolitanism offer a straight choice between 'nonnational emotion or concern and patriotic American identity', thereby occluding the possibility that such a position is itself tacitly universalising a particular perspective in the guise of ecumenicalism: an American identity writ large on a global scale.[29]

What is the political value of Rushdie's position? At best it has none, save for a residual rhetorical value that attempts to outmanoeuvre the politics of fear promoted by the US administration's 'war on terror', for which the permeability of borders represents a national security threat. Talking about boundary crossing in existential rather than political terms may be rhetorically useful because if such transgression is part of human 'nature' then why are some persecuted and others not? The reason, of course, is political and because Rushdie vacates the political in favour of the philosophical his strategy, in effect if not intent, is an endorsement of the status quo. *The Ground Beneath Her Feet* correspondingly concludes with the desire for 'ordinary human life' but situates it in the enclosed comfort of contemporary American domesticity. At worst, however, Rushdie's shift represents not only an abdication of the 'terrible, unquiet fuss' of 'Outside the Whale' in favour of quietism but is also complicit with the hegemonic forces that insulate 'ordinary [American] life' from the ravages of globalisation.[30] As such it reinforces the very boundaries that it would hope to erase.

NOTES

1 Salman Rushdie, *The Ground Beneath Her Feet* (London: Jonathan Cape, 1999); *Fury* (London: Jonathan Cape, 2001), hereinafter GF and F in citations.
2 Parts of GF are also set in London and Mexico; *Fury* also has scenes in London, Cambridge and a fictional island called Lilliput-Blefescu, which is modelled loosely on Fiji.
3 Salman Rushdie, 'The Attacks on America' (October 2001), in *Step Across This Line: Collected Non-Fiction 1992–2002* (London: Jonathan Cape, 2002), p. 391.
4 Salman Rushdie, Interview in *Le Monde* (1 October 1999).
5 Rushdie, 'Rock Music' (April 1999), in *Step Across This Line*, p. 300.
6 Fredric Jameson and Masao Miyoshi (eds.), *The Cultures of Globalization* (Ithaca: Duke University Press, 1998).
7 See also Mariam Pirbhai, 'The Paradox of Globalization as an "Untotalizable Totality" in Salman Rushdie's *The Ground Beneath Her Feet*', *International Fiction Review* 28.1–2 (2001), pp. 55–6.
8 Nico Israel, *Outlandish: Writing Between Exile and Diaspora* (Stanford: Stanford University Press, 2000), p. 126.
9 Sabina Sawhney and Simona Sawhney, 'Reading Rushdie after September 11, 2001', *Twentieth-Century Literature* 47.4 (2001), p. 433.
10 Rushdie, 'Globalization' (March 1999), in *Step Across This Line*, pp. 297–8.
11 Salman Rushdie, 'In Good Faith' (1990), in *Imaginary Homelands* (London: Granta, 1991), p. 394.
12 Israel, *Outlandish*, p. 135.
13 James Wood, 'The Nobu Novel: Salman Rushdie's *Fury*', *The New Republic* (24 September 2001), p. 33.
14 *Ibid.*, p. 36.
15 The result, in Homi Bhabha's words, is a 'hallucination of nearness which abolishes a sense of distance ... and in so doing ... is both a familiar presence and a phantasmic icon'. Cited in Elisabeth Bronfen, 'Celebrating Catastrophe', *Angelaki: Journal of the Theoretical Humanities* 7.2 (2002), p. 178.

16 See Stuart Hall, 'Encoding/Decoding' in Stuart Hall, Dorothy Hobson, Andrew Lowe and Paul Wills (eds.), *Culture, Media, Language* (London: Hutchinson, 1980), pp. 128–38.
17 Judith Leggatt, 'Other Worlds, Other Selves: Science Fiction in Salman Rushdie's *The Ground Beneath Her Feet*', *ARIEL: A Review of International English Literatures* 33.1 (2002), p. 116.
18 Rushdie, 'Step Across This Line', in *Step Across This Line*, p. 434.
19 Salman Rushdie, *Shame* (London: Jonathan Cape, 1983), p. 86.
20 Rushdie, 'Imaginary Homelands', in *Imaginary Homelands*, pp. 12 and 19; note also the change in emphasis between 'myths', as used in *Shame*, and 'scam' or 'brainwashing'.
21 Rushdie, 'In Good Faith', in *Imaginary Homelands*, p. 394.
22 Salman Rushdie, 'Out of Kansas', in *Step Across This Line*, p. 33.
23 Rushdie, 'Step Across This Line', p. 425.
24 *Ibid.*, p. 425.
25 *Ibid.*, pp. 407–8.
26 The collection of essays by the Social Text collective attempts to change this dominant paradigm. See Pheng Cheah and Bruce Robbins (eds.), *Cosmopolitics: Thinking and Feeling Beyond the Nation* (Minneapolis: University of Minnesota Press, 1998).
27 Bruce Robbins, 'Introduction: Part 1', Cheah and Robbins (eds.), *Cosmopolitics* (1998), p. 2.
28 Timothy Brennan, *At Home in the World: Cosmopolitanism Now* (Cambridge, Mass.: Harvard University Press, 1997), p. 26.
29 *Ibid.*, p. 23.
30 Rushdie, 'Outside the Whale' (1984), in *Imaginary Homelands*, p. 101.

GUIDE TO FURTHER READING

This bibliography is organised into the following sections:

Works by Salman Rushdie

Fiction

Grimus (First published London: Victor Gollancz, 1975; London: Vintage, 1996).

Midnight's Children (First published London: Jonathan Cape, 1981; London: Vintage, 2006).

Shame (First published London: Jonathan Cape, 1983; London: Vintage, 1995).

The Satanic Verses (First published London: Viking, 1988; London: Vintage, 1998).

Haroun and the Sea of Stories (First published Harmondsworth & London: Penguin/Granta, 1990; 1991).

East, West (First published London: Jonathan Cape, 1994; London: Vintage, 1995).

The Moor's Last Sigh (First published London: Jonathan Cape, 1995; London: Vintage, 1996).

'The Firebird's Nest', *New Yorker* (23 and 30 June 1997), pp. 122–7. Reprinted in Gordimer, Nadine (ed.), *Telling Tales* (New York: Picador USA, 2004), pp. 45–64. Also published as a special edition by Rainmaker Editions, Las Vegas, Nevada, 2004.

The Ground Beneath Her Feet (First published London: Jonathan Cape, 1999; London: Vintage, 2000).

Fury (First published London: Jonathan Cape, 2001; London: Vintage, 2002).

Shalimar the Clown (London: Jonathan Cape, 2005).

Non-fiction

'Anti-Americanism has Taken the World by Storm', *Guardian* (6 February 2002).

'The Empire Writes Back with a Vengeance', *The Times* (3 July 1982), p. 8.

Imaginary Homelands: Essays and Criticism 1981–1991 (1st edn London: Granta, 1991; 2nd edn Harmondsworth & London: Penguin/Granta, 1992).

'Ironic if Bush Himself Causes Jihad', *Sydney Morning Herald* (10 September 2002), www.smh.com.au/articles/2002/09/09/1031115997448.html

The Jaguar Smile: A Nicaraguan Journey (First published London: Pan Books, 1987; London: Vintage, 2000).

'A Liberal Argument for Regime Change', *Washington Post* (1 November 2002), p. A35.

Step Across This Line: Collected Non-Fiction 1992–2002 (First published London: Jonathan Cape, 2002; London: Vintage, 2003).

'Where is the Honour in this Vile Code that Condemns Women to Die in Shame?' *The Times* (18 July 2005), p. 16.

The Wizard of Oz (London: British Film Institute, 1992).

Television, screenplays and play adaptations

Rushdie, Salman, 'The Riddle of Midnight: India, August 1987', Channel 4 Television (27 March 1988). The script is reprinted in *Imaginary Homelands*.

Rushdie, Salman, *The Screenplay of Midnight's Children* (London: Vintage, 1999).

Rushdie, Salman, Simon Reade and Tim Supple (adaptors), *Salman Rushdie's Midnight's Children* (London: Vintage, 2003).

Supple, Tim and David Tushingham (adaptors), *Salman Rushdie's Haroun and the Sea of Stories* (London: Faber & Faber, 1998).

Anthology

Rushdie, Salman and Elizabeth West (eds.), *The Vintage Book of Indian Writing 1947–1997* (London: Vintage, 1997); published in the USA as *Mirror Work: 50 Years of Indian Writing* (New York: Owl Books, 1997).

Interviews and collections of interviews

Amis, Martin, 'Rendezvous with Rushdie', *Vanity Fair* (December 1990), pp. 160–3.

Chauhan, Pradyumna S. (ed.), *Salman Rushdie Interviews: A Sourcebook of his Ideas* (Westport, Conn. & London: Greenwood Press, 2001).

Fenton, James, 'Keeping up with Salman Rushdie', *New York Review of Books* (28 March 1991), pp. 26–34.

Haffenden, John, *Novelists in Interview* (London: Methuen, 1985).

Jaggi, Maya, 'The Last Laugh', *New Statesman and Society* (8 September 1995), pp. 20–1.

Nasta, Susheila (ed.), *Writing Across Worlds: Contemporary Writers Talk* (London & New York: Routledge, 2004).

Reder, Michael (ed.), *Conversations with Salman Rushdie* (Jackson, Miss.: University of Mississippi Press, 2000).

Secondary material

Bibliography

Kuortti, Joel, *The Salman Rushdie Bibliography: A Bibliography of Salman Rushdie's Work and Rushdie Criticism* (Frankfurt am Main: Peter Lang, 1997).

Rushdie and his work

Afzal-Khan, Fawzia, *Cultural Imperialism and the Indo-English Novel: Genre and Ideology in R. K. Narayan, Anita Desai, Kamala Markandaya and Salman Rushdie* (University Park, Pa.: Pennsylvania University Press, 1993).

Banerjee, Mita, *The Chutneyfication of History: Salman Rushdie, Michael Ondaatje, Bharati Mukherjee and the Postcolonial Debate* (Heidelberg: Universitätsverlag C. Winter, 2002).

Bell, John Clement, *Satire and the Postcolonial Novel: V. S. Naipaul, Chinua Achebe, Salman Rushdie* (New York & London: Routledge, 2003).

Bloom, Harold (ed.), *Bloom's Modern Critical Views: Salman Rushdie* (Philadelphia: Chelsea House Publishing, 2002).

Booker, M. Keith (ed.), *Critical Essays on Salman Rushdie* (New York: G. K. Hall, 1999).

Brennan, Timothy, *Salman Rushdie and the Third World: Myths of the Nation* (Basingstoke & London: Macmillan, 1989).

Clark, Roger Y., *Stranger Gods: Salman Rushdie's Other Worlds* (Montreal & London: McGill-Queen's University Press, 2001).

Cundy, Catherine, *Salman Rushdie* (Manchester: Manchester University Press, 1997).

Dutheil de la Rochere, Martine Hennard, *Origin and Originality in Rushdie's Fiction* (Bern: Peter Lang, 1999).

Fletcher, D. M. (ed.), *Reading Rushdie: Perspectives on the Fiction of Salman Rushdie*, Cross/Cultures 16 (Amsterdam & Atlanta: Rodopi, 1994).

Goonetilleke, D. C. R. A., *Salman Rushdie* (Basingstoke: Macmillan Press, 1998).

Gorra, Michael, *After Empire: Scott, Naipaul, Rushdie* (Chicago & London: University of Chicago Press, 1997).

Grant, Damian, *Salman Rushdie* (Plymouth: Northcote House in association with the British Council, 1999).

Hassumani, Sabrina, *Salman Rushdie: A Postmodern Reading of his Major Works* (Madison: Fairleigh Dickinson University Press, 2002).

Kuortti, Joel, *Fictions to Live In: Narration as an Argument for Fiction in Salman Rushdie's Novels* (Frankfurt am Main & New York: Peter Lang, 1998).

Mittapalli, Rajeshwar and Joel Kuortti (eds.), *Salman Rushdie: New Critical Insights*, 2 vols. (New Delhi: Atlantic Publishers, 2003).

Parmeswaran, Uma, *The Perforated Sheet: Essays on Salman Rushdie's Art* (New Delhi: Affiliated East–West Press, 1988).

Reynolds, Margaret and Jonathan Noakes, *Salman Rushdie: The Essential Guide* (London: Vintage, 2003).

Sanga, Jaina C., *Salman Rushdie's Postcolonial Metaphors: Migration, Translation, Hybridity, Blasphemy and Globalization* (Westport, Conn. & London: Greenwood Press, 2001).

Sawhney, Sabina and Simona Sawhney (eds.), 'Salman Rushdie – Special Issue', *Twentieth Century Literature: A Scholarly and Critical Journal* 47:4 (Winter 2001), pp. 431–618.

Popular culture and Rushdie

Chakravarty, Sumita S., *National Identity in Indian Popular Cinema 1947–1987* (Austin, Tex.: Texas University Press, 1993).

Desai, Jigna, *Beyond Bollywood: The Cultural Politics of South Asian Diasporic Film* (New York & London: Routledge 2004).

Dwyer, Rachel, *All You Want Is Money, All You Need Is Love: Sexuality and Romance in Modern India* (London & New York: Cassell, 2000).

Dwyer, Rachel and Christopher Pinney (eds.), *Pleasure and the Nation: The History, Politics and Consumption of Public Culture in India* (Delhi: Oxford University Press, 2001).

Ghosh, Bishnupriya, *When Borne Across: Literary Cosmopolitics in the Contemporary Indian Novel* (New Brunswick, N.J. & London: Rutgers University Press, 2004).

Mishra, Vijay, *Bollywood Cinema: Temples of Desire* (New York & London: Routledge, 2002).

Feminism and Rushdie

Deszcz, Justyna, 'Salman Rushdie's Attempt at a Feminist Fairytale Reconfiguration in *Shame*', *Folklore* 115:1 (April 2004), pp. 27–44.

Grewal, Inderpal, 'Salman Rushdie: Marginality, Women, and *Shame*', *Genders* 3 (November 1988), pp. 24–42.

Kuortti, Joel, 'Feminization of Narrative and Shame', *Zenith: A Literary Magazine* 7 (2001–2), pp. 45–9.

Parameswaran, Uma, 'Purdah in Salman Rushdie, Attia Hosain and Rama Mehta' in Jain, Jasbir and Amina Amin (eds.), *Margins of Erasure: Purdah in the Subcontinental Novel in English* (New Delhi: Sterling, 1995), pp. 33–48.

Phillips, Kathy J., 'Salman Rushdie's *The Satanic Verses* as a Feminist Novel' in Bacchilega, Cristina and Cornelia N. Moore (eds.), *Constructions and Confrontations: Changing Representations of Women and Feminisms, East and West: Selected Essays* (Honolulu, HI: University of Hawaii Press, 1996), pp. 103–8.

Salih, Sabah A., 'The Space of the Woman in Salman Rushdie's *The Satanic Verses*', *Notes on Contemporary Literature* 32:3 (May 2002), pp. 2–3.

Grimus

Cundy, Catherine, ' "Rehearsing Voices": Salman Rushdie's *Grimus*', *The Journal of Commonwealth Literature* 27:1 (1992), pp. 128–38.

Dell'Aversano, Carmen, 'Worlds, Things, Words: Rushdie's Style from *Grimus* to *Midnight's Children*' in Linguanti, Elsa, Francesco Casotti and Carmen Concilio (eds.), *Coterminous Worlds: Magical Realism and Contemporary Post-Colonial Literature in English* (Amsterdam: Rodopi, 1999), pp. 61–9.

Johansen, Ib, 'The Flight from the Enchanter: Reflections on Salman Rushdie's *Grimus*', *Kunapipi* 7:1 (1985), pp. 20–32.

Syed, Mujeebuddin, 'Warped Mythologies: Salman Rushdie's *Grimus*', *ARIEL: A Review of International English Literature* 25:4 (October 1994), pp. 135–51.

Midnight's Children

Afzal-Khan, Fawzia, 'Myth De-Bunked: Genre and Ideology in Rushdie's *Midnight's Children* & *Shame*', *South Asian Review* 17:14 (December 1993), pp. 76–84.

Bader, Rudolf, 'Indian Tin Drum', *International Fiction Review* 11:2 (Summer 1984), pp. 75–83.

Batty, Nancy, 'The Art of Suspense: Rushdie's 1001 (Mid-)Nights', *ARIEL: A Review of International English Literature* 18:3 (July 1987), pp. 49–65.

Bharucha, Rustom, 'Rushdie's Whale', *The Massachusetts Review* 27:2 (1986), pp. 221–37.

Dingwaney, Anuradha, 'Author(iz)ing *Midnight's Children* and *Shame*: Salman Rushdie's Constructions of Authority' in Nelson, Emmanuel S. (ed.), *Reworlding: The Literature of the Indian Diaspora* (Westport, Conn. & London: Greenwood Press, 1992), pp. 157–68.

Durix, Jean-Pierre, 'Magic Realism in *Midnight's Children*', *Commonwealth Essays and Studies* 8:1 (Autumn 1985), pp. 57–63.

Hawes, Clement, 'Leading History by the Nose: The Turn to the Eighteenth Century in *Midnight's Children*', *MFS: Modern Fiction Studies* 39:1 (Spring 1993), pp. 147–68.

Heffernan, Teresa, 'Apocalyptic Narratives: The Nation in Salman Rushdie's *Midnight's Children*', *Twentieth Century Literature: A Scholarly and Critical Journal* 46:4 (Winter 2000), pp. 470–91.

Hogan, Patrick Colm, '*Midnight's Children*: Kashmir and the Politics of Identity', *Twentieth Century Literature: A Scholarly and Critical Journal* 47:4 (Winter 2001), pp. 510–44.

Kirpal, Viney, '*Midnight's Children* and the Allegory of History', *ARIEL: A Review of International English Literature* 26:2 (April 1995), pp. 41–62.

'Postcolonial Ekphrasis: Salman Rushdie Gives the Finger Back to the Empire', *Contemporary Literature* 38:2 (Summer 1997), pp. 232–59.

Kirpal, Viney (ed.), *The New Indian Novel in English: A Study of the 1980s* (New Delhi: Allied Publishers Ltd, 1990).

Kortenaar, Neil Ten, *Self, Nation, Text in Salman Rushdie's Midnight's Children* (Montreal & Kingston, Canada: McGill-Queen's University Press, 2004).

Merivale, Patricia, 'Saleem Fathered by Oskar: Intertextual Strategies in *Midnight's Children* and *The Tin Drum*', *ARIEL: A Review of International English Literature* 21:3 (July 1990), pp. 5–21.

Mishra, Vijay and Bob Hodge, 'What is Post(-)colonialism?', *Textual Practice* 5:3 (1991), pp. 399–414.

Mukherjee, Meenakshi (ed.), *Rushdie's Midnight's Children: A Book of Readings* (New Delhi: Pencraft, 2003).

Prasad, G. J. V., 'Writing Translation: The Strange Case of the Indian English Novel' in Bassnett, Susan and Harish Trivedi (eds.), *Post-Colonial Translation: Theory and Practice* (London: Routledge, 1999), pp. 41–57.

Rege, Josna E., 'Victim into Protagonist? *Midnight's Children* and the Post-Rushdie National Narratives of the Eighties', *Studies in the Novel* 29:3 (Fall 1997), pp. 342–75.

Riemenschneider, Dieter, 'History and the Individual in Anita Desai's *Clear Light of Day* and Salman Rushdie's *Midnight's Children*', *World Literature Written in English* 23:1 (Winter 1984), pp. 196–207. Also published in *Kunapipi* 6:2 (1984), pp. 53–66.

Rushdie, Salman, '*Midnight's Children* and *Shame*', *Kunapipi* 7:1 (1985), pp. 1–19.

Singh, Sujala, 'Secularist Faith in Salman Rushdie's *Midnight's Children*', *New Formations: A Journal of Culture/Theory/Politics* 41 (Autumn 2000), pp. 159–72.

Su, John J., 'Epic of Failure: Disappointment as Utopian Fantasy in *Midnight's Children*', *Twentieth Century Literature: A Scholarly and Critical Journal* 47:4 (Winter 2001), pp. 545–68.

Swann, Joseph, ' "East Is East and West Is West?" Salman Rushdie's *Midnight's Children* as an Indian Novel', *World Literature Written in English* 26:2 (Autumn 1986), pp. 353–62.

Syed, Mujeebuddin, '*Midnight's Children* and its Indian Con-Texts', *The Journal of Commonwealth Literature* 29:2 (1994), pp. 95–108.

Trivedi, Harish, 'Post-Colonial Hybridity: *Midnight's Children*' in Allen, Richard and Harish Trivedi (eds.), *Literature and Nation: Britain and India, 1800–1990* (London: Routledge in association with the Open University, 2000), pp. 154–65.

Trousdale, Rachel, ' "City of Mongrel Joy": Bombay and the Shiv Sena in *Midnight's Children* and *The Moor's Last Sigh*', *Journal of Commonwealth Literature* 39:2 (June 2004), pp. 95–110.

Wilson, Keith, '*Midnight's Children* and Reader Responsibility', *Critical Quarterly* 26:3 (Autumn 1984), pp. 23–37.

Shame

Abrioux, Cynthia Carey, 'In the Name of the Nation: Salman Rushdie's *Shame*', *Commonwealth Essays and Studies* 18:1 (Autumn 1995), pp. 48–55.

Ahmad, Aijaz, 'Salman Rushdie's *Shame*: Postmodern Migrancy and the Representation of Women' in *In Theory: Classes, Nations, Literatures* (London & New York: Verso, 1992).

Albertazzi, Silvia, 'In the Skin of a Whale: Salman Rushdie's "Responsibility for the Story"', *Commonwealth Essays and Studies* 12:1 (Autumn 1989), pp. 11–18.

Ben-Yishai, Ayelet, 'The Dialectic of Shame: Representation in the Metanarrative of Salman Rushdie's *Shame*', *MFS: Modern Fiction Studies* 48:1 (Spring 2002), pp. 194–215.

Booker, M. Keith, 'Beauty and the Beast: Dualism as Despotism in the Fiction of Salman Rushdie' in Fletcher, D. M. (ed.), *Reading Rushdie: Perspectives on the Fiction of Salman Rushdie*, Cross/Cultures 16 (Amsterdam & Atlanta: Rodopi, 1994), pp. 237–54.

Brennan, Timothy, '*Shame*'s Holy Book', *The Journal of Indian Writing in English* 16:2 (July 1988), pp. 210–25.

Chandra, Suresh, 'The Metaphor of *Shame*: Rushdie's Fact-Fiction', *Commonwealth Review* 1:2 (1990), pp. 77–84.

Durix, Jean-Pierre, 'The Artistic Journey in Salman Rushdie's *Shame*', *World Literature Written in English* 23:2 (Spring 1984), pp. 451–63.

Fletcher, D. M., 'Rushdie's *Shame* as Apologue', *The Journal of Commonwealth Literature* 21:1 (1986), pp. 120–32.

Grewal, Inderpal, 'Salman Rushdie: Marginality, Women and Shame', *Genders* 3 (November 1988), pp. 24–42.

Moss, Stephanie, 'The Cream of the Crop: Female Characters in Salman Rushdie's *Shame*', *International Fiction Review* 19:1 (1992), pp. 28–30.

Parameswaran, Uma, 'Salman Rushdie's *Shame*: An Overview of a Labyrinth' in Kirpal, Viney (ed.), *The New Indian Novel in English: A Study of the 1980s* (New Delhi: Allied Publishers Ltd, 1990), pp. 121–30.

'Unravelling Sharam: Narrativisation as a Political Act in Salman Rushdie's *Shame*', *Wasafiri* 39 (Summer 2003), pp. 55–61.

Raza, Hima, 'Unravelling *Sharam* as a Metaphor for *Mohajir* Identity in Salman Rushdie's *Shame*', *SOAS Literary Review* 4 (Spring 2005), pp. 1–24.

Sharpe, Jenny, 'The Limits of What Is Possible: Reimagining Sharam in Salman Rushdie's *Shame*', *Jouvert: A Journal of Postcolonial Studies* 1:1 (1997), 18 paragraphs, electronic publication http://social.chass.ncsu.edu/jouvert/

Srivastava, Aruna, ' "The Empire Writes Back": Language and History in *Shame* and *Midnight's Children*', *ARIEL: A Review of International English Literature* 20:4 (October 1989), pp. 62–78.

Suleri, Sara, 'Salman Rushdie: Embodiments of Blasphemy, Censorships of Shame', *The Rhetoric of English India* (Chicago & London: The University of Chicago Press, 1992), pp. 174–206.

Teverson, Andrew, 'Salman Rushdie and Aijaz Ahmad: Satire, Ideology and *Shame*', *The Journal of Commonwealth Literature* 39:2 (2004), pp. 45–60.

The Satanic Verses

Al-Raheb, Hani, 'Salman Rushdie's *The Satanic Verses*: Fantasy for Religious Satire', *Literary Criterion* 27:4 (1992), pp. 31–41.

Aravamudam, Srinivas, ' "Being God's Postman Is No Fun, Yaar": Salman Rushdie's *The Satanic Verses*', *Diacritics: A Review of Contemporary Criticism* 19:2 (Summer 1989), pp. 3–20.

'Fables of Censorship: Salman Rushdie, Satire and Symbolic Violence', *Western Humanities Review* 49:4 (Winter 1995), pp. 323–9.

Bader, Rudolf, '*The Satanic Verses*: An Intercultural Experiment by Salman Rushdie', *International Fiction Review* 19:2 (1992), pp. 65–75.

Balasubramanian, Radha, 'The Similarities between Mikhail Bulgakov's *The Master and Margarita* and Salman Rushdie's *The Satanic Verses*', *International Fiction Review* 22:1–2 (1995), pp. 37–46.

Ball, John Clement, ' "A City Visible but Unseen": The (Un)Realities of London in South Asian Fiction', *Journal of Comparative Literature and Aesthetics* 21:1–2 (1998), pp. 67–82.

Bardolph, Jacqueline, 'Language Is Courage: *The Satanic Verses*', *Commonwealth Essays and Studies* 12:1 (Autumn 1989), pp. 1–10.

Bhabha, Homi K., 'DissemiNation: Time, Narrative and the Margins of the Modern Nation' in Bhabha, Homi K. (ed.), *The Location of Culture* (London & New York: Routledge, 1994), pp. 139–70.

'How Newness Enters the World: Postmodern Space, Postcolonial Times and the Trials of Cultural Translation' in *The Location of Culture* (London & New York: Routledge, 1994), pp. 212–35.

Booker, M. Keith, '*Finnegans Wake* and *The Satanic Verses*: Two Modern Myths of the Fall', *Critique* 32:3 (Spring 1991), pp. 190–207.

Brennan, Tim, 'Rushdie, Islam, and Postcolonial Criticism', *Social Text* 31–32 (1992), pp. 271–5.

Brians, Paul, 'Notes for Salman Rushdie: *The Satanic Verses*' (13 February 2004) electronic publication www.wsu.edu/~brians/anglophone/satanic_verses

Cavanaugh, Christine, 'Auguries of Power: Prophecy and Violence in *The Satanic Verses*', *Studies in the Novel* 36:3 (Fall 2004), pp. 393–404.

Erickson, John, *Islam and Postcolonial Narrative* (Cambridge: Cambridge University Press, 1998).

Finney, Brian, 'Demonizing Discourse in Salman Rushdie's *The Satanic Verses*', *ARIEL: A Review of International English Literature* 29:3 (July 1998), pp. 67–93.

Fokkema, Aleid, 'Post-Modern Fragmentation or Authentic Essence? Character in *The Satanic Verses*' in Barfoot, C. C. and Theo D'haen (eds.), *Shades of Empire in Colonial and Post-Colonial Literatures* (Amsterdam: Rodopi, 1993), pp. 51–63.

Gane, Gillian, 'Migrancy, the Cosmopolitan Intellectual, and the Global City in *The Satanic Verses*', *MFS: Modern Fiction Studies* 48:1 (Spring 2002), pp. 18–49.

Gurnah, Abdulrazak, 'Displacement and Transformation in *The Enigma of Arrival* and *The Satanic Verses*' in Lee, A. Robert (ed.), *Other Britain, Other British: Contemporary Multicultural Fiction* (London: Pluto Press, 1995).

Hämeen-Anttila, Jaakko, 'Qur. 53:19, the Prophetic Experience and *The Satanic Verses* – a Reconsideration', *Acta Orientalia* 58 (1997), pp. 24–34.

'Rushdie's Dastan-E-Dilruba: *The Satanic Verses* as Rushdie's Love Letter to Islam', *Diacritics: A Review of Contemporary Criticism* 26:1 (Spring 1996), pp. 50–73.

Jussawalla, Feroza, 'Post-Joycean Sub-Joycean: The Reverses of Mr. Rushdie's Tricks in *The Satanic Verses*' in Kirpal, Viney (ed.), *The New Indian Novel in English: A Study of the 1980s* (New Delhi: Allied Publishers Ltd, 1990), pp. 227–38.

'Globalization, Postcoloniality, and the Problem of Literary Studies in *The Satanic Verses*', *MFS: Modern Fiction Studies* 48:1 (Spring 2002), pp. 50–82.

Kuortti, Joel, '"Nomsense": Salman Rushdie's *The Satanic Verses*', *Textual Practice* 13:1 (Spring 1999), pp. 137–46.

Kuortti, Joel, '"To Be Born Again ...": Reading Salman Rushdie's *The Satanic Verses*' in Bennett, Andrew (ed.), *Reading Reading: Essays on the Theory and Practice of Reading* (Tampere, Finland: University of Tampere, 1993), pp. 69–82.

Mann, Harveen Sachdeva, '"Being Borne Across": Translation and Salman Rushdie's *The Satanic Verses*', *Criticism: A Quarterly for Literature and the Arts* 37:2 (Spring 1995), pp. 281–308.

Mishra, Vijay, 'Postcolonial Differend: Diasporic Narratives of Salman Rushdie', *ARIEL: A Review of International English Literature* 26:3 (July 1995), pp. 7–45.

Mishra, Vijay and Bob Hodge, 'What is Post(-)colonialism?' *Textual Practice* 5:3 (1991), pp. 399–414.

Mookerjea, Sourayan, 'Irradiations of History: The Author, Cosmopolitanism and *The Satanic Verses*', *World Literature Written in English* 32–3:2–1 (1992–3), pp. 107–21.

Mufti, Aamir, '*The Satanic Verses* and the Cultural Politics of "Islam": A Response to Brennan', *Social Text* 31–2 (1992), pp. 277–82.

Myers, David, 'From Satiric Farce to Tragic Epiphany: Salman Rushdie's *The Satanic Verses*', *Commonwealth Review* 2:1–2 (1990–1), pp. 144–67.

Nasta, Susheila, 'Writing Home: "Unfinished Business" in Salman Rushdie and *The Satanic Verses*' in *Home Truths: Fictions of the South Asian Diaspora in Britain* (Basingstoke: Palgrave, 2002), pp. 132–70.

Petersson, Margareta, *Unending Metamorphoses: Myth, Satire and Religion in Salman Rushdie's Novels* (Lund: Lund University Press, 1996).

Rombes, Nicholas D. Jr., '*The Satanic Verses* as a Cinematic Narrative', *Literature/Film Quarterly* 11:1 (1993), pp. 47–53.

Sawhney, Simona, 'Satanic Choices: Poetry and Prophecy in Rushdie's Novel', *Twentieth Century Literature: A Scholarly and Critical Journal* 45:3 (Fall 1999), pp. 253–77.

Seminck, Hans, *A Novel Visible but Unseen: A Thematic Analysis of Salman Rushdie's The Satanic Verses*, Studia Germanica Gandensia 33 (Gent: Seminarie voor Duitse Taalkunde, 1993).

Sharma, Shailja, 'Salman Rushdie: The Ambivalence of Migrancy', *Twentieth Century Literature: A Scholarly and Critical Journal* 47:4 (Winter 2001), pp. 596–618.

Spivak, Gayatri C., 'Reading *The Satanic Verses*', *Third Text* 11 (Summer 1990), pp. 41–60.

The *Satanic Verses* affair and the *fatwa*

Abdallah, Anouar, et al., *For Rushdie: Essays by Arab and Muslim Writers in Defense of Free Speech* (New York: G. Braziller, 1994).

Ahmed, Akbar, *Postmodernism and Islam: Predicament and Promise* (London: Routledge, 1992).

Ahsan, M. M. & A. R. Kidwai (eds.), *Sacrilege versus Civility: Muslim Perspectives on The Satanic Verses Affair* (Leicester: Islamic Foundation, 1991).

Akhtar, Shabbir, *Be Careful with Muhammad! The Salman Rushdie Affair* (London: Bellew, 1989).

Alibhai, Jasmin, 'Satanic Betrayals', *New Statesman and Society* (24 February 1989), p. 12.

Appignanesi, Lisa and Sara Maitland (eds.), *The Rushdie File* (London: ICA and Fourth Estate, 1990).

Bhabha, Homi, 'The Third Space' in Rutherford, J. (ed.), *Identity: Community, Culture, Difference* (London: Lawrence & Wishart, 1990).

Bowen, David (ed.), *The Satanic Verses: Bradford Responds* (Bradford: Bradford and Ilkley Community College, 1992).

Cohn-Sherbok, Dan, *The Salman Rushdie Controversy in Interreligious Perspective* (Lewiston, Lampeter: E. Mellon Press, 1990).

Donald, James and Ali Rattansi (eds.), *Race, Culture and Difference* (London: Sage Publications in association with the Open University, 1992).

Easterman, Daniel, *New Jerusalems: Reflections on Islam, Fundamentalism and the Rushdie Affair* (London: Grafton, 1992).

Jussawalla, Feroza, 'Resurrecting the Prophet: The Case of Salman, the Otherwise', *Public Culture* 2 (1989), pp. 106–17.

Kuortti, Joel, *Place of the Sacred: The Rhetoric of the* Satanic Verses *Affair* (Frankfurt am Main: Peter Lang, 1997).

Lee, Simon, *The Cost of Free Speech* (London: Faber, 1990).

Majid, Anouar, 'Can the Postcolonial Critic Speak? Orientalism and the Rushdie Affair', *Cultural Critique* 32 (Winter 1995–6), pp. 5–42.

McDonough, Steve (ed.), *The Rushdie Letters: Freedom to Speak, Freedom to Write* (Dingle, Co. Derry: Brandon, 1993).

Miller, Don F. (ed.), 'Beyond the Rushdie Affair – Special Issue', *Third Text* 11 (Summer 1990), pp. 3–144.

Modood, Tariq, *Not Easy Being British: Colour, Culture and Citizenship* (London: Trentham Books, 1992).

Mufti, Aamir, 'Reading the Rushdie Affair: "Islam," Cultural Politics, Form' in Burt, Richard and Jeffrey Wallen (eds.), *The Administration of Aesthetics: Censorship, Political Criticism, and the Public Sphere* (Minneapolis: University of Minnesota Press, 1994), pp. 307–39.

Rutherford, Jonathan, *Identity: Community, Culture and Difference* (London: Lawrence & Wishart, 1990).

Ruthven, Malise, *A Satanic Affair: Salman Rushdie and the Rage of Islam* (London: Chatto and Windus, 1990).

Sardar, Ziauddin and Merryl Wyn Davies, *Distorted Imagination: Lessons from the Rushdie Affair* (London: Grey Seal and Kuala Lumpur: Berita, 1990).

Webster, Phillip, Ben Hoyle and Ramita Navai, 'Ayatollah Revives Death Threat on Salman Rushdie', *The Times* (20 January 2005), p. 4.

Webster, Richard, *A Brief History of Blasphemy: Liberalism, Censorship and the* Satanic Verses (Southwold: The Orwell Press, 1990).

Haroun and the Sea of Stories

Aklujkar, Vidyut, 'Haroun and the Sea of Stories: Metamorphosis of an Old Metaphor', *Commonwealth Novel in English* 6:1–2 (Spring–Fall 1993), pp. 1–12.

Baena, Rosalía, 'Telling a Bath-Time Story: *Haroun and the Sea of Stories* as a Modern Literary Fairy Tale', *Journal of Commonwealth Literature* 36:2 (2001), pp. 65–76.

Chandran, Mini, 'Fabulation as Narrative in *Haroun and the Sea of Stories*', *Jouvert: A Journal of Postcolonial Studies* 7:1 (Autumn 2002), 23 paragraphs. Electronic publication http://social.chass.ncsu.edu/jouvert/

Cundy, Catherine, 'Through Childhood's Window: *Haroun and the Sea of Stories*' in Fletcher, D. M. (ed.), *Reading Rushdie: Perspectives on the Fiction of Salman Rushdie*, Cross/Cultures 16 (Amsterdam: Rodopi, 1994), pp. 335–41.

Durix, Jean-Pierre, '"The Gardener of Stories": Salman Rushdie's *Haroun and the Sea of Stories*', *Journal of Commonwealth Literature* 29:1 (1993), pp. 114–22.

Goonetilleke, D. C. R. A., '*Haroun and the Sea of Stories* and Rushdie's Partial/Plural Identity', *World Literature Written in English* 35:2 (1996), pp. 13–27.

Krishnan, R. S., 'Telling of the Tale: Text, Context, and Narrative Act in Rushdie's *Haroun and the Sea of Stories*', *International Fiction Review* 22:1–2 (1995), pp. 67–73.

Merivale, Patricia, 'The Telling of Lies and "The Sea of Stories": "Haroun", "Pinocchio" and the Postcolonial Artist Parable', *ARIEL: A Review of International English Literature* 28:1 (January 1997), pp. 193–208.

Mukherjee, Meenakshi, 'Politics and Children's Literature: A Reading of *Haroun and the Sea of Stories*', *ARIEL: A Review of International English Literature* 29:1 (January 1998), pp. 163–77.

Rangachari, Latha and Evangelini Manickam, 'The Story Teller Silenced: A Study of Rushdie's *Haroun and the Sea of Stories*', *Literary Criterion* 30:4 (1995), pp. 15–24.

Sen, Suchismita, 'Memory, Language, and Society in Salman Rushdie's *Haroun and the Sea of Stories*', *Contemporary Literature* 36:4 (Winter 1995), pp. 654–75.

Teverson, Andrew S., 'Fairy Tale Politics: Free Speech and Multiculturalism in *Haroun and the Sea of Stories*', *Twentieth Century Literature: A Scholarly and Critical Journal* 47:4 (Winter 2001), pp. 444–66.

East, West

Carey-Abrioux, Cynthia, '"Coming Unstuck": Salman Rushdie's Short Story "The Courter"' in Bardolph, Jacqueline (ed.), *Telling Stories: Postcolonial Short Fiction in English* (Amsterdam: Rodopi, 2001), pp. 315–22.

Challakere, Padmaja, 'Migrancy as Paranoid Schizophrenia in Salman Rushdie's *East, West*', *South Asian Review* 20:17 (December 1996), pp. 66–74.

Rauwerda, Antje M., '*East, West*: Rushdie Writes Home', *South Asian Review* 24:2 (2003), pp. 133–48.

The Moor's Last Sigh

Baker, Stephen, '"You Must Remember This": Salman Rushdie's *The Moor's Last Sigh*', *Journal of Commonwealth Literature* 35:1 (2000), pp. 43–54.

Ball, John Clement, 'Acid in the Nation's Bloodstream: Satire, Violence, and the Indian Body Politic in Salman Rushdie's *The Moor's Last Sigh*', *International Fiction Review* 27:1–2 (2000), pp. 37–47.

Cantor, Paul A., 'Tales of the Alhambra: Rushdie's Use of Spanish History in *The Moor's Last Sigh*', *Studies in the Novel* 29:3 (Fall 1997), pp. 323–41.

Didur, Jill, 'Secularism Beyond the East/West Divide: Literary Reading, Ethics, and *The Moor's Last Sigh*', *Textual Practice* 18:4 (2004), pp. 541–62.

Greenberg, Jonathan, '"The Base Indian" or "The Base Judean"?: Othello and the Metaphor of the Palimpsest in Salman Rushdie's *The Moor's Last Sigh*', *Modern Language Studies* 29:2 (Fall 1999), pp. 93–107.

Henighan, Stephen, 'Coming to Benengeli: The Genesis of Salman Rushdie's Rewriting of Juan Rulfo in *The Moor's Last Sigh*', *Journal of Commonwealth Literature* 33: 2 (1998), pp. 55–74.

Loomba, Ania, ' "Local-Manufacture Made-in-India Othello Fellows": Issues of Race, Hybridity and Location in Post-Colonial Shakespeares' in Loomba, Ania and Marti Orkin (eds.), *Post-Colonial Shakespeares* (London: Routledge, 1998), pp. 143–63.

Moss, Laura, ' "Forget Those Damnfool Realists!": Salman Rushdie's Self-Parody as the Magic Realist's "Last Sigh" ', *ARIEL: A Review of International English Literature* 29:4 (October 1998), pp. 121–39.

Schultheis, Alexandra W., 'Postcolonial Lack and Aesthetic Promise in *The Moor's Last Sigh*', *Twentieth Century Literature: A Scholarly and Critical Journal* 47:4 (Winter 2001), pp. 569–96.

Trousdale, Rachel, ' "City of Mongrel Joy": Bombay and the Shiv Sena in *Midnight's Children* and *The Moor's Last Sigh*', *Journal of Commonwealth Literature* 39:2 (June 2004), pp. 95–110.

Weiss, Timothy, 'At the End of East/West: Myth in Rushdie's *The Moor's Last Sigh*', *Jouvert: A Journal of Postcolonial Studies* 4:2 (Winter 2000), 47 paragraphs. Electronic publication http://social.chass.ncsu.edu/jouvert/

The Ground Beneath Her Feet

Bronfen, Elisabeth, 'Celebrating Catastrophe', *Angelaki: Journal of the Theoretical Humanities* 7:2 (August 2002), pp. 175–86.

Cabaret, Florence, 'Writing as Translation in *The Ground Beneath Her Feet*', *Commonwealth Essays and Studies* 24:2 (Spring 2002), pp. 47–57.

Falconer, Rachel, 'Bouncing Down to the Underworld: Classical Katabasis in *The Ground Beneath Her Feet*', *Twentieth Century Literature* 47:4 (Winter 2001), pp. 467–509.

Ganapathy-Dore, Geetha, 'An Orphic Journey to the Disorient: Salman Rushdie's *The Ground Beneath Her Feet*', *World Literature Written in English* 38:2 (2000), pp. 17–27.

Israel, Nico, *Outlandish: Writing Between Exile and Diaspora* (Stanford: Stanford University Press, 2000).

Leggatt, Judith, 'Other Worlds, Other Selves: Science Fiction in Salman Rushdie's *The Ground Beneath Her Feet*', *ARIEL: A Review of International English Literature* 33:1 (January 2002), pp. 105–26.

Linguanti, Elsa and Viktoria Tchernichova (eds.), *The Great Work of Making Real: Salman Rushdie's The Ground Beneath Her Feet* (Pisa, Italy: ETS, 2003).

Fury

Brouillette, Sarah, 'Authorship as Crisis: Salman Rushdie's Fury', *Journal of Commonwealth Literature* 40:1 (2005), pp. 137–56.

Deszcz, Justyna, 'Solaris, America, Disneyworld and Cyberspace: Salman Rushdie's Fairy-Tale Utopianism in *Fury*', *Reconstruction: A Culture Studies eJournal* 2:3 (Summer 2002), 47 paragraphs, Electronic publication: http://reconstruction.eserver.org/023/deszcz.htm

Wood, James, 'The Nobu Novel: Salman Rushdie's *Fury*', *The New Republic* (24 September 2001), pp. 32–6.

INDEX

Cambridge Companions to ...

AUTHORS

Edward Albee edited by Stephen J. Bottoms

Margaret Atwood edited by Coral Ann Howells

W. H. Auden edited by Stan Smith

Jane Austen edited by Edward Copeland and Juliet McMaster

Beckett edited by John Pilling

Aphra Behn edited by Derek Hughes and Janet Todd

Walter Benjamin edited by David S. Ferris

William Blake edited by Morris Eaves

Brecht edited by Peter Thomson and Glendyr Sacks (second edition)

The Brontës edited by Heather Glen

Frances Burney edited by Peter Sabor

Byron edited by Drummond Bone

Albert Camus edited by Edward J. Hughes

Willa Cather edited by Marilee Lindemann

Cervantes edited by Anthony J. Cascardi

Chaucer, second edition edited by Piero Boitani and Jill Mann

Chekhov edited by Vera Gottlieb and Paul Allain

Coleridge edited by Lucy Newlyn

Wilkie Collins edited by Jenny Bourne Taylor

Joseph Conrad edited by J. H. Stape

Dante edited by Rachel Jacoff (second edition)

Charles Dickens edited by John O. Jordan

Emily Dickinson edited by Wendy Martin

John Donne edited by Achsah Guibbory

Dostoevskii edited by W. J. Leatherbarrow

Theodore Dreiser edited by Leonard Cassuto and Claire Virginia Eby

John Dryden edited by Steven N. Zwicker

George Eliot edited by George Levine

T. S. Eliot edited by A. David Moody

Ralph Ellison edited by Ross Posnock

Ralph Waldo Emerson edited by Joel Porte and Saundra Morris

William Faulkner edited by Philip M. Weinstein

Henry Fielding edited by Claude Rawson

F. Scott Fitzgerald edited by Ruth Prigozy

Flaubert edited by Timothy Unwin

E. M. Forster edited by David Bradshaw

Brian Friel edited by Anthony Roche

Robert Frost edited by Robert Faggen

Elizabeth Gaskell edited by Jill L. Matus

Goethe edited by Lesley Sharpe

Thomas Hardy edited by Dale Kramer

Nathaniel Hawthorne edited by Richard Millington

Ernest Hemingway edited by Scott Donaldson

Homer edited by Robert Fowler

Ibsen edited by James McFarlane

Henry James edited by Jonathan Freedman

Samuel Johnson edited by Greg Clingham

Ben Jonson edited by Richard Harp and Stanley Stewart

James Joyce edited by Derek Attridge (second edition)

Kafka edited by Julian Preece

Keats edited by Susan J. Wolfson

Lacan edited by Jean-Michel Rabaté

D. H. Lawrence edited by Anne Fernihough

Primo Levi edited by Robert Gordon

David Mamet edited by Christopher Bigsby

Thomas Mann edited by Ritchie Robertson

Herman Melville edited by Robert S. Levine

Christopher Marlowe edited by Patrick Cheney

Arthur Miller edited by Christopher Bigsby

Milton edited by Dennis Danielson (second edition)

Molière edited by David Bradby and Andrew Calder

Nabokov edited by Julian W. Connolly

Eugene O'Neill edited by Michael Manheim

George Orwell edited by John Rodden

Ovid edited by Philip Hardie

Harold Pinter edited by Peter Raby

Sylvia Plath edited by Jo Gill

Edgar Allan Poe edited by Kevin J. Hayes

Ezra Pound edited by Ira B. Nadel

Proust edited by Richard Bales

Pushkin edited by Andrew Kahn

Philip Roth edited by Timothy Parrish

Salman Rushdie edited by Abdulrazak Gurnah

Shakespeare edited by Margareta de Grazia and Stanley Wells

TOPICS